What Is Sociolinguistics?

Linguistics in the World

Linguistics in the World is a textbook series on the study of language in the real world, enriching students' understanding of how language works through a balance of theoretical insights and empirical findings. Presupposing no or only minimal background knowledge, each of these titles is intended to lay the foundation for students' future work, whether in language sciences, applied linguistics, language teaching, or speech sciences.

What Is Sociolinguistics? by Gerard Van Herk

What Is Sociolinguistics?

Gerard Van Herk

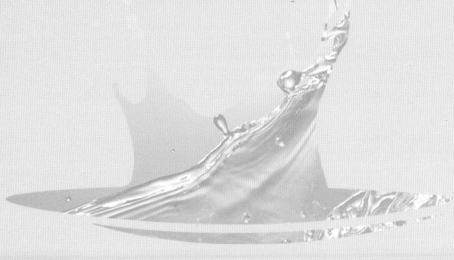

WILEY-BLACKWELL

A John Wiley & Sons, Ltd., Publication

Blackwell Publishing was acquired by John Wiley & Sons in February 2007. Blackwell's publishing program has been merged with Wiley's global Scientific, Technical, and Medical business to form Wiley-Blackwell.

Registered Office
John Wiley & Sons Ltd, The Atrium, Southern Gate, Chichester, West Sussex, PO19 8SQ, UK

Editorial Offices
350 Main Street, Malden, MA 02148-5020, USA
9600 Garsington Road, Oxford, OX4 2DQ, UK
The Atrium, Southern Gate, Chichester, West Sussex, PO19 8SQ, UK

For details of our global editorial offices, for customer services, and for information about how to apply for permission to reuse the copyright material in this book please see our website at www.wiley.com/wiley-blackwell.

Library of Congress Cataloging-in-Publication Data
Van Herk, Gerard.
   What Is Sociolinguistics / Gerard Van Herk.
      p.   cm. – (Linguistics in the world)
   Includes bibliographical references and index.
   ISBN 978-1-4051-9319-1 (hardcover) – ISBN 978-1-4051-9318-4 (paperback)
   1. Sociolinguistics.
   I. Title.
   P40.V354 2011
   306.44–dc23   2011034986

A catalogue record for this book is available from the British Library.

Set in 10/13 pt Minion by Toppan Best-set Premedia Limited
Printed and bound in Singapore by Markono Print Media Pte Ltd

6   2015

Brief Contents

Contents

Boxes

Research in the Spotlight

Companion Website

This text has a comprehensive companion website which features a number of useful resources for instructors and students alike.

For instructors

- PowerPoint slides to accompany each chapter
- Description and notes for each set of chapter slides
- A list of useful links to relevant online material

For students

- A list of useful links to relevant online material
- The book's extensive glossary in full

Visit www.wiley.com/go/vanherk to access these materials.

Acknowledgments

Funnily enough, a personalized book like this actually depends more than most textbooks on the work and judgments of other people. Somebody has to make it accessible, tell me when I've gone too far, and catch all the errors that are staring me in the face.

I'd like to thank:

- Annie Rose, Julia Kirk, and especially Danielle Descoteaux at Wiley-Blackwell;
- Jenn Thorburn, James Bulgin, Suzanne Power, Evan Hazenberg, Matt Hunt Gardner, and Rachel Deal at the Memorial University Sociolinguistics Laboratory; and
- students in sociolinguistics courses at Memorial and at the University of Victoria, who were guinea pigs for earlier drafts of the book.

And I'd like to thank and apologize to:

- everybody who's ended up getting mentioned in this book just because they had the misfortune of knowing me;
- everybody who put up with my drama and/or slackness during my writing, including my colleagues at Memorial and especially Willem, Max, Lidia, Becky, and Christine; and
- everybody I forgot to thank by name!

1 Introduction

In this chapter:

- Types of sociolinguistics
- The background of the discipline
- Personalizing sociolinguistics
- How this book works

I'm sitting here in Newfoundland, in Canada, writing a book about sociolinguistics, and you're out there somewhere, starting to read it. If you were here and could hear me talk – especially if you were Canadian, especially if you had some training – you could tell a lot about me. For example, you'd know which **speech community** I originally came from. When I speak English, most people can tell I'm North American (I pronounce *schedule* with a [sk] sound), Canadian (I rhyme *shone* with *gone*, not *bone*), and probably from Québec (I drink *soft drinks* and keep my socks in a *bureau*). When I speak French, it's clear that I'm from Québec (I pronounce *tu* like *tsu*), from the southwest (I pronounce *garage* like *garawge*), and definitely English (I say *so* a lot, and I have a particular pronunciation of the letter r that English Québecers use to avoid sounding "too English").

You could also tell where I fit into my speech community. I'm the child of immigrants – if you were really good, you'd know that one of them was from the north of England

speech community
A group of people who are in habitual contact with one another, who share a language variety and social conventions, or sociolinguistic norms, about language use.

(I have an unusual r when I speak English, almost like a w). I'm probably under 80 (I pronounce *whale* and *wail* the same), but I'm definitely not young (I almost never end sentences with a question-like rising intonation). Once you knew I was middle-aged, you could tell I was male, and either straight or straight-sounding (I don't use a lot of *so* to mean *very*, I pitch my voice fairly deep and don't often have "swoopy" pitch patterns). Those are just some of the obvious things – there are more specific but hard-to-hear distinctions, like the exact way I pronounce my vowels, that could tell you even more. And if I was wherever you are, I could probably tell a lot about *your* speech community and where you fit into it. The fact that we can do this is one of the things that interest sociolinguists.

But there's more. I'm writing a textbook, and you're probably reading it because you have to (for a university course, most likely). So you have certain expectations, given your past experiences with higher education and previous textbooks that you've read, and I have certain obligations to you (and to my publisher). If I want to appear competent, I should use academic language, but if I don't want to discourage you, I shouldn't go overboard with linguistic terminology. Maybe I should work hard to make this book more accessible than other textbooks. At the same time, I have to get all this past your prof, who knows your school and its students far better than I do, and who at some point had to read this book and decide if it was suitable for your course, and who might not have much patience for my attempts at accessibility. The fact that we're aware of what's expected (linguistically) from this particular interaction is also the kind of thing that interests sociolinguists.

And all of this – the way we talk, the writing and reading of textbooks – happens in a broader social context, the result of decisions made by societies and those who govern them. I grew up going to an English-language school because earlier Canadian governments decided to protect English language rights in Québec (sometimes to a greater degree than French language rights elsewhere in Canada). Maybe I use my "not too English" r when I speak French because my generation doesn't want to be associated with the English speakers before us, the ones who didn't try too hard to speak French-sounding French. As for the textbook, somebody more powerful than either of us decided that you needed a particular kind of education for whatever it is you're doing, and that it involved a course in sociolinguistics, and maybe that it would happen in English, whether that's convenient for you or not. So here we are. And all that, too, is the kind of thing that interests sociolinguists.

types of sociolinguistics

So, what is sociolinguistics? The usual answer is something like "The scientific study of the relationship(s) between language and society." Which is true enough. A more useful answer for someone new to the field, though, might be "It depends who you ask." As in any hyphenated or blended field, the umbrella term *sociolinguistics* covers researchers working all across the spectrum, from very linguistic to very socio. Socio-linguists can study how the language practices of one community differ from those of the next, as described in chapters 2 (communities), 3 (place), and 6 (ethnicity). We can study the relationship in a particular community between language use and social categories like class and status (chapter 4), gender and sexuality (chapter 7), and ethnicity (chapter 6), whether we perceive those categories as relatively fixed or open to active performance and construction (chapter 7, identity). We can study the relationship between social and linguistic forces and language change (chapter 5, time). We can also choose to study how language can reveal social relationships, such as how each of us, as social beings, adapts our language to suit the situation and the audience (chapters 8, style, and 9, interaction). We can study the relationships between different languages within and across communities (chapters 10, multilingualism, and 11, language contact). We can study how people feel about language and language diversity (chapter 12, attitudes), and how their societies manifest those attitudes through language planning and policy (chapter 13), especially in the domain of educa-tion (chapter 14).

And, of course, we understand that all these forces interact, and that the distinct research traditions that we've developed to deal with them can all be brought to bear on a single sociolinguistic situation (as in chapter 15). You'll see as we work our way through the book that those research traditions can be quite distinct. Sociolinguists looking at the status of different languages in a country might never mention the actual linguistic details of the languages in question. Sociolinguists working on change in the vowel system of a language might never mention the changing status of the language. Different subdisciplines have different ideas, not only about what's worth studying, but also about what would count as valid evidence in that study. This, in turn, drives their choice of research methods. So in the chapters that follow, we'll look at some of those research traditions and methods – where possible, under the chapter headings where they're most relevant.

social category
A way of grouping people by traits that are relatively fixed, such as class, gender, or ethnicity, or open to active performance and construction, like identity.

social relationships
How each of us, as social beings, adapt our language to suit the situation and the audience. Often contrasted with social characteris-tics, the socially relevant traits that we are seen to possess.

background: the history of sociolinguistics

Deciding exactly when sociolinguistics began is like arguing about when the first rock "n" roll record was made. It's entertaining for the participants, but it gives you only a slight understanding of how things got to where they are today. For many people, the first systematic study of the relationship between language variation and social organiza-tion is described in a 1958 article by the sociologist John L. Fischer. Fischer was studying how New England schoolchildren used "g-dropping," alternating between *running* and *runnin'*. He found statistically significant correlations between each linguistic form and a student's sex and social class. In other words, rather than free variation, in which the choice between forms is completely arbitrary and unpredictable, he found structured variation, in which the choice between forms is linked to other factors. In fact, it's pos-sible to push the birth of sociolinguistics back ever further – Louis Gauchat's work on

free variation
A term used when the speaker's choice between forms (or variants) is completely arbitrary and unpredictable. Opposite of structured variation.

structured variation
A term used when the speaker's choice between forms (or variants) is linked to other factors. Opposite of free variation.

the French dialects of Charney, Switzerland (1905!), correlates language variation with the age and sex of the people he spoke to.

If you're not committed to the idea that you need lots of numbers to do sociolinguistics, you can see that people have spent centuries observing the relationship between some linguistic forms and the kind of people who use them. For example, over 200 years ago, the grammarian James Beattie observed that extending where you could use an -s on the end of verbs (as in *the birds pecks*) was found "in the vernacular writings of Scotch men prior to the last century, and in the vulgar dialect of North Britain to this day: and, even in England, the common people frequently speak in this manner, without being misunderstood" (Beattie 1788/1968: 192–3). So here we see awareness of language variation ("people *frequently* speak in this manner"), as well as the regional and social correlates (the north, "common people"). Generally, though, earlier linguistic work assumes categoricity (that linguistic rules always apply), and assumes that all variation is free variation. Writing aimed at a broader public, like grammars and usage manuals, often just assumes that all variation is, well, wrong. Jackson (1830), for example, categorizes a variety of non-standard language features as "low," "very low," "exceedingly low," "vilely low," or "low cockney," as well as "ungentlemanly," "filthy," "ridiculous," "disrespectful," "blackguard-like," "very flippant," or "abominable." (More on this kind of thing in chapter 12 on language attitudes.)

But in the same way that there's a difference between Jackie Brenston's *Rocket 88* and an actual genre that people called rock 'n' roll, there's a difference between using sociolinguistic-like methods and the organized research tradition called sociolinguistics. Many of us would trace the birth of modern sociolinguistics as a subdiscipline to the work of William Labov, starting in the early 1960s. In several groundbreaking studies in Martha's Vineyard (off the coast of Massachusetts) and in New York's Lower East Side and Harlem, Labov (1963, 1966) used recordings of natural (or natural-like) speech, correlated with sociologically derived speaker characteristics, to examine in detail the relationship between how people spoke and how they fit into their sociolinguistic community.

This work was interesting enough that nearly 50 years later it's still a model and an inspiration for variationist researchers like me, who look at the correlations between language variation and social and linguistic characteristics. But it also benefited from being the right stuff in the right place at the right time. Technological advances like portable recording equipment and computers made this type of research feasible. Social activism raised interest in the language and status of cultural and class minority groups. And a modernist approach to social problems encouraged the application of findings from the social sciences to improving the school performance of children from marginalized groups.

Since that time, sociolinguistics has widened its geographic, methodological, and theoretical scope, in dialogue with such fields as linguistic anthropology, applied linguistics, gender and ethnic studies, dialectology, phonetics, and the sociology of language. At the boundaries, the dividing lines between these fields and sociolinguistics can be blurry. This is especially true of the relationship between sociolinguistics and the

---

categorical

The opposite of probabilistic, categorical rules are absolute, that is, they apply every time that they can apply.

---

variationist

A researcher who focuses on variationist sociolinguistics.

sociology of language, most closely associated early on with the work of Joshua Fishman, which focuses on the role of language(s) in social organization. Rather than looking at how social forces can shape language, the sociology of language considers how society and language also interact at a strictly social level. In other words, society can treat language the same way it treats clothing, the arts, or business, as a thing to be debated and regulated. (Much more on this in chapter 13 on language as a social entity and chapter 14 on language and education.)

sociology of language
The branch of sociology concerned with language. Unlike sociolinguistics, this approach studies the social contexts of language without recourse to analysis of linguistic structure.

Personalizing sociolinguistics: Author's introduction

Hi, my name's Gerard.

I grew up in Québec, speaking English, just as that Canadian province's French-speaking majority was finally gaining control of the tools of linguistic power. I later lived in Toronto, a city with a large immigrant population, before moving to Newfoundland, where almost everybody speaks English, but the local dialect is highly distinct and diverse.

In each of those places, the relationship between language and society is central to public discourse. In fact, we sometimes joke that Québec has seven million linguists, but only a hundred of them get paid. In each of the places I've lived, a person's language variety is tightly linked to identity and ideology, to their perceived role in society, and to their access to education, work, and power. But in each place, those things play out differently, or involve different aspects of language and society.

Québec has in many ways been defined by the fluctuating relationship between French and English, going back to the conquest of New France by the British over 200 years ago. The dominant discourse there is about the perilous status of the French language. In Toronto, more than half the city's inhabitants were born in another country, and most residents speak at least two languages. The dominant sociolinguistic discourses are about multiculturalism and multilingualism, and about access to English and the benefits it may bring. In Newfoundland, which didn't join Canada until 1949, the dominant sociolinguistic discourse is about the relationship between standard (mainland) speech and local identity, played out in attitudes toward the local dialects and how people use them. I'll draw examples from these and other sociolinguistic situations as we work through the book, and we should all keep in mind that a change in a social situation (for example, economic improvements in a region) will lead to changes in the sociolinguistic situation (for example, the status of the dialect of that region).

In terms of my academic background, I've studied and taught in university departments devoted to education, applied linguistics, and theoretical linguistics. So in the same way that multilingual people are often very conscious of what's odd about each of their languages, I'm very aware of the specific strengths and interests of different approaches to language and society. That will probably reflect itself in how this book is written.

And, for what it's worth, I still remember how stressful it was to switch from one subdiscipline to another as a student. So I'll try to keep the jargon to a minimum. Linguists in particular will notice that I often simplify linguistic terminology (or mention it only briefly), in order to keep all the readers in the loop. I'll also try to pick examples that don't need a lot of terminology to start with. I don't think this will affect our discussions – usually, it's not the mechanics of (say) vowel height that we care about here. We're more interested in a community's *interpretation* of that vowel height.

My research interests and experiences are mostly in varieties of English – from the various places I've lived, as well as Caribbean creoles and early African American English. I'm also interested in how people use language to create identities, especially with respect to gender and local-ness. From a "meta" perspective, I'm interested in research methods, the educational implications of sociolinguistics, and making our work accessible to non-linguists. Luckily, lots of very talented people are interested in these topics, so the book will be full of examples, from my own work as well as that of students, colleagues, and friends. I hope my familiarity with the background to a piece of research will make it easier to discuss its strengths and weaknesses, as well as the methodological decisions that went into creating it.

summing up

Sociolinguistics is the study of the relationship between language and society, but that study can take very different forms depending on who's doing it and what they're interested in finding. Modern sociolinguistics has been shaped by technological advances in recording and handling language data, theoretical interest in bridging disciplines, and researchers' interest in using our findings to address issues of social concern.

Where to next?

We could argue that the label "sociolinguistics" makes more sense when applied to research closer to the socio (sociology) side. Some variationist work, such as that on changing vowel sounds, or my own work on earlier African American English, has very little social component, and even the people doing it are sometimes uncomfortable with the label. Variationists have suggested (only slightly facetiously) that their work would be better described simply as "linguistics." Some sociolinguistics books (by Labov and Fasold) are even divided into multiple volumes — one for the socio end of things, one for the linguistic end.

A younger generation of sociolinguists seems to be moving toward the middle of the spectrum. Even researchers who focus very much on linguistic content are bringing in new ideas from sociology and anthropology.

How this book works

I assume that you, the reader, have limited experience with sociolinguistics. I mean, really, why else would you be reading a book called *What Is Sociolinguistics?* You might have a background in theoretical linguistics, or in applied linguistics, or in education; you might have a completely different background from other readers of the book. So I'm going to assume you're a smart, well-educated person, but I'll try to use examples that make sense even if you don't know much about the fine linguistic details.

The chapter topics will try to cover the major sub-areas of sociolinguistics. These seem to be the breakdowns that people in the field are most comfortable with, but obviously, they overlap, and some material can be covered from more than one perspective. In fact, several studies are mentioned more than once. When the connections between topics and chapters seem particularly important, I'll point them out. But you can safely assume that almost anything covered in one chapter has some connection to material from elsewhere. In fact, you might find it rewarding to frequently ask yourself, "How could my understanding of this topic (say, planning educational language policy) be enriched by considering some other topic (say, gender and identity)?" After we've made it through all these sub-areas, the final chapter will consider a single language variety, African American English, and discuss how people from different areas might approach doing research on it.

Each chapter will introduce some of the main theoretical positions and assumptions, research traditions, and findings in that area.

- The chapters also include:
  - *Definitions* of common sociolinguistic terms. The terms are **in color** in the text and many are defined in the margin. The glossary at the back of the book provides a complete list of definitions, and includes some other important sociolinguistic terms.
  - *"Where to next?"* boxes, where I talk about where research in a particular field seems to be heading.
  - *Exercises* that you can do on your own or in groups. Many of these involve doing some research on your own.

○ *Discussion* questions that are intended to help you elaborate or evaluate what you've read in relation to your own experiences and beliefs.

○ *Other resources* sections that list some books, web-sites, films, etc. that will tell you more about the topics covered in the chapter. Full information on print and online sources is found in the bibliography at the back of the book.

• Many chapters expand on that with a *spotlight*, introducing a piece of writing that I think is especially relevant. These are a mix of classics and more recent buzz-worthy articles, and my discussion is intended to make it easier for people with a limited background in the area to read the original article.

• Some chapters include a description of research *methods*, as different areas often involve different kinds of research.

The book is also written in a very personal style (the text section of the book starts with the word "I" and ends with the word "Gerard"). I think you'll get more out of it if you *read* it in a personal style. Ask yourself: How does this topic or idea work where you live? Who do you know who's like this? Has something like this ever happened to you? Does the research coincide with your experiences? Are you going to have to re-think some of your beliefs? Do things work differently in your community? (If they do, let me know!)

exercises

1. If you have access to online versions of scholarly journals, get an article or two (ideally about a similar topic or community) from the journals *Language Variation and Change* and either *Language in Society* or the *International Journal of the Sociology of Language*. Search the articles (electronically, if possible) for the relative frequency of words from each of these groups:
   (a) *identity, culture, gender, performance, situate, problematize, social capital*
   (b) *quantitative, variation, change, operationalize, results, correlation, statistical, significance, significant*
   Which journal included more of the words from (a)? From (b)? What does this suggest about the focus of each journal?

   (For an easy and attractive version of this exercise, input each article into a software program that generates collages of the most frequently used words in a text, such as Wordle, http://www.wordle.net/create. Think about how the two collages differ.)

2. Using a source such as scholarly journals, the internet, or talking to somebody from one of the communities involved, seek out descriptions of (or opinions about) the sociolinguistic situation in one of the places I mentioned in the author introduction (Québec, Toronto, Newfoundland). How does their description differ from mine?

3. A discursively written textbook like this one can be intimidating for some students, as it's hard to tell which material is more important, and what might end up on a test. Read over the chapter and try to write test questions that could be answered by – and interesting to – an undergraduate student (with a C average, a B average, an A average, or an A+ average), or a graduate student in either linguistics, education, or language policy and planning. (You might find this to be a useful study tool for each chapter, especially if a bunch of you get together on it.)

4. Using the author's introduction above as a rough model, write your own sociolinguistic autobiography. How does the way you speak differ from other people you know? What might account for this? What are your research interests? What social forces might influence them? Don't worry about technical terms. To spark some ideas, ask people around you about the way you speak; or, if necessary, define yourself negatively (e.g., "In my speech community, upper-class people do X and recent immigrants do Y. I don't do either.").

5. Get two (or more) of the sociolinguistics textbooks mentioned in "Other resources." Look over their tables of contents and compare the chapter titles in each book. Which topics deserve a chapter in one book, but not another? What do you think accounts for the differences? Can you see where particular material might be covered in different chapters in different books?

6. As you read through this book and any other assigned readings, keep track of places where sociolinguists' claims are different from what *you* think about how language and society work. Consider how you feel about each mismatch: is it "Wow, I never thought of it like that!" or is it "These people are clearly deluded, because they disagree with me"?

discussion

1. Where you live, are there language features (pronunciation, grammatical constructions, particular words or word meanings) that people associate with particular groups (women, young people, people from a particular neighborhood, non-native speakers)? What are they? (And when you read the previous sentence, did you think, "Hey! Why is he asking about language associated with women or young people, rather than men, or old people?" What does that tell you about who we tend to see as the default setting, or **unmarked** group?)

unmarked
The opposite of marked, that is, a feature that does not get noticed.

2. What would *you* expect a course (and a textbook) about sociolinguistics to cover? You might find it useful to write notes about this, put them away, and consult them at the end of your course or reading.

3. Early in the chapter, I refer to the fact that I'm writing this book and you're reading it as an "interaction." How is this like other interactions? How is it different?

4. Have a look at the table of contents for this book. Which of the chapters do you expect to find the most (or least) interesting? Why?

other resources

There are many existing sociolinguistic textbooks out there, many of them very good. Almost all treat particular studies (e.g., Labov in Martha's Vineyard) in greater detail than I do here. Most of them require some knowledge of linguistic terminology, but if you can get past your understandable anxiety over reading something where you don't understand every word, you should be fine.

I've tried to list some from roughly the most linguistic to the most social:

Chambers, J. K., Peter Trudgill, and Natalie Schilling-Estes, eds. *The Handbook of Language Variation and Change* (2002).
Milroy, Lesley, and Matthew Gordon. *Sociolinguistics: Method and Interpretation* (2003).
Chambers, J. K. *Sociolinguistic Theory: Linguistic Variation and its Social Significance* (1995, 2009).
Meyerhoff, Miriam. *Introducing Sociolinguistics* (2006).
Holmes, Janet. *An Introduction to Sociolinguistics* (1992).
Mesthrie, Rajend, Joan Swann, Ana Deumert, and William Leap. *Introducing Sociolinguistics* (2009).
Trudgill, Peter. *Sociolinguistics: An Introduction to Language and Society* (1983).
Coulmas, Florian. *Sociolinguistics: The Study of Speakers' Choices* (2005).
Romaine, Suzanne. *Language in Society: An Introduction to Sociolinguistics* (2000).
Wardhaugh, Ronald. *An Introduction to Sociolinguistics* (2006).
Coulmas, Florian, ed. *The Handbook of Sociolinguistics* (1997).

There are also some collections of major readings in sociolinguistics:

Coupland, Nikolas, and Adam Jaworski, eds. *The New Sociolinguistics Reader* (2009).
Meyerhoff, Miriam, and Eric Schleef, eds. *The Routledge Sociolinguistics Reader* (2010).
Paulston, Christina Bratt, and G. Richard Tucker, eds. *Sociolinguistics: The Essential Readings* (2003).
Trudgill, Peter, and Jenny Cheshire, eds. *The Sociolinguistics Reader. Vol. 1: Multilingualism and Variation* (1998).

Scholarly journals include:

Language Variation and Change, http://journals.cambridge.org/action/displayJournal?jid=LVC (accessed August 30, 2011).
Journal of Sociolinguistics, http://www.wiley.com/bw/journal.asp?ref=1360-6441 (accessed August 30, 2011).
Language in Society, http://journals.cambridge.org/action/displayJournal?jid=LSY (accessed August 30, 2011).

For an accessible (autobiographical!) introduction to Bill Labov and his work, try "How I got into linguistics, and what I got out of it," http://www.ling.upenn.edu/~wlabov/Papers/HowIgot.html (accessed August 16, 2011).

E. F. K. Koerner's *Toward a History of American Linguistics* (2002) includes a chapter on the theoretical roots of modern sociolinguistics.
Jackie Brenston and his Delta Cats' *Rocket 88* (1951) is available in re-issue.

Language and Society   2

Years ago, my family was walking the narrow roads of Thorpe, a village in northern England, and a car nearly clipped us. We joked that that would be one way to lose weight. Ever since, we've referred to cars passing too close to us as the "Thorpe Diet." Nobody else knows what we're talking about, of course.

You may also have "inside jokes" like this, turns of phrase or odd meanings for words that only make sense to close friends or family, people who have shared particular experiences with you. This is kind of how sociolinguists think about language use – within any group, shared experiences or understandings of the world lead us to use language in a particular way, and to define or reinforce our place in the group by drawing on those possible ways of using language.

In chapter 1, I proposed that we define sociolinguistics as the study of the relationship between language and society. In this chapter, I'd like to expand on that by looking at how sociolinguists define "language" and "society." As you'll see, doing that will bring

What Is Sociolinguistics?, First Edition. Gerard Van Herk.
© 2012 Gerard Van Herk. Published 2012 by Blackwell Publishing Ltd.

back another definition from the first chapter – "It depends on who you ask." Or, better yet, "It depends on what you want to find out."

defining "language" in sociolinguistics

When sociolinguists talk about "language," we mean language as it is actually used. That doesn't sound very profound, but it actually sets us apart from both normal people and some other branches of linguistics.

sociolinguists vs. other linguists

If you work in mainstream ("theoretical") linguistics, you may take issue with the previous sentence, with its implication that other linguists don't necessarily look at language as it's actually used. You may say, "Wait a minute. Theoretical linguists look at real language all the time. We do fieldwork, learning from native speakers of a language." Fair enough. What I'm really talking about here is the object of study, the actual data that each discipline uses to build theoretical claims.

Mainstream linguists usually elicit translations ("How would you say this in your language?") and grammaticality judgments ("Can you say this in your language?") from native speakers of a language. Then they develop a set of rules or constraints that together make up the grammar of that language. They're interested in describing how language is represented in the mind – a **mentalist** approach. This requires some abstraction – the producer of language in this framework is the "ideal speaker-listener, in a completely homogeneous speech community" (Chomsky 1965: 3). It also involves a distinction between **competence** – what speakers know *about* language – and **performance** – what they actually come out with (which might be full of false starts, errors, hesitations, and other such "noise," as well as switches between dialects). In this theoretical framework, it wouldn't make sense to just record people talking and use that to explain linguistic structure. For one thing, you'd need to filter out all the "noise" to get at people's underlying competence; for another, some of the linguistic constructions that would let you decide between theoretical models are so infrequent in daily speech that you'd need to record forever. (If you're a linguistics student, you may have noticed the oddness of some theoretically important sentence constructions when you tried running them past your friends.)

The sociolinguistic approach, on the other hand, is **empiricist** – we only trust evidence that we find out there in the real world. We assume that it's our job to describe and explain what we hear people saying (ideally, by recording them). Sure, there will be some noise, some *ums* and *uhs* and sentences that just peter out, but on the whole, we find that everyday speech is far more structured than people think. (In fact, the idea that real speech is hesitant and meandering originally came partly from studies of the language of professors. Hmmm.)

mentalist
The philosophy or approach that describes how language is represented in the mind.

competence
A distinction drawn by Chomsky (1965) (vs. performance) that refers primarily to what speakers know about language.

performance
What speakers actually produce when speaking (which might be full of false starts, errors, hesitations, and other such "noise," as well as switches between dialects).

empiricist
The philosophy or approach that knowledge comes through sensory experience.

Of course, this means that we end up studying different linguistic features than our mainstream linguist friends, and we study them using different techniques. Most of the time, we record people (especially nowadays). We develop tools to represent what we've recorded in ways that work for us. Many sociolinguists undertake detailed analysis of relatively short stretches of interaction to investigate how participants are constructing their places in the relationship (see chapter 9). In my subfield, on the other hand, we look at frequently occurring language features in long stretches of speech, we count stuff and look for correlations, and we describe our findings in terms of tendencies, or probabilities, rather than absolute rules. In all this, we see ourselves as falling somewhere between other branches of linguistics and other areas of the social sciences.

sociolinguists vs. normal people

standard
The codified variety of a language, that is, the language taught in school, used in formal writing, and often heard from newscasters and other media figures who are trying to project authority or ability.

non-standard
Varieties of a language other than the standard.

descriptive
A non-evaluative approach to language that is focused on how language is actually used, without deciding if it is "right" or "wrong." Contrasted with prescriptive.

prescriptive
An approach to language that is focused on rules of correctness, that is, how language "should" be used. Contrasted with descriptive.

Many normal people (that is, non-linguists) reserve the term *language* for what we linguists usually call the **standard** variety – the language taught in school, used in formal writing, and often heard from newscasters and other media figures who are trying to project authority or ability. Other varieties of the language – the ones which linguists would call **non-standard** – are often described by non-linguists as "dialects." There are almost always value judgments attached to this practice. Many people see the standard as good, pure, clear, and rule-governed – a "real language" – while "dialects" are broken, chaotic, limited, or impermanent. Linguists (of all stripes) try to avoid these kinds of value judgments. Our approach is **descriptive** (how people actually talk), rather than **prescriptive** (how people "should" talk).

Claiming that there's no "right" way to talk can be an unpopular idea, especially, ironically, among people taking their first sociolinguistics course. If you've made it this far in the educational system, then you, like all of us, have been steeped in the ideology of the standard language for years. You're probably pretty skilled at using Standard English (and when you're not, you feel bad about it). You may have had to change your way of speaking to succeed, or to avoid discrimination. You've been rewarded (I imagine) for following the rules of spelling and grammar and punctuation, and for knowing what type of language is appropriate in a particular context. Your career path might involve passing on that knowledge, to children or non-native or disfluent speakers. And now here come the sociolinguists, telling you that there's no such thing as a mistake? You may be thinking, "It's going to be a long semester . . ."

Let me clarify. When I say that our approach is not prescriptive, I don't mean that we're hopelessly idealistic, or deliberately confrontational. We know that certain ways of talking will limit the opportunities of their speakers. In fact, the attitudes toward some language varieties and the social limitations imposed on their speakers, as well as the linguistic consequences of those forces, are the things that we describe and try to explain. They're social or linguistic fact. But to study language and society, we need to be clear that certain language features are not objectively wrong; they're just, as I said above, different ways of saying the same thing. It would be bad science to assume otherwise, and other fields don't do it. Presumably, geologists don't worry about whether (say) feldspar is worse than diamonds; it's just different. Of course, feldspar has a lower *social* evaluation, as a geologist might discover after buying a feldspar engagement ring.

language vs. dialect

When I tell normal people that I study local language use, they have a lot of terms for the language I look at: dialect, slang, accent, bad language, etc. Sociolinguists use most of the same terms (OK, not "bad"). But for us, each of these terms has a distinct meaning. Linguists (and not just sociolinguists) usually use the criterion of **mutual intelligibility** to determine whether people are speaking "the same language" or not. If people from two different places – say, Hamilton, New Zealand, and Hamilton, Canada – can understand each other, then they're speaking the same language, and the systematic differences in their speech reflect different **dialects**, or (regional) subsets of the same language.

    In practice, though, things are messier than this. First off, what does it mean to "understand" somebody who speaks a different language variety? If you've traveled much, or lived somewhere with a lot of visitors, you've almost certainly been in a situation where you couldn't always understand your **interlocutor** (the person you were speaking with). I remember a few years back, soon after Hurricane Katrina, being in a restaurant in Columbus, Ohio, full of Gulf Coast expatriates. An elderly woman at the next table struck up a conversation with me about her time in Columbus, and how expensive she found the city. We spoke for about ten minutes, until her daughter came back and told her to stop talking to strangers. After they left, my table-mate (a fellow Canadian) confessed that he hadn't been able to understand her side of the conversation at all. This may have been partly because he hadn't spent much time in the south, or because he didn't expect to understand somebody of a different age, sex, ethnicity, and nationality. If that were the case, we might say that intelligibility was affected by **social distance** between the speaker and the overhearer.

    I've also been the one who didn't understand another English speaker. In fact, since moving to Newfoundland, I've been in several situations where I've had a hard time understanding somebody from the island, especially older men. And I study Newfoundland English for a living! Usually this happens during sudden topic shifts, or when I have no context to work from. One of my old profs tells a story about an extreme version of this. He was waiting for a train in London late one night when the man sitting next to him leaned over and said, with great emotion, something like "Medooksdid." My prof asked him to repeat this, and the man did, several times, getting more upset each time. Finally he opened his suitcase, pointed to a dead duck inside, and said, very slowly, "Me

mutual intelligibility
If people speaking different varieties (of languages or dialects) can understand each other, their varieties are mutually intelligible.

dialect
A term that tends to refer to subvarieties of a single language. Non-linguists sometimes use the term as a synonym for accent, though dialects can differ in terms of not only pronunciation but also words, word and sentence structure, and meaning.

interlocutor
The person with whom you are speaking.

social distance
Degree of intimacy or familiarity between interlocutors.

dook's did!" If my prof had been confronted with the evidence in the first place, he almost certainly would have understood "My duck's dead."

A second problem with using mutual intelligibility to decide whether something is a language or a dialect is that this is simply not how things work in the real world. For example, speakers of Swedish, Norwegian, and Danish can (more or less) understand each other's languages. Non-linguists think of these as three different languages because they're found in three different countries (and perhaps also because they're found in European countries, and tied up with issues of nineteenth-century nationalism). The variously attributed relevant saying here is, "A language is a dialect with an army and a navy." In other words, a way of speaking is seen as a separate language when various subgroups of speakers have the political power to convince people that they're distinct. The same naming practices happen in other situations where speakers of similar varieties see themselves as distinct for social reasons. For example, the language varieties spoken by Serbs and Croats in the former republic of Yugoslavia are mutually intelligible, although each has some distinct vocabulary. Since the breakup of Yugoslavia in the early 1990s, Serbian and Croatian (and, more recently, Bosnian) have been considered distinct languages by many of their speakers – helped along in this case by the fact that they have different writing systems, reflecting different religious and educational histories. A similar state of affairs is found with Hindi and Urdu in the Indian subcontinent.

The Chinese situation, on the other hand, is the opposite – spoken Cantonese and Mandarin are *not* mutually intelligible, but they are usually described as Chinese "dialects" because they are spoken in the same country, and because words of similar meaning in each language are usually written using similar characters (table 2.1). Here, political and social forces work to encourage a focus on similarities, rather than differences.

Table 2.1.   A comparison of some language features in two "dialects" of Chinese.

English	Mandarin	Cantonese	written the same?
'Hong Kong'	xiang1gang3	hoeng1gong2	yes
'A is taller than B'	A bi3 B gao1 A than B tall	A gou1 gwo3 B A tall more B	partly
'umbrella'	yu3san3	ze1	no

Source: Adapted from Zhang (n.d.).

And sometimes, languages are "invisible." Kachru and Bhatia (1978) describe a situation in parts of India where the local variety (distinct enough for linguists to consider it as a separate language) might not be considered a language at all. So when census takers come around and ask people what language they speak, people instead name the language that they occasionally use in formal situations: Hindi. This was especially true just after Indian independence, when nationalist feeling was at its strongest; in that census, reported Hindi use spiked.

Other naming issues: Dialect, slang, accent, variety . . .

This might be a good place to clear up a couple of other naming problems related to dialects. Non-linguists often call non-standard varieties slang. To us linguists, however, "slang" refers only to *words* – either words that are new to the language, or old words or phrases with new meanings. Slang is usually associated with younger speakers – in fact, a good indicator that a slang term is finished is when middle-aged university professors like me start using it. Most slang is "faddish" or short-lived – you don't hear many people saying *far out* or *the bee's knees* any more, and if I put any current slang in the book, it'll be outdated by the time you read it. Not all slang dies out, though. *Mob*, *freshman*, and *glib* all started out as slang, but have become part of the standard language, and only a generation ago mainstream news media used to give a definition whenever they used the then-obscure slang term *ripoff*. Unlike slang, a dialect is usually distinct in multiple linguistic domains – lexicon (word choice), morphology (word structure), syntax (sentence structure), and phonology/phonetics (pronunciation).

A second term sometimes used by non-linguists to describe dialects is accent, a word that linguists reserve to describe pronunciation. Although dialects usually include distinct accent features, dialect and accent boundaries don't have to match. For example, many people speak Standard English (in terms of grammar and lexicon), but with an accent reflecting their social or regional background – think of Martin Luther King, Jr., BBC regional newsreaders, or CBC editorialist Rex Murphy. The reverse situation (standard accent, non-standard grammatical features) is much less common, and often sounds strange to us. This was used to comedic effect a few years back in a popular online video, which featured a Standard English-accented Gilbert and Sullivan version of "Baby Got Back."

Many sociolinguists avoid the naming problem by using the value-neutral term variety for any subset of a language. They'll talk about the standard variety, as well as regional, class, or ethnic varieties. Others reclaim the term *dialect*, and speak of the standard dialect, as well as regional dialects, sociolects, or ethnolects. They'll often say, "Everybody has a dialect."

Another way that sociolinguists differ from linguists (and many normal people) is that we think of language as existing at the level of the group. Sure, we understand that each human learns language individually and stores it in an individual brain, but we stress that our language gets its meaning through interaction with others, as we negotiate understanding, decide how to present ourselves to others, and express belonging (or not-belonging!). In its strongest form, some sociolinguists lay out our theoretical viewpoint by saying that, linguistically, there's no such thing as the individual – the way we talk comes from our membership in a group or groups. (Although sometimes I think that when we express it that strongly, we do it just to goad people from other research traditions.) As a result, we tend to study language from as many people as it takes to figure out what's going on, generally focusing on individual speakers only when their behavior lets us better understand the boundaries of a group or its linguistic norms.

what is "society"?

So sociolinguists think of language as a social object that gets its meaning and power through speakers' participation in language-using groups. But what do we really mean by "social" in this context? More specifically, what exactly are the social groups that matter in determining what people are doing with language at any particular time?

For sociolinguists who study language policy (chapter 13), this question is often already answered in some kind of official sense. There are specific social and political entities that are responsible for different domains of language. In Canada, for example, most decisions about language – official languages, language in education – are made at the provincial level, and there might be specific agencies responsible for some aspect of language (for example, the *Office Québécois de la langue française* in Québec).

It's a different kind of question for sociolinguists like me, who look at language structure. Let's take my last social interaction as an example – I've just been down the hall talking to my colleague Paul about some research he's working on. Why did we talk the way we did – our accents, our grammar, our word choices? Did we sound the same because we're both Canadian, male, native English speakers, professors? A little different because we're from different provinces in Canada, our parents are from different countries, and he's younger than I am? Were we adapting our speech to each other, or the topic or setting? A researcher studying specific interactions, maybe from an **ethnographic** viewpoint, would say that all those variables can be considered in a single framework – they're all things that could affect the form of the conversation, and we can investigate the relative influence of each component (see chapter 9). A scholar of language variation, though, would probably assume that a lot of the language that Paul and I brought to our conversation is fairly consistent, reflecting our cumulative past linguistic experiences. For example, I probably don't change my vowels when I talk about sociolinguistics, or when I'm in Paul's office.

So, how do we want to think about our similarities and differences? We could say that Paul and I are both from the same group, speakers of Canadian English, and the way we talk reflects our shared understanding of how that group uses English (and what kind of language is appropriate for that kind of interaction between our kind of people). In other words, we're from the same **speech community**. Or we could say that the different groups of people that each of us has interacted with over the years – our **social networks** – have reinforced particular sociolinguistic norms. Or we could drill down to a more local level, and say that because all the people in our lab get together regularly to talk about sociolinguistic methods, our language (and other stuff we do) ends up taking on particular social meanings related to that group, our **community of practice** (CofP).

This gives us three different (although possibly complementary) models for thinking about how our social surroundings influence our linguistic choices. Social networks and communities of practice are both ideas from other disciplines that sociolinguists have adapted. Speech community, on the other hand, is much more of a discipline-specific concept, which traces its origins to the early days of modern sociolinguistics, especially the work done by Bill Labov in the 1960s in New York City's Lower East Side.

In fact, speech community is so much a part of my theoretical understanding of how language is socially organized that I find it hard to define (perhaps because the term's been used in linguistics, even outside sociolinguistics, for at least 80 years, and with slightly different intent by different researchers). A common definition is that a speech community is a group of people who share social conventions, or **sociolinguistic norms**, about language use. These norms (a combination of expressed attitudes and variable linguistic behavior) are shared by all members of a speech community, which is why sociolinguists study the language of the community, not the speech (or perceptions of the speech) of a single speaker. This broad definition lets us talk about speech communities of very different sizes. English Montréal is a speech community – its members

ethnography
A branch of anthropology that deals with the scientific description of individual cultures.

speech community
A group of people who are in habitual contact with one another, who share a language variety and social conventions, or sociolinguistic norms, about language use.

social network
The different groups of people that each of us has interacted with over the years.

community of practice (CofP)
Unit of analysis that looks at a smaller analytical domain than social networks. A community of practice is characterized by mutual engagement, a jointly negotiated enterprise, and a shared repertoire.

sociolinguistic norms
A combination of expressed attitudes and variable linguistic behavior shared by all members of a speech community.

share norms about what to call sweet fizzy drinks and whether *marry* and *merry* are pronounced the same (they're not). But in a sense, "all speakers of English" are a (very big) speech community – we share norms about putting adjectives before nouns, for example (*red car*, not *car red*).

How do we know whether a particular bunch of language-using people are a speech community? It's important to note that a speech community is something that the researcher *discovers*, through an analysis of language use (and attitudes). Labov (1966) determined that New York City could be described as a speech community by showing that New Yorkers shared norms about particular language features. For example, they knew that r-lessness (pronouncing *car* as something like *cah*) was a local feature with very little prestige, and they avoided it (or at least tried to) in situations where they were paying more attention to their speech (such as when repeating an answer or reading word lists). Even rebelling against these perceptions, as some speakers did, qualified people as members of the speech community – you have to know the norms in order to resist them. Labov also determined, though, based on linguistic evidence, that African American New Yorkers did not share the same linguistic norms, and thus should be considered part of a different speech community. (Later work showed remarkable similarities in the vernacular speech of African Americans in different cities, suggesting that speakers of African American English formed a distinct speech community.)

Of course, this means we're using language to define a social entity, and the concept of the speech community has been criticized on these grounds. In practical terms, though, the definition is not entirely language-determined and applied after the fact; when researchers first decide to study a group that might meet the definition of a speech community, we use non-language criteria (such as region) to decide who we'll talk to. I mean, there was such a thing as "New York City" even before Labov determined its speech community status.

And even if we *did* use nothing but language norms to define a social group, that could be interesting as a concept. In fact, some early sociolinguistic studies suggested that our findings might help social scientists in other fields – that shared linguistic norms might reveal previously obscure connections or affiliations between people and groups. As far as I know, nobody's really followed up on this, which might be for the best – otherwise by now marketers would be targeting people on the basis of their verb marking strategies.

There are, of course, some aspects of how society affects language that the speech community model isn't really set up to address. What if you don't have a consensus – if different subgroups in a community (e.g., different classes) have different ideas about what counts as a prestigious form? And what's the actual mechanism by which language features (especially innovative ones) spread through a community? The idea of social networks was imported into sociolinguistics from social anthropology to address these issues. It's central to Lesley and James Milroy's description of patterns of language change in urban Belfast in the 1980s (Milroy 1980). The term "social networks" is well known nowadays in the sense of social networking websites, but that's only marginally related to what we're talking about here. The term as used in the social sciences refers to the fact that we build networks (personal communities, in a sense) to deal with life, and as our everyday problems change, so do our personal networks. Each of us partici-

dense
A term used to describe the number of connections within a social network. In a low-density network, people know a central member but not each other. In a high-density network, members know and interact with each other.

multiplex
A term used to describe social networks in which members have multiple connections with one another. The opposite of a uniplex network.

pates in multiple networks; our networks are connected through the members that they share, and some of our connections are stronger than others. If your background is in education, you've probably seen social network diagrams used to describe classroom interactions, with lines of varying thicknesses representing the frequency and strength of connections between students.

Social network theory is often used to investigate why people who might share some social characteristic (such as class or region) nevertheless behave differently linguistically, especially with respect to participation in language change. What the Milroys found was that new language features are much slower to take root in **dense** and **multiplex** social networks – those where a few people interact with each other often (the "dense" part) and in multiple ways (the "multiplex" part). If your neighbors are also your friends, and your co-workers, and your in-laws, the intensity and frequency of your contacts with them will reinforce your traditional way of speaking (figure 2.1). In this model, change is brought into the community by people with looser ties, those who work or go to school or hang out elsewhere.

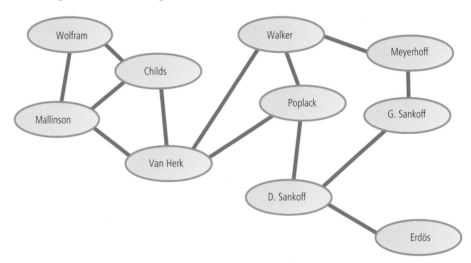

Figure 2.1.   A simple social network diagram. In this case, the links are between people who have co-authored papers.

Although originally developed to investigate how language changes (or doesn't) within a single language (and speech community), social network theory has been useful to investigate how and why people shift from one language to another, for example in immigrant situations, or when a local minority language is in decline. Li (1994) describes a situation in Tyneside, in England, in which Chinese immigrants and their children are far more likely to keep up their Chinese if they are part of a tight local network associated with the True Jesus Church. Edwards (1992) shows that African American Detroiters have higher rates of use of African American English speech features if they participate in local neighborhood culture. And Hoffman and Walker (2010) look at how the children of immigrants in Toronto are less likely to pick up on changes happening in local English if they live and work in enclave communities like Chinatowns.

Compared to the speech community model, which privileges shared knowledge and norms, the social network model allows a larger role for interaction and **speaker agency**, the ability of speakers to control what they do and to make conscious choices. Even further in this direction is the third model, the community of practice (CofP). This idea, adapted from research on social learning (e.g., Lave & Wenger 1991), looks at a smaller analytical domain. A CofP is defined as a group with mutual engagement in a jointly negotiated enterprise, involving (or leading to) a shared repertoire. The best-known application of the idea in sociolinguistics is found in the work of Penelope Eckert (Eckert & McConnell-Ginet 1992), who spent (a lot of) time in a Michigan high school to understand the groups (the *burnouts* and the *jocks*) that formed there, and the coalescing language behavior associated with each (Eckert 1989). In fact, the CofP framework has been especially appropriate for research on adolescents and gender, in situations where participants are actively and collaboratively negotiating their identity and group memberships.

Maybe the idea to take away here is that these three models of linguistically relevant social groupings are **heuristics**, guidelines for how to approach a research problem, and that the thing that you want to study affects your choice of how to conceptualize the "society" end of things. The CofP framework (and, to a lesser extent, social network theory) assumes, more than a speech community model, that group members do a lot of conscious work to build and maintain linguistic identities. These models are especially useful to explain local language behaviors (within small groups).

But how do we start local, as with people in a particular high school developing social meaning around how they pronounce their vowels, and get to vowel changes shared by most of the people in a huge area? This has been a particular concern for researchers looking at widespread language changes. Maybe in some cases, large-scale developments result from large linguistic or social forces that are not related to speaker agency, and that get social meaning only after they hit a certain level of public awareness. Maybe simple contact between dialects is enough for a change to "take" sometimes, and whichever variant is most common in the dialect mix wins out. But CofPs may still play a role in larger changes. As the social meaning of some variants disperses through a community, and as sociolinguistically aware young people age and disperse, the variants may become associated with broader social categories like region or class. If this continues, or spreads outward, then language change will happen as people align themselves with (or in opposition to) these social meanings.

In particular, innovations might spread between communities through **brokers**, people who participate in multiple communities of practice and bring ideas from one into the other. Wenger (1998: 189) describes the job of brokering as "complex. It involves processes of translation, co-ordination and alignment between perspectives. It requires enough legitimacy to influence the development of a practice, mobilise attention and address conflicting interests." In other words, it's not enough to just belong to a community, or to have a bunch of loose ties. You need to have enough clout in your multiple communities or networks that what you bring in from one group catches on with the others. It's interesting that Labov's recent work (in a speech community framework) describes the type of people who influence language change (Labov 2001: 356, 384), and those people sound a lot like Wenger's description of brokers.

speaker agency
The ability of speakers to control what they do and to make conscious choices.

heuristic
Guidelines for how to approach a research problem.

brokers
People who participate in multiple communities of practice and bring ideas from one into the other, that is, people who introduce innovations to their social networks.

Method: Variationist sociolinguistics

As the name implies, variationist sociolinguists like me are interested in linguistic **variation**, roughly defined as "different ways of saying the same thing." For example, most younger speakers of English have more than one verb form that they can use for reporting speech, at least in casual conversation: "He *said*, 'Look! A bee!' and *I'm like*, 'Oh my god! Where?'" Sociolinguists have found that there are distinct linguistic and social constraints on who uses each form, for what purpose, and how often.

Much of our work is **quantitative**, looking at how often people use a particular linguistic feature. Obviously, we can't tell this unless we have a good record of what was actually said, by whom, for what purpose, and so on, and this almost always means that we need sound recordings to do our work. It also means that we need to minimize how much our presence (and recording equipment) is influencing how people talk when we record them.

As in other branches of linguistics, the needs of researchers determine how the research proceeds. But we usually do it something like this:

1. *Find the speech community.* We may investigate our local community, or we may have a specific community in mind, one that can contribute to our knowledge of a particular issue (ethnicity, isolation, etc.). We then find **informants** (also known as **consultants** or participants), people from the speech community who are willing to be recorded. Sometimes these informants are a random sample; sometimes one informant leads us to another, and so on (a "snowball sample").

2. *Collect data.* Investigating variation in language use usually calls for large amounts of fairly natural language. This can come from existing material (such as letters), but often we use **sociolinguistic interviews**, with questions that encourage informants to forget that someone from a university is recording their every word. Time-tested questions include *Were you ever in a situation where you thought, "This is it, I'm going to die"?* and *Did you ever get blamed for something you didn't do?* And,

of course, there are particular questions that work well in each community. Sometimes, we elicit more formal speech by having informants read written passages or word lists.

3. *Analyze the data you collect.* Find a **variable**, something that can be done more than one way in the community. Some variables, such as the differences between vowels, are **gradient**, with a full range of values possible. These are plotted through acoustic analysis, with separate vowel plots developed for each segment of the community (or even for each informant). Other variables, such as the choice between *going to* and *will* for future marking, are **discrete**, with easily distinguishable separate **variants**. These are usually coded for variant and a range of social or linguistic factors.

Consider an example from the Ottawa Intensifier Project's work on online subcultures. The variable that we studied was intensifiers — the words people use before adjectives to mean *very*. We found nearly 10,000 sentences with adjectives, and coded each one for variant used (*very, really, way, so, totally,* etc.). We also coded for factors that might influence the choice of variant: location of adjective in the sentence, type of adjective (physical property, human characteristic, etc.), sex of the informant (where known), and subculture (hip-hop fan, country fan, nerd, etc.). Each sentence ended up looking something like this:

ravmc   That's a really kickass song.

The coding string on the left means that the variant used was *really*, the adjective (*kickass*) occurred in <u>a</u>ttributive position (before a noun) and was a <u>v</u>alue judgment, and the sentence was written by a <u>m</u>ale <u>c</u>ountry fan. When we examined which variants went with which factors, we found really nice variation depending on gender and subculture (for example, tween girls are definitely leading a change toward the use of *so*). We also found shared linguistic factors, no matter who was using a variant (for example, hardly anyone used *so* when the adjective was before a noun, as in *That was a so cool movie*).

Linguists use the principle of mutual intelligibility to distinguish a language from a dialect, but speakers and governments may apply different criteria. Sociolinguists label distinct subsets of a language as dialects or varieties, reserving terms like slang or accent for specific linguistic domains. We study language in use, at the level of the social group. Depending on our research interests and assumptions, we may define the social group as a speech community, social network, or community of practice, each of which implies a greater level of speaker agency in linguistic interactions.

Where to next?

There are two big (and possibly competing) pulls in how sociolinguists consider language use these days. One approach, which we might label the telescope view, uses quantitative methods (and improving technology) to conduct large-scale studies of large data sets. People using this approach, influenced by the growing discipline of corpus linguistics, work to develop statistical methods, automated data extraction and analysis, and database building methods. This approach is especially well suited to investigating language changes that are widespread or that occur over a long period of time. Another approach, which we could call the microscope view, uses mostly qualitative methods to conduct small-scale, intensive studies of particular communities of practice. People using this approach, influenced by anthropology, work to develop conversation analysis tools and to identify locally significant social distinctions. There's some hope, though, that the two approaches can work together. For example, the (telescope) Ottawa Intensifier Project found quantitative evidence that nerds, in particular, actively distance themselves linguistically from other youth subcultures, confirming the findings of Bucholtz's (1999) well-known (microscope) study of nerd girls in high school.

corpus linguistics
A linguistic research method based on the quantitative analysis of collections of naturally occurring language data, usually very large.

qualitative
Usually smaller-scale intensive research, using methods like interviewing and ethnography, that aims to study meanings and motivation, rather than large-scale quantitative frequencies or correlations.

conversation analysis
Among other things, this method looks at the sequential organization of conversation and how participants manage the conversation using strategies like turn-taking.

1. Ask people if they can think of any inside jokes, things that only make sense (or are funny) to a small group of people who know the "back story." These might include strange definitions, things that refer back to a particular event, or unusual pronunciations of a word (for some reason, lots of families seem to have at least one of these that results from how somebody in the family pronounced something when they were very young). Write them down; look for common traits among the things people tell you.

2. Using whatever source you like (or that your prof is OK with), such as scholarly journals, the internet, or talking to somebody from one of the communities involved, seek out descriptions of

(or opinions about) similarities and differences between the language varieties in one of the following groups:

(a)   Serbian, Croatian, Bosnian

(b)   Russian, Ukrainian, Belarusian

(c)   Hindi, Urdu

(d)   Danish, Swedish, Norwegian

(e)   Swiss German, Standard German

(f)   Canadian or Louisiana French, French from France

(g)   Haitian Creole, French

(h)   Jamaican Creole ("patwa"), British English

(i)   standard Arabic, local Arabic

Write down or record what you find. Did your source include value judgments – of either a language variety or its speakers? What do you conclude about how a social situation influences the status assigned to the language varieties involved?

3.   Use an internet search engine (such as Google) to see how many hits you get for each of the following phrases (put them in quotation marks):

(a)   "European languages"

(b)   "European dialects"

(c)   "African languages"

(d)   "African dialects"

For each continent, calculate the ratio of "language" to "dialect" references (divide European languages hits by European dialects hits, and divide African languages hits by African dialects hits). Which continent's language varieties get called "languages" more often? Care to guess why?

4.   Sociolinguists look outside our field for many ideas about how social groups work. Read (Wikipedia will do) about one of the major concepts discussed in this chapter (social identity, social network, community of practice) to get a sense of how it's discussed outside sociolinguistics. Does what you read help you understand the ideas in this chapter? Or does it just get messier?

5.   Not every community or network qualifies as a community of practice. In your opinion, which of the following do?

(a)   a group of engineers working on similar problems

(b)   the people who gather to smoke outside your school or workplace

(c)   people who have lived on the same block for many years

(d)   students in a residence

(e)   a network of surgeons exploring novel techniques

(f)   a group of education students who meet on a plane trip and discuss teaching

(g)   a youth gang

(h)   a "stitch and bitch" group

6.   Compare and contrast at least three different definitions of *speech community* (e.g., Bloomfield 1926; Gumperz 1968; Hymes 1972; Labov 1972b; Santa Ana & Parodi 1998). How might these definitions relate to what you consider to be your own speech community?

discussion

1. Have you ever been in a situation where you were speaking to somebody with a different dialect or accent, and you just couldn't understand each other? How did you deal with the situation?
2. What speech community/communities, social network(s), and community/communities of practice do you belong to? Are there any social groups that you belong to that might affect your language, but don't qualify as classic examples of any of these group types?
3. Introducing linguistic innovations seems to be mostly the job of brokers (in CofP terminology), people with loose or weak ties (in social networks terminology). In the circles you move in, who might qualify? How much do *you* move back and forth between communities? Would you be a good broker? Why, or why not?
4. Starting university is a time of developing new networks and communities, even new identities, and there are presumably linguistic consequences. This is especially salient for people who go to university in a different town. Often on their first trip "back home," students are told by the locals that their speech has changed, so they end up doing a sort of dialect switching, with varying levels of success. (In fact, sociolinguists may try to avoid recording these people, assuming that university time has messed up the regularity of their speech.) Has this happened to you, or to people you know? What happened? Can you think of other, parallel situations (maybe joining the military, or a new church, or starting a new job)?
5. A few of us have been talking lately about another idea from sociology: **communities of choice**. We assume that people have more control over their community membership(s) than they used to, partly due to social and geographic mobility, but also thanks to the internet, which lets you find or build communities not restricted by place. Do you think technological advances have changed our idea of what counts as a community? If so, how? And would you expect these changes to have linguistic consequences?
6. Can any of the three models of social organization – speech community, social networks, communities of practice – be applied to bilingual groups? Would they need to be adapted? How might your answer change depending on the kind of bilingual group you were thinking of?

communities of choice
Communities that people choose to belong to, as opposed to communities of circumstance.

other resources

For expanded discussions of *speech community*, *social networks*, and *community of practice*, see the relevant chapters in *The Handbook of Language Variation and Change* (2002) edited by J. K. Chambers, Peter Trudgill, and Natalie Schilling-Estes.

There are book-length treatments of speech community (Labov's *The Social Stratification of English in New York City*, 1966), social network (Milroy's *Language and Social Networks*, 1980), and community of practice (Eckert's *Linguistic Variation as Social Practice*, 2000).

For a guide to the methods of the kind of variationist research that I do, try Tagliamonte's *Analysing Sociolinguistic Variation* (2006).

For a look at how many sociolinguists feel about the introspective methods of mainstream linguistics, read "The linguist as lame," pp. 290–4 of Labov's *Language in the Inner City: Studies in the Black English Vernacular* (1972a).

For a short, readable background of communities of practice, try Penelope (Penny) Eckert's home page, at http://www.stanford.edu/~eckert/csofp.html (accessed August 17, 2011).

3 Place

Once I was hitchhiking in northeastern West Virginia, and I got a lift from a family with very strong local accents. We chatted as we drove along, and I found I had to work really hard to follow the conversation. After a while, the dad said to me, "You're not from 'round here, are you?" I confessed that I was, in fact, a Canadian. "I thought so," he said. "You sure talk funny." And he was right. If we had been in Canada, of course, then *he* would have been the one who talked funny.

how regional differences develop

Geographical location is probably the most-studied social factor affecting language variation (and really, any study of a speech community implies a physical location). If it's true that we talk *like* who we talk *with*, it makes good sense that we share linguistic features with our neighbors. But how did we end up sounding so different in some places (like neighboring valleys in Switzerland or Newfoundland), and so alike in others

What Is Sociolinguistics?, First Edition. Gerard Van Herk.
© 2012 Gerard Van Herk. Published 2012 by Blackwell Publishing Ltd.

(like across about 3,000 miles of central and western Canada)? The forces that contribute to distinct dialects include varying points of origin, migration, linguistic and dialect contact, and isolation.

english, for example

The story of English (or Englishes) offers a quick look at how regional linguistic diversity can develop. In Europe, where much early dialect study was done, countries long settled by speakers of the same language have had the time to develop distinct regional varieties. These varieties reflect settlement patterns that are often over a thousand years old. For example, the major traditional dialect areas of England pretty much match the areas conquered and settled by different groups – Angles, Saxons, and Jutes – about 1,500 years ago. In effect, English was regionally variable from the start, as those groups brought over related but distinct Germanic dialects from northern Europe. Toss in influence from the Norse, who settled/conquered the northeastern half of England; the French-speaking Norman conquerors, who replaced the Saxon upper classes (and a lot of vocabulary) with their own; and the speakers of Welsh, Scottish, and (later) Irish Gaelic, who colored the language of their conquerors with features of their original languages, and you get a Britain with a lot of regional diversity. On top of that (sociologically speaking), impose the increasing and outward-spreading influence of the variety spoken in the political and educational center of the country, and by about the year 1600 you're well on the way to the complex regional and social mix that, over time, exported itself through colonization, trade, and cultural weight to a large part of the world.

Ireland's first English speakers were Norman invaders in the late 1100s, within an area in the east known as the Pale (thus the expression "beyond the Pale"). In the 1500s and early 1600s, more English speakers arrived through land confiscation, and English slowly spread westward, still heavily influenced by Irish Gaelic. In Scotland, the local variety of English, often called Scots, was so distinct that some researchers believe it would have eventually become a separate language if not for the political union of Scotland and England in the 1600s. Newfoundland, England's oldest North American colony, was settled by fishermen from southwestern England (the "West Country") and southeastern Ireland. Caribbean Englishes (or the creoles that predate or influence them) began to develop at about the same period from contact between African slaves and Europeans from roughly the same areas that settled Newfoundland.

In the USA, the New England area was settled largely by people from East Anglia (figure 3.1). People who settled along the coast farther south came mostly from the south of England; their African slaves were exposed to that variety of English, and in many cases to Caribbean varieties as well. Later arrivals in America, who moved into the inland Appalachian area, came largely from the north of England and from northern Ireland (sometimes known as Scots-Irish). In each area, each group of settlers introduced the speech patterns of their home areas. Presumably some mixing took place;

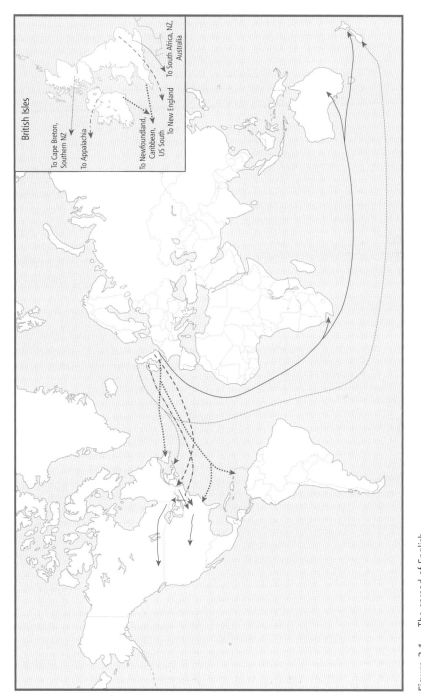

British Isles

To Cape Breton, Southern NZ

To Appalachia

To Newfoundland, Caribbean, US South

To New England

To South Africa, NZ, Australia

Figure 3.1.   The spread of English.

dialect leveling
The process by which the regional features of the speech of a group of people converges toward a common norm over time.

perhaps some of the differences between dialects were worn down over time, a process known as **dialect leveling**.

By the time of the American Revolution, 1776–83, three major dialect areas had developed in the eastern USA: a Northern variety in New England and the Hudson valley, the Midland dialect of Pennsylvania, and the Southern dialect. These varieties were already becoming distinct from British English and from each other. After the revolution, Americans who remained loyal to Britain moved north, bringing their dialects (especially Midland and New England) to what would later become eastern Canada. As waves of English-speaking settlers moved westward, they took their dialects with them. The dialect of central Canada spread across the Prairies; the three major American dialects spread west, blurring and merging as they went, so that dialect maps of North America show a "fanning out" from the east, and a general mixed dialect in the western USA (figure 3.2).

As an aside: Dialect leveling

New Zealand English, which was formed more recently than North American varieties and thus can be studied through archival recordings, sheds some light on how dialect leveling works (Trudgill 2004). Researchers there describe a three-stage process: the original settler generations kept their home dialects, the next generation chose somewhat randomly from all the linguistic options available, and the third generation leveled out the diversity in favor of the most frequent variant in most cases. Probably something similar happened in North America, centuries before dialectologists and tape recorders were around to document it.

The southern British colonies – Australia, New Zealand, and South(ern) Africa – were settled by English speakers later, mostly in the 1800s and largely from southern England, including a large Cockney component (especially for Australia). Despite their shorter English-speaking histories and similar English-speaking immigrant groups, each of these three varieties of English has developed distinct features, perhaps partly due to relative isolation from other varieties.

These areas together comprise what the linguist Braj Kachru (1985) has described as the **inner circle** of English, places where English is an official language and the first language of most people. In the **outer circle**, we find countries where English is historically important as the result of colonial history and plays an institutional role, including former British colonies in Africa (Nigeria, Kenya, Tanzania) and South Asia (India, Pakistan, Bangladesh), as well as the Philippines and the non-English-speaking areas of Canada and South Africa. In these places, other languages also play a large role in public life, and English is not the first language of the majority. In the **expanding circle**, we find countries like China where English doesn't have an official role, but is still widely spoken, as a foreign language, to tourists, or as a shared language of communication.

As an aside: The r-ful truth about American English

A good example of colonial-era variation is "r-lessness" (which makes British English *far* sound like *fah* to most North Americans). By 1776, r-lessness was spreading across the south of England, and this was reflected in North American patterns. New England and the coastal South were settled by British immigrants from the south of England and maintained social and economic ties with England, so they were r-less (and, to some extent, still are). Other North American dialects were (and still are) "r-ful" (also called **rhotic**), reflecting their settlement from parts of Britain that r-lessness hadn't yet reached and their lack of sustained contact with (southern) England.

rhotic
A term used to describe English dialects in which the /r/ following a vowel is pronounced. Also known as *r-ful*.

Sociolinguists who work on language variation usually focus on inner circle varieties (partly because we assume that the linguistic regularity of non-standard varieties grows

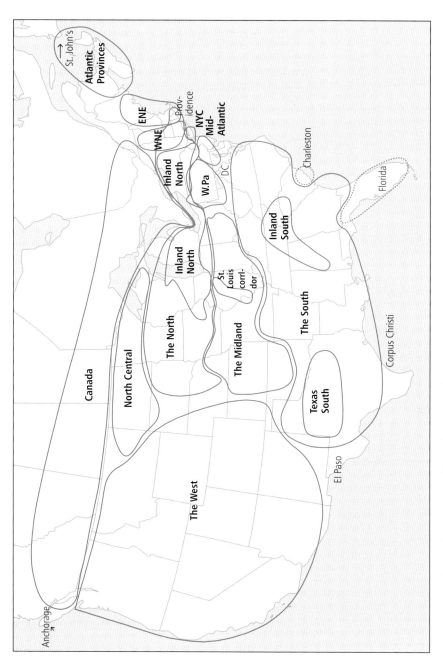

Figure 3.2.   Major North American English dialect areas (Labov et al. 2006).

out of native-speaker competence). Sociolinguists who work on the role of language in society, though, are more likely to include the outer and expanding circles. They may have a point – although historically it makes sense to think of English as a thing from England that spread to a bunch of colonies and then around the world, a look at the number of people speaking English today suggests a different balance. There are probably more people speaking English (at least sometimes) in the outer and expanding circles than in the inner circle, and within the inner circle over two thirds of all English speakers are in a single country, the USA.

In the inner circle countries, even in the middle of great change, the dialect distinctions laid down over the centuries remain strong today. For example, the geographic boundaries of the (fairly recent) Northern Cities Shift, described in more detail in chapter 5, are fairly close to those described by dialect geographers of past generations (Labov et al. 2006).

english worldwide: linguistic features

I'm always impressed by people who can accurately identify a speaker's origin from a tiny sample of speech. (Many of these people are fictional and/or British, such as George Bernard Shaw's Henry Higgins, who says "I can place any man within six miles. I can place him within two miles in London. Sometimes within two streets.") Although some claims may be exaggerated, there are clearly real-world speech characteristics associated with different regions.

The highly simplified list in table 3.1 demonstrates a few distinct features of the more or less Standard variety of each region's English. A few things to note:

- I often describe a variety by how it differs from its closest neighbor or relative, because that's easier.
- I'm usually describing tendencies – not everybody in the USA says "different than."
- I use **lexical sets** (Wells 1982; and see table 3.2), in which a term like "the STRUT vowel" is shorthand for "all the words that in most varieties of English are pronounced with the same vowel as in the word *strut*."
- Unless your prof tells you otherwise, you probably shouldn't try to memorize all these distinctions. Just try saying the things out loud, to see if you recognize them or use them in your own English.

lexical set
A way of identifying vowels using a set of words in which they occur as opposed to a linguistic symbol.

As you read through this list, you might have thought, "What? You mean there are people who *don't* say all these things that I take for granted?" (It's happened to me – once while listening to a sociolinguistics conference paper, I learned that not all English speakers call an art opening a *vernissage*.) On the other hand, you might have thought, "Hey, I'm not from that place, but I say those things!" Given the partly shared histories of these language varieties, and the increase in social and regional mobility over the years, this would make sense. On the other hand, people are proud of their region, and appear to be increasingly willing to use local features to resist the globalization of language.

Table 3.1. English worldwide.

region	pronunciation	grammar	lexicon
New World			
USA (non-Southern)	mostly "r-ful"; often keep the THOUGHT and PALM word classes distinct (though how they're actually pronounced varies widely by region)	prefer the simple past (*I already ate*) in some places where British Englishes prefer the present perfect (*I have already eaten*); avoid *shall*; use *different than*	see exercise 1 below
USA (Southern)	pronounce MOUTH and many PRICE words as **monophthongs**, so that *crowd* and *mine* sound like *crahd* and *mahn*; the final vowel in happY is similar to the final vowel in commA, as when Elvis pronounces *baby* as "bay-buh"	second person plural pronoun *y'all*; for many speakers, double modal verbs, as in *I might could do that*; *fixin' to* to mark future verbs	*stealing sugar* (baby-snuggling), *heap of* (a lot of)
Canada	often similar to (non-Southern) American, but merge THOUGHT and PALM word classes, so that *caught* and *cot* sound the same (also found in the western USA, and apparently spreading); and **Canadian Raising** – pronounce some MOUTH words (linguists: the ones before voiceless consonants) different from others (so that Americans think Canadians say *oot and aboot* for *out and about*)	basically a mix of British and American usages	*acclamation* (elected without opposition), *riding* (political district)
Caribbean	mix of r-less and r-ful countries; monophthongize FACE and GOAT (see "Scotland"); "stopped" /th/ (*that thing* as *dat ting*) more socially widespread than in other Englishes	we all argue about whether to describe Caribbean English grammatical features as creole or not – so see chapter 11	*suck-teeth* (like tsk, tsk on steroids), *cut-eye* (disapproving sweeping gaze)
Old World			
England	mostly r-less; mostly distinguish THOUGHT and PALM (although with pronunciations of each that are different from what Americans do); happY final vowel similar to US Southern; in the north, STRUT and FOOT merge	use *shall, whilst, different from*	see exercise 1 below

monophthongs
A pure vowel sound, spoken in a single place of articulation, with no change in quality, for example, *bat* as opposed to *bite*.

Canadian Raising
A phonological process found in Canadian English (and some other varieties), in which the MOUTH and PRICE vowels (see table 3.2) are pronounced differently when preceding a voiceless consonant in the same syllable, in words like *hike* and *stout*.

Table 3.1.   (*Continued*)

region	pronunciation	grammar	lexicon
Scotland	r-ful; distinguish *wh* words (like *whale*) from *w* words (like *wail*); merge THOUGHT and PALM word classes; monophthongize FACE and GOAT vowels (non-linguists: something like *fehss* and *goht*)	*needs washed* for *needs to be washed*; wider use of *-ing* (*I'm needing some help*)	*wee* (small), *bairn* (child)
Ireland	as for Scotland (although it's a different R); plus, in the south, "clear" /l/ (the /l/ in *pill* is pronounced with the tongue farther forward), "slit fricative" /t/ (so that *get* is a bit like *getch*); in the north, "palatalized" /k/ and /g/ (so that *garden* is a bit like *gyarden*)	*I'm after eating* for *I have just eaten*; in the south, *does be eating* for *regularly eats*	*soft day* (drizzly day), *craic/crack* (good times)
Southern Hemisphere			
Australia	r-less; distinct FACE and MOUTH (so that *mate* sounds a bit like *might*, *mouth* a bit like *math*); KIT a bit like other varieties' FLEECE (*feesh and cheeps*)	close to England – perhaps more often use *different to*	*outback* (remote area), *g'day* (hello)
New Zealand	r-less in most areas; KIT a bit like other varieties' commA (*fush and chups*), DRESS near others' FACE or KIT, TRAP near others' DRESS; NEAR and SQUARE vowels are merging (so that *beer* and *bear* sound the same)	close to England	*togs* (swimwear), *kia ora* ('hello', from Maori, literally "be healthy")
South Africa	r-less; KIT, DRESS, and TRAP close to New Zealand	close to England	*bakkie* (pickup truck), *robot* (traffic light)

For example, in Newfoundland, younger speakers seem to be building a local identity through traditional grammar and pronunciation features (Van Herk et al. 2008). And in nearby Cape Breton Island, young men are adopting a pronunciation of word-final /t/ that in the past has been associated with local older women (Parris 2009). This kind of expansion of the social range of a local feature is also described for young Cajun men in Louisiana by Dubois and Horvath (1999).

Table 3.2. Lexical sets.

lexical set	examples	lexical set	examples
KIT	ship, big, dim	THOUGHT	taut, awe, broad
DRESS	fret, ebb, hem	GOAT	moat, soul, home
TRAP	bad, cab, spam	GOOSE	who, group, tune
LOT	stop, rob, swan	PRICE	ride, tribe, fine
STRUT	cub, rub, hum	CHOICE	boy, void, coin
FOOT	full, look, could	MOUTH	out, noun, crowd
BATH	staff, clasp, dance	NEAR	beer, fear, fierce
CLOTH	cough, long, gone	SQUARE	care, bear, fair
NURSE	hurt, nerd, work	START	star, harp, farm
FLEECE	seed, key, please	NORTH	war, core, form
FACE	freight, train, steak	FORCE	floor, coarse, bore
PALM	calm, bra, father	CURE	poor, tour, sure

Note: Wells (1982) describes varieties of English by referring to word groups, or lexical sets. Although different varieties of English may have different ways of pronouncing a particular vowel, pretty well all of them will pronounce all the words with the "same" vowel (from a speaker's perspective) in the same way. So "the KIT vowel," in this sense, means "the vowel in all the words that you pronounce with the same vowel as in the word *kit*." In this table, the word in capitals is the name that Wells gives to each lexical set, while the words in the "examples" columns are from that set, sometimes with very different spellings of the vowel sound.

physical isolation
A dialect or language can be physically or geographically isolated from others, for example, by being on an island.

linguistic isolation
When speakers of a dialect or language are cut off from other varieties and have retained older features, so that their variety has developed differently from their sister ones.

isolation

Speech communities that are isolated in some way often preserve older ways of speaking, just as they might preserve traditional music or farming methods. The isolation involved can be **physical**, isolated from *everybody*; **linguistic**, isolated from speakers of the same or a similar language; or **social**, isolated by conventions or attitudes. These communities can act as a sort of linguistic "time machine" for us – as long as we're cautious enough to remember that even isolated speech communities change over time, perhaps in ways very different from mainstream speech.

social isolation
A dialect or language can be socially isolated by conventions or attitudes, for example, by class or race prejudice.

physical isolation: the case of newfoundland english

Newfoundland was settled very early, by North American standards; its settlers came largely from two clearly defined areas (southwestern England and southeastern Ireland); most immigration occurred before the mid-1800s; and the island is a long way from other heavily populated areas. As a result, Newfoundland English has retained many

As an aside: Shibboleths

When the pronunciation of a single word becomes a stereotype of a speech community, as with *b'y* in Newfoundland, linguists call it a **shibboleth**. Many varieties of English have their own shibboleths: Jamaicans supposedly always say *mon* for *man*; Pittsburghers say *dahntahn* for *downtown*; Canadians say *oot and aboot*. In fact, many Newfoundlanders do say *b'y* (from *boy*, which is pronounced something like *bye* in the local dialect). It's a marker of solidarity in casual speech (in the same way that many Jamaicans, among others, use *man*).

In fact, shibboleths can often be reclaimed by their speakers and turned into markers of local identity (like *dahntahn* and *b'y*). Many speakers of Irish English, for example, pronounce *idiot* as *eejit*, although they probably wouldn't pronounce *idiom* as *eejom*. In effect, *eejit* has become a separate word from *idiot* for those speakers, with its own special meaning.

shibboleth
When the pronunciation of a single word becomes a stereotype of a speech community, such as Jamaicans supposedly saying *mon* for *man*.

after perfect
A grammatical means of describing a (usually recent) completed event in Irish (and consequently Newfoundland) English.

distinct speech features that have disappeared or diminished elsewhere. Of equal interest to linguists, individual communities in Newfoundland were often isolated from each other, and were settled by people from only one of the two input populations, so that Newfoundland English is not only distinct compared to other North American varieties, but also highly regionally variable within Newfoundland itself (Schneider 2005).

Several features of the dialect are widely known outside Newfoundland. Many mainland Canadians – comedians, for example – believe they can "sound like a Newfoundlander" by adding the word *b'y* to the end of every utterance.

There are other pronunciation features that traditional Newfoundland English speakers do more than other Canadians: pronouncing /th/ sounds like [t] or [d] (so that *that thing* sounds like *dat ting*), deleting *h* at the beginning of words ('*Olyrood* for *Holyrood*), and deleting the final consonant in a cluster of them (*pos'* for *post*).

Newfoundland English also retains some of the distinct grammar brought over by the original settlers. Location can be marked with phrase final prepositions, as in the often quoted *Stay where you're to till I comes where you're* at. Object pronouns can use subject forms, as in *They see we*. The plural *-s* suffix is sometimes absent, as in *two pound*, and the verbal *-s* suffix is found with a range of subjects: *I goes, you goes, all the people goes*. This salient feature has surfaced recently on Newfoundland t-shirts (figure 3.3). Many Newfoundlanders also use the **after perfect**, saying *I'm after doing it* for *I have just done it*.

Figure 3.3. In Newfoundland, the verbal suffix *-s* appears in many places, including with first person subjects and on t-shirts.

The *Dictionary of Newfoundland English* lists thousands of distinct Newfoundland lexical items. Many are regionally restricted, near-obsolete, or associated with particular industries (http://www.heritage.nf.ca/dictionary, accessed August 17, 2011). Some nautical terms have spread into broader use, such as *gaff* to mean *steal*. Others describe specifically Newfoundland phenomena: *slob ice* is loose chunks of ice floating on the surface of the water; *glitter* is a shiny coating of freezing rain, and *scruncheons* are glorious bits of crisp-fried salt pork fat, used as a garnish.

Newfoundland English has retained so many older features that linguists are now beginning to use it in comparative work. Scholars of Irish and southwestern Englishes look to Newfoundland English for evidence of earlier stages of those varieties (Clarke 2004). And the historical and linguistic parallels with Caribbean creoles and African American English may shed light on how those varieties developed.

linguistic isolation: the case of québec french

Québec French is so distinct, and so filled with interesting variation, that it is actually one of the language varieties most studied by sociolinguists. In fact, several major theoretical concepts in sociolinguistics have been developed through work on this variety (Sankoff & Laberge 1978; and see chapter 4).

Like Newfoundland English, Québec French is a good example of how isolated language varieties can retain older features of a language, while undergoing some language changes of their own. Until 1763, the linguistic history of New France was remarkably similar to that of Newfoundland – early settlement from specific regions of Europe (especially northwestern France) to an area far away, and a sudden cessation of immigration. For more than two centuries, however, French in North America has been isolated linguistically, rather than physically. The metaphor of an island of French surrounded by a sea of English is often heard, and English influence is sometimes invoked to explain why the French spoken in Québec (and elsewhere in Canada) is different from the European standard variety.

Certainly some English words have been borrowed into Québec French. A restaurant in Québec might give you a *bill* (rather than a *facture*) for your order of *bines* ('beans') and *toast* (rather than *feves* or *haricots* and *roties*). On the other hand, Québecers park in a *terrain de stationnement*, while in France they use the English loan word *parking*. And people in both Québec and France look forward to *le weekend*. Other distinct Québec French forms reflect retention of older forms (*archaïsmes*), such as *flambe* for 'flame' (rather than the European *flamme*). In some cases, words have developed distinct meanings in Québec French. These include *traversier*, which means 'ferry' in Québec and 'crossing' in France; *ma blonde*, which means 'my girlfriend' in Québec and 'my blonde' in France; and *dépanneur*, which means 'repairman' in France but 'convenience store' in Québec (in both French and English).

Some grammatical differences observed in Canadian French, although sometimes attributed to contact with English, seem to represent either processes that started centuries ago, or the kind of change that can happen without language contact. For example, recently unearthed early recordings by folklorists show that the loss of *ne* in casual speech, as when people say *Je sais pas* instead of *Je ne sais pas* for 'I don't know', was widespread even among speakers born as early as 1846. Some differences between Québec French and France French may reflect differences in social structure rather than region, such as when Québecers use the informal *tu* (rather than formal *vous*) ('you') in more contexts (more on that in chapter 9).

As a Québecer visiting Paris for the first time, I quickly realized how many pronunciation features of my French were distinctive. I pronounced *père* ('father') like *pyre*, not *pair*. I pronounced *poule* ('hen') more like *pull* than *pool*. I pronounced *oui* ('yes') like *way*, not *wee*. Most noticeable of all, I pronounced /t/ and /d/ as [ts] and [dz] before some vowels, so that I said *tsu dzis* where they said *tu dis* ('you say'). Well, actually, most of them said *vous dites*, and considered my use of *tu* a bit over-friendly. They also wondered how *ma blonde* could have dark hair.

Linguistic isolates are more common than you might think. Around the world, languages and language varieties, cut off from their sources, have kept older features and developed along their own paths. In the Dominican Republic, the African American community of Samaná has spoken English since 1824, surrounded by Spanish speakers. Western Louisiana preserves Acadian French. Mennonite communities in North America speak an earlier form of German. And in Turkey, the descendants of Jews who fled the Spanish Inquisition five centuries ago still speak a form of medieval Spanish (Gordon 2005). We also see a weaker and shorter-lived version of linguistic isolation in immigrant neighborhoods, whose members often find when revisiting their original homelands that language has moved on without them.

social isolation: the case of african nova scotian english

After the American Revolution and again after the War of 1812, groups of African Americans who had fought for the British settled in Canada's Maritime provinces. Some moved on, to found Freetown in Sierra Leone, and some eventually integrated into the surrounding White communities. Several communities remained separate, however. The best-known of these is North Preston, near Dartmouth, Nova Scotia, which to this day is populated almost entirely by descendants of those original African American settlers. The community remained separated from the surrounding communities by limited road and transportation services and by racial segregation (some Nova Scotia schools remained segregated until 1964). When older Preston residents were interviewed in the early 1990s, many retained distinct speech features that their ancestors had presumably brought to Canada with them. These included features widespread in

African American English in the USA, such as deletion of the copula, or *be* word (as in *he gonna go*). They also used older English forms not found in most contemporary North American English, Black or White, such as verbal *-s* marking (*I goes*). Researchers found similar forms in the speech of people in the social isolate of North Preston, the linguistic isolate of Samaná, and 70-year-old recordings from former American slaves (Poplack & Tagliamonte 2001). Not only that, but the linguistic factors influencing the forms were similar, suggesting that the language of these isolated communities was living evidence of the African American English of earlier centuries.

the social meaning of space

Contemporary sociolinguists are developing different ways to think of space. For example, we borrow ideas from cultural geographers to distinguish between physical distance and social perceptions of distance. Some places seem "closer" because we can easily travel there thanks to highways, or the routes followed by airlines, buses, or ferries. For example, the Northern Cities Shift, a vowel change which mostly affects cities in the American Midwest, seems to be creeping down Interstate 55 to St. Louis. And some linguistic innovations, especially in Britain, seem to spread first from big city to big city, "jumping over" intervening small towns, and only later diffuse into the surrounding regions. This makes sense if you think of the innovations in a social networks framework – maybe lots of loose ties between cities (football fans, club-goers, students) lead to easy transmission of features between those same cities. This also suggests that people in cities might see themselves as urban first and inhabitants of their region second, and that might have interesting social implications. But it also represents a new way for language change to spread, compared to past centuries. Back then, innovative language features seem to have spread outward, usually from a high-prestige urban area, like waves (some of the variability found in North American English originally resulted from people immigrating in the middle of a wave of British language change).

In many cases, physical and social barriers encourage residents to remain within (and thus speak with) their own community. In Petty Harbour, a small Newfoundland town where my colleagues and I are doing research (Childs et al. 2011), the north side of the harbor used to be Irish Catholic, and the south side was English Anglican, and there were even different paths into town depending on your religion. In Montréal, the neigh-borhoods of Westmount (wealthy, English) and St-Henri (working-class, French) are separated by train tracks (as in the expression "wrong side of the tracks"), a highway, and a hill, encouraging the persistence of two linguistic solitudes. In Detroit, if you refer to Eight Mile Road, locals know that you're describing a racial boundary, not just a piece of asphalt. It's interesting that this particular barrier is sociological, not physical (as in, there are no physical barriers to crossing the road). Perhaps because of that, people need to talk about and name the boundary, so that community members are aware of the sanctions against crossing.

David Britain's (1991) work in the Fens, in eastern England, shows how social and physical ideas of space can interact to affect language. The towns of Wisbech and King's Lynn are only 22 km (14 miles) apart, but several traditional pronunciation and grammar features persist in King's Lynn, but not in Wisbech. The boundary between old and new features runs roughly halfway between the two towns (figure 3.4). Britain shows how people on the old-features side of this boundary are linked to King's Lynn for work, shopping, and entertainment (as also reflected by the local bus routes), while those on the new-features side are linked in the same ways to Wisbech. Interactions between these two networks are also blocked by rivers, drainage channels, and negative stereotypes of each other.

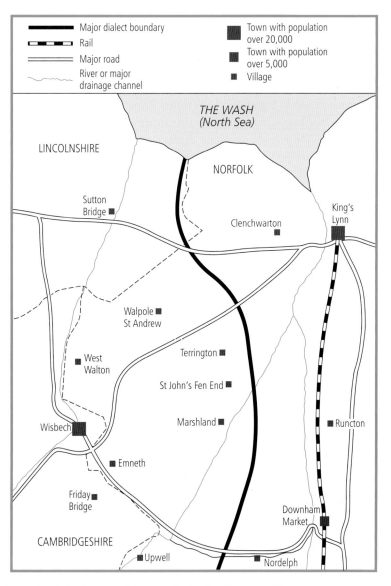

Figure 3.4.   Boundaries between dialect areas in the Fens (Britain 2002).

Social factors influence not just our perceptions of distance, but also how we think about place itself. When people talk about a place (including its language), they often mean a collection of social characteristics, not just a physical location. Look at the term *Cockney*, used for hundreds of years to describe the inhabitants of a region and the language they speak. It technically refers only to central London (within the sound of the bells of the Bow church, some say), but it has strong social connotations – urban, working-class, low-prestige, street-smart. And these connotations have been around for a while – even back in 1803, when Joshua Pegge wrote the amazing but little-known *Anecdotes of the English Language: Dialect of London* about Cockney, some reviewers assumed that the book was a joke. Why would anyone write about the historical pedigree and internal logic of *Cockney*?

The same attribution of social meanings to places is found today. At the local level, you can probably name neighborhoods in your hometown that have particular class or ethnic or linguistic associations. Some social scientists say that neighborhood is a better indicator of where you fit into the social system than class is, given that neighborhoods often gather together people who share multiple social traits. Notice, for example, that junk mail is different in different neighborhoods, as advertisers

> ## As an aside: Imaginary dialects
>
> One way that the social meaning of place can have socio-linguistic implications is that if people feel that a particular place is different enough, then they think that it must be linguistically different, as well. If you ask Barbadians about differences in speech, they'll tell you that people in the parish of St. Lucy sound different . . . probably because St. Lucy is the farthest from the capital, and is very rural. But if you record Barbadians from different areas, the dialect that actually sounds different is from St. Andrew (which was originally settled by many people from Scotland). Some New Zealanders will tell you that there's a distinct accent in Southland, the most southerly area of the country. That may have been true in earlier generations, but younger Southlanders today sound much like other New Zealanders (Meyerhoff 2006).
>
> Another imaginary dialect idea is that isolated varieties sound *exactly* like earlier languages, rather than just retaining some features. Media people are in love with this idea, occasionally doing crazy stuff like getting people in coastal North Carolina to read Shakespeare for the cameras.

target a particular "kind" of person. Differences between neighborhoods are reinforced by economic and political phenomena, such as the location of gated communities, subsidized housing, or the catchment area of schools. In fact, given that high school is such a time of identity creation and affirmation, the high school you attend often proclaims a great deal about both your neighborhood and your social status. So when Elvis Presley gave his first interview on Memphis radio in 1954, R&B DJ Dewey Phillips made sure to ask him which high school he went to, so that listeners would know that he was white.

Recently, dialect scholars have taken greater interest in how regional language identities are **reified** (made into a "thing") through a process they call **enregisterment** (Agha 2003). How is it that the language features that make up (say) "Pittsburghese" first are not noticed at all, then are seen as class features, and then eventually become a way of showing that you're from Pittsburgh? Johnstone (2009: 159) traces the "process by which particular linguistic forms become linked with 'social' meaning" in this context through such things as t-shirts featuring local language or sayings. Regional identity (including regional language) is often built up through cultural products (mugs, shirts, joke books, dialect dictionaries aimed at the general public, websites, bumper stickers), affiliations with a particular sports team (*Rider Pride*, *Toon Army*, *Steeler Nation*) and against their hated rivals, and naming practices. *Scouse, Yooper, Caper*, and other such names describe

reified
Made into a concrete thing.

enregisterment
A process through which a linguistic feature or repertoire becomes a socially recognized register.

the inhabitants and language of recognized regions, but the names themselves act to make that perception of region part of local discourse.

Of course, studying enregisterment as it happens implies that the regions or language varieties involved *didn't* previously have a distinct identity, and so maybe the successful products of enregisterment work precisely because the target audience is hungry for validation. A nice example of this is found in the "I am Canadian" commercials (1994–8) for Molson breweries. The first, best-known commercial features a podium speaker who dismisses supposed stereotypes of Canadians (including rejecting outdated dialect features), then boasts (to an ironically overblown soundtrack) of Canada's good points, almost all of them through contrast (direct or implied) with the USA. The commercial was extremely successful when first issued, getting ovations at hockey games, and still provokes rabid discussion on YouTube sites.

Distinct regional and national varieties (the things most people think of as "dialects") presumably first acquired much of their social meanings during urbanization and associated population movements. Language varieties that had been left alone to develop their own distinct personalities for generations were suddenly brought into contact, as poor workers from rural areas and other countries moved into cities looking for work.

These groups started at the bottom of the social scale in their new homes, and their distinct language features marked them out for discrimination and the negative connotations applied to low-prestige varieties everywhere. In America, the lower status of Southern varieties after the Civil War was reinforced as Appalachian, Ozark, and African American job seekers migrated northward and westward in the early twentieth century. Irish English was associated with the desperate migration in the early nineteenth century, when millions of rural Irish ended up at the bottom of the social ladder in eastern North America. In Greece, the early twentieth century saw the influx to Athens of Greek speakers from Asia Minor, many of whom settled in the waterfront area of Piraeus. In situations like these, broad regional varieties are reinterpreted in their new homes as social varieties (see chapter 4), with varying levels of prestige. They can also be reinterpreted as *local* regional varieties as their speakers end up in (linguistically bounded) neighborhoods.

As an aside: The people in the neighborhood

It would be simplistic to assume that the social meanings of places can be reduced solely to a question of prestige and wealth. Neighborhoods develop complex social meanings, both for their inhabitants and for outsiders. They can be safe and supportive home bases from which participants can negotiate the wider society, or social networks that ease new arrivals into the community. We see the sociolinguistic consequences of this in the immigrant enclaves briefly described in the previous chapter.

Urban neighborhoods often develop positive connotations of toughness or street smarts for outsiders. Their local music, often rooted in traditions brought from elsewhere, develops a sheen of cool, as with rebetiko in Greece or blues, country, jazz, soul, funk, or hip-hop in America. In the same way, language associated with these communities can acquire positive value, especially for mainstream youth. We see the importance of sociolinguistic "street cred" in the work of Peter Trudgill (1972) on **covert prestige**, described in more detail in chapter 4.

More recently, sociolinguists are noting a growth in the use of (sometimes watered-down) urban varieties as a sort of "escape hatch" from the old distinction between local

covert prestige
A norm or target that speakers unconsciously orient to, with a sort of hidden positive evaluation that speakers give to other (presumably non-standard) forms. The linguistic equivalent of *street credibility*.

Place features as social features: Talk like a pirate

Place can actually represent other salient social characteristics, such as ethnicity or class, and this can work the other way around, too – what we see as social features can actually represent place. This is especially clear in the case of migration – what a particular community sees as class or ethnic features might just be the way migrants talked back home.

Here's a stranger case: pirate talk. English speakers have a shared idea of what pirates are supposed to sound like, maybe because "pirate talk" is a named register, maybe thanks to International Talk Like A Pirate Day (September 19!) and Robert Louis Stevenson's *Treasure Island*, with that archetypal pirate-talker Long John Silver. In fact, "pirate" language features such as big Rs, invariant *be*, plural *ye*, and rhyming *tie* and *toy* are found in the dialects of southwestern England, which was the home of many of the sailors (and slavers, and pirates) of the British Empire (and of Long John Silver in the book). These speech features also made it to Newfoundland and parts of the Caribbean and the coastal US South. In Barbados, the slang terms for local White people include *Redlegs* (if your ancestors were kilt-wearing, sunburned Scots) and *Peglegs* (if they were pirates).

(rural) dialects on the one hand and standard language on the other. For example, younger adults in small towns in the north of England might not want to talk like Grandma ('cause Grandma's not cool), but they don't want to talk posh like the queen ('cause the queen's not so cool either). In many cases, they'll adopt the language features of the nearest large city, leading to a clumping of tiny dialect areas into bigger ones. These clumped varieties are usually called **supralocal** ("above the local").

Even farther from the local, many speakers are adopting a sort of "London Lite" variety, which includes some features of urban London speech (such as pronouncing *milk* as *miwk*), but not others (such as pronouncing *think* as *fink*). You sometimes see this variety referred to as "Estuary English," after the Thames Estuary. Not too posh, not too "street," it seems to be spreading across age, class, and gender (British prime minister David Cameron's wife Samantha has described how she deliberately toned down her upper-class accent into something closer to Estuary English). Similar situations are described for the Netherlands and Denmark (Smakman 2006; Gregersen et al. 2009).

You might expect something like this to happen in the USA as well, but there are complications. First, many urban speech features are associated specifically with African American English, and so their adoption involves the problematic **crossing** of an ethnic boundary (thus the term "wigger" – see chapter 6's discussion of crossing). Second, as Thomas Paul Bonfiglio points out in the very readable *Race and the Rise of Standard American* (2002), the obvious urban candidate, New York English, doesn't enjoy high status in America, a situation that he traces back to a hundred-year-old distrust of immigrants (and by extension their major city of settlement). However, if Estuary English can develop out of low-status Cockney, it's possible that a similar urban lite variety could develop out of New York English. Or maybe California will act as a competing influence; readers of the future may have a better handle on this.

supralocal
A term used to refer to the level "above the local," in which speakers adopt the language features of the nearest large city.

crossing
When speakers use language features or linguistic styles associated with another ethnic group (cf. Rampton 1995).

Method: Dialect geography

Sociolinguistics shares a lot with **dialectology**, the study of regional differences in language. In fact, some people have called sociolinguistics "urban dialectology," and you could say that dialectology was the first distinct branch of linguistics to really take a social distinction (where people were from) into account. Early linguistics had a major historical focus, and linguists turned to the study of traditional rural dialects, because those dialects preserved older speech features and thus held many clues to earlier stages of the language, especially with respect to sound changes. From there, the field branched out to study other areas of the grammar, especially the lexicon.

Sociolinguists and dialectologists share some goals and methods. We both tend to be interested in the language of a particular place (a speech community), language in use, "authentic" speech, and defining a language variety in terms of how it might differ from the standard. A major difference is that in the past dialectologists or dialect geographers have been interested in the most divergent, traditional language of a community, assuming that other forms resulted from later movement toward the standard. Sociolinguists, on the other hand, are interested in the full range of forms in a community (and their social evaluation). The two fields have influenced each other over the years, and we often end up at each other's conferences and writing books together. Dialectologists now study social and ethnic varieties (see chapter 6), and the Canadian dialectologist/sociolinguist Jack Chambers uses the term *dialect topography* to describe a form of dialect geography that takes into account the social "lie of the land."

The goals of dialect geography and dialectology have been to show where particular speech features are found, and to discover the boundaries between dialect regions. But dialect geography has also tried to find the most traditional speech in each region, on the assumption that regional dialects are most distinct when they haven't been influenced by their neighbors, or by mainstream language. These goals tend to lead to specific methods.

1. Find the speakers in a region with the least outside influence. Traditionally, these have been rural older men who've spent their whole lives in the same area, sometimes known as **NORMs** (non-mobile older rural males).
2. With each speaker, run through a (very long!) questionnaire of lexical features known to show regional differentiation. You probably know a few of these already – do you say *running shoes*, *tennis shoes*, or *sneakers*? *Hoagies*, *grinders*, *subs*, or *hero sandwiches*? *Soda*, *pop*, or *soft drink*?
3. Record each speaker's responses. In the days before tape recorders, fieldworkers would write these responses down, and make notes on pronunciation.
4. Tabulate the results from lots of questionnaires. Map out each variant. If you can, draw boundaries between different areas. For example, you might find a boundary between *sneaker* users and *running shoe* users somewhere in eastern North America. These boundary lines are called **isoglosses**.
5. Use your accumulated data to propose dialect areas and boundaries. If you find a lot of isoglosses in the same place (an **isogloss bundle**), it seems likely that you've found a boundary between dialect areas.

Dialect studies in the early and mid-twentieth century collected huge amounts of data, more than could be analyzed with the technology of the time. Dialectologists are still analyzing that earlier material today, using advanced computer modeling.

summing up

dialectology
The study of regional differences in language.

What we call *place* is not simply a GPS coordinate, or geographic accident. Each regional language variety is a product of historical and social forces particular to that place. It reflects the language of the original inhabitants, the language of later settlers (in the case of immigration, colonization, or conquest), the status of each contributing variety and of the region itself, the degree and type of contact with other varieties, the distinct products and practices of the region, the cumulative social and identification choices of its speakers, and a complex interaction with economic, political, attitudinal, and educational forces. Every generation has greater exposure to the language of other places, through advances in travel and communications technology. Although observers have been predicting the death of regional differences in language for at least 150 years, we still manage to sound different from our distant neighbors. It's still the people we talk with regularly who have the greatest impact on the way we speak.

NORMs
An acronym for "non-mobile older rural males." These speakers are believed to have retained the most traditional speech and are consequently the focus of many dialectology studies.

isogloss
An imaginary boundary or line drawn on a map that separates particular linguistic features, for example, the line across England separating northerners who pronounce the STRUT and FOOT vowels roughly the same from southerners who don't.

isogloss bundle
Many isoglosses occurring in the same area, likely representing a major dialect boundary.

Where to next?

Research on place seems to be heading in two directions at the same time. On the one hand, mapping software is becoming more and more powerful, and ordinary people are more familiar with mapping tools. In linguistics, this leads to increasingly complex and precise quantitative mapping research from the number-crunching end of the field. At the same time, though, anthropologically leaning linguists are refining and elaborating the multifaceted social meanings of place, and how place relates to aspects of people's identity performance. The two approaches don't have to be mutually exclusive – cultural geographers, for example, can be counted on to give us rich and nuanced explanations of neighborhood dynamics that lend themselves to representation through mapping.

exercises

1. In this story, the underlined words have distinctive British English meanings.

    As I left the <u>lift</u>, the <u>caretaker</u> stopped me. "I was just about to <u>knock you up</u>," he said. "The <u>estate agents</u> just <u>rang</u>, and they'd like to show your <u>flat</u>. You'll have to <u>sort out</u> all that <u>rubbish</u>." The flat looked like a <u>dustbin</u> and smelled of <u>spirits</u>. <u>Sweets</u>, <u>draughts</u>, <u>rubbers</u>, and <u>biros</u> covered the table. <u>Dungarees</u>, <u>trousers</u>, <u>vests</u>, and <u>pants</u> were all over the <u>cupboard</u>. Where had that <u>nappy</u> come from? Or that <u>dummy</u>? Whose <u>torch</u> was that? Whose <u>wellies</u>? The kitchen was even worse. <u>Courgettes</u>, bits of <u>aubergine</u>, <u>biscuit</u> crumbs, and empty <u>crisp packets</u> littered the floor. <u>Treacle</u> was everywhere.
       It was too much. I took the lot down to the <u>pavement</u>, tossed it in my <u>boot</u>, and left it under the <u>flyover</u> next to the <u>chemist's</u>. I doused it in <u>petrol</u> and lit a match.

    Try to "translate" the story into North American English.
    After you translate it:
    (a) If you're not British or North American, which of the underlined words do you use? If you don't use an underlined word, what word do you use instead?
    (b) If you're North American, which underlined words were you somewhat familiar with, maybe through media or books? Are any of them words that you've read in books, only vaguely understood, and never looked up?

(c) If you're British, are there any underlined words (or specific meanings) here that you didn't realize might be unfamiliar to speakers of another variety of English? Are there any underlined words that you don't use yourself? What words do you use instead?

2. This exercise will be more fun if you can find people from a lot of different places. Survey five people (or more). Find out where they're from, and what they call:
    (a) a sweetened fizzy drink
    (b) a long padded piece of furniture, usually with arms, that seats several people
    (c) rubber-soled shoes that you'd wear in the gym
    (d) not going to school when you're supposed to
    (e) a sandwich, usually filled with cold meat or cheese, served on a long bun
    (f) the covered area in front of the front door of a house, usually up a couple of steps
    Report on what you discover.

3. Using the list of words given below, ask at least five people:
    (a) How do you pronounce this word?
    (b) Do you know of any other pronunciations for this word? What are they?
    (c) Who uses these other pronunciations?
    Word list: *herb, lever, lieutenant, news, student, missile, leisure, marry, merry, ice, man.*
    Report on what you discover.

4. Watch some television (on the internet, maybe). Look for shows (older or recent) whose location matters, such as *Dukes of Hazzard, Ballykissangel, Heartbeat, Coronation Street, EastEnders, Under One Roof* (the Singaporean one), or *Republic of Doyle.* What distinct language features do you notice? If you come from one of the places (supposedly) represented by these shows, how do you feel about the idea that your people speak like that? Do you ever feel like kicking people who say, "Wow, you sound just like the people on . . ."?

5. Ask people who travel or move a lot if they have any stories about misunderstandings due to words meaning different things in different places. If they can't think of any, try prompting them with words like *togs, rashers* (of bacon), *bent, thongs, trainers,* or some of the words from exercise 1.

6. Ask people about stereotypes associated with Irish English and Australian English. See if you get different stereotypes from old and young people.

7. There are several websites that feature recordings of people from different places, usually all reading the same text (Google *dialect recordings* to find them). Listen to recordings from a few different places, ideally with somebody who has lived or visited different places than you have. What distinct pronunciation features do you notice? Are there more pronunciation differences in vowels, or consonants? Do you and your fellow listener(s) notice different things?

8. The examples given in the section on isolation are all drawn from a Canadian context. If you're from another country, can you think of parallel examples from your country? Are there specific local conditions that influence the possibility of parallel examples? For example, is physical isolation limited by the fact that your country is tiny and flat?

9. Get together with a few people and try to correctly produce all the regional pronunciations in table 3.1. Don't be afraid to exaggerate!

1. Does anybody still use the word *Cockney*? Do you know any other terms for people from a particular place (as distinct from a particular ethnicity)?
2. Were you ever in a situation where people could tell where you were from by the way you talk? What accent or other linguistic features gave you away?
3. Can you think of any regional shibboleths?
4. Can you think of movies, theater, or TV shows where actors have portrayed somebody from a different dialect area and either succeeded so well that they fooled you, or failed miserably? What about *House*? Matt Damon in *Invictus*? Craig Ferguson in *The Drew Carey Show*? Brad Pitt in anything?
5. What assumptions about somebody's character or social status would you make if they claimed not to understand speakers of Appalachian English, Scots English, Canadian English, "posh" British English, Indian English, or Scouse?
6. How many neighborhoods can you name in your town? (Don't count the lame names given by real estate developers or city planners, like Happy Acres, unless people in your town actually use them.) How many neighborhood names refer to the origins of their inhabitants?
7. Do people where you live name regions for their telephone or postal area codes? For example, do they talk about "people from the 905"? Are there social values associated with particular area codes?
8. Where you live, can you buy t-shirts with the local dialect's name or nickname for your town or its inhabitants? How about shirts with local dialect terms? Which terms make it onto t-shirts?
9. What other shibboleths can you think of? Do they serve as identity markers? Are any of them associated with social characteristics other than place, such as class, gender, or ethnicity?
10. Can you think of any other words like *eejit* in the shibboleths box, where a particular (local) pronunciation of a word doesn't mean the same thing as the standard pronunciation? Caribbean people, what's the difference between *workin'* and *wukkin*?

David Britain's description of his work in the Fens is easy to read in his chapter in J. K. Chambers, Peter Trudgill, and Natalie Schilling-Estes, eds, *The Handbook of Language Variation and Change* (2002).

John Wells introduced the idea of lexical sets in *Accents of English* (1982). On his website, he says, "I sometimes think that a century from now my lexical sets will be the one thing I shall be remembered for. Yet I dreamt them up over a weekend" (http://phonetic-blog.blogspot.com/2010/02/lexical-sets.html, accessed August 17, 2011)

For more on the influence of hip-hop culture and language worldwide, try Alastair Pennycook's 2007 book *Global Englishes and Transcultural Flows*, Alim et al.'s *Global Linguistic Flows: Hip Hop Cultures, Youth Identities, and the Politics of Language* (2009), or the Local Noise website at http://localnoise.net.au (accessed August 17, 2011). Sarkar and Winer's multilingualism "spotlight" reading (see chapter 10) is also about this topic.

Chambers and Trudgill's *Dialectology* (1980) is a look at the discipline by two big names who do both dialectology and sociolinguistics.

Overviews of Englishes around the world include Kortmann et al.'s *Handbook of Varieties of English. Vol. 2* (2004), Kachru et al.'s *Handbook of World Englishes* (2006), Mesthrie and Bhatt's *World Englishes: The Study of New Linguistic Varieties* (2008), and Schneider's *Postcolonial English* (2007). Several sites let you listen to accents of English from around the world; one such site is the Speech Accent Archive, at http://accent.gmu.edu/browse_atlas.php (accessed August 17, 2011). You can still easily find the video series *The Story of English* (PBS, 1986). The hairstyles and politics (and slang!) are out of date, but the footage of Englishes from all over is interesting. The PBS series *Do You Speak American?,* http://www.pbs.org/speak (accessed August 17, 2011) is a sort of update, restricted to the USA.

The BBC Voices website at http://www.bbc.co.uk/voices (accessed August 17, 2011) will give you access to all kinds of regional British English, as well as language-related news.

Pretty well every major variety of English has a book about it, one or more dictionaries, and one or more books about some particularly interesting aspect of the variety. For example, for American English, Wolfram and Schilling-Estes' *American English: Dialects and Variation* (2006) is a sociolinguistically informed look, Labov et al.'s (2006) *Atlas of North American English: Phonetics, Phonology, and Sound Change* is a gigantic study of sound differences, and Finegan and Rickford's *Language in the USA: Themes for the Twenty-First Century* (2004) deals with English and other languages. You can look at maps showing the regional distribution of many American lexical variants (words) according to dialect survey results at http://www4.uwm.edu/FLL/linguistics/dialect/maps.html (accessed August 17, 2011).

Journals:

American Speech, http://americanspeech.dukejournals.org (accessed August 17, 2011).
English World-Wide, http://www.benjamins.com/cgi-bin/t_seriesview.cgi?series=eww (accessed August 17, 2011).

4 Social Status

In this chapter:

- Class and status
- Determining class
- Social mobility
- Status and standards

So far, we've looked at social factors that apply to pretty well everyone in a community. The kinds of change, isolation, and contact that we've discussed affect entire regional groups. For the next few chapters, we'll look at what language variation tells us about distinctions within communities. These distinctions include class, ethnicity, age, and gender, among others, as well as the interactions between them. In this chapter, we'll expand on the idea of social status and class.

Let's start where some people say sociolinguistics started, with Fischer's 1958 study of schoolchildren in New England. Fischer found that "g-dropping" (saying *jumpin'* and not *jumping*) wasn't random, as most linguists had previously assumed most variation to be. Although there were no absolute (categorical) rules for when it happened, there were clear probabilistic constraints – that is, g-dropping was more likely in some contexts. Fischer found linguistic constraints on g-dropping in his data: it was less common with formal verbs like *criticizing* than with informal verbs like *running*. But he also found clear social constraints. Boys g-dropped more often than girls, working-class students g-dropped more often than middle-class students, and everybody (but especially middle-class students) g-dropped more often during formal conversations. The distinctions were quite clear, as you can see in table 4.1.

categorical
Categorical rules apply every time that they can apply.

probabilistic
The opposite of categorical, probabilistic constraints are not absolute but rather tendencies in one direction.

linguistic constraint
A linguistic factor that governs the use of a particular variant.

social constraint
A social factor like sex or age that governs the use of a particular variant.

What Is Sociolinguistics?, First Edition. Gerard Van Herk.

Table 4.1.   Rates of g-droppin' among New England youth, across social groups and styles.

social group and style	-ing (number)	-in' (number)
speakers preferring each variant (in formal contexts):		
boys	5	7
girls	10	2
middle-class	8	4
working-class	7	5
uses of each variant by one speaker, by formality:		
test	38	1
formal interview	33	35
informal interview	24	41

Source: Adapted from Fischer (1958: 484, tables 1, 3, and 4).

status
Social positions that society assigns to its members, or the differences between social groups, in terms of the prestige associated with them by others.

variable
The abstract representation of a source of variation, realized by at least two variants, for example, *gonna* and *will* are variants of the variable *future temporal reference*.

So right there, you have the basic ideas that sociolinguists have expanded on ever since: most societies are divided into groups with different **status**. Some linguistic functions are **variable** – that is, they can be expressed in two or more ways (called **variants**). Sometimes, linguistic variation seems to have no social meaning at all (for example, the choice between *Give her the potato* and *Give the potato to her*). But often, one of the variants becomes associated with higher-status groups and acquires **prestige** (or, more likely, another one becomes associated with lower-status groups and acquires **stigma**). If we study that particular variable, we'll find that higher-status people use the prestige form more often, and that when people are in formal situations, or paying more attention to their speech, they're more likely to use the prestige form. G-dropping is stigmatized, even though we all do it sometimes.

OK, now let's spend the rest of the chapter messing with that by challenging assumptions and expanding ideas, just the way sociolinguistics has for fifty years.

determining social class or status

variant
The different expressions, or actual realizations, of a variable, for example, pronouncing the suffix *-ing* as "ing" or "in."

prestige
Variants associated with higher-status groups are considered prestige forms.

stigma
A negative association, something viewed pejoratively.

First off, how do we determine status? The idea that a (western, industrialized) society is composed of different classes can be traced back to Karl Marx (Marx and Engels 1848), who identified two antagonistic classes: capitalists (who owned the means of production) and the proletariat (who worked for the capitalists). But the class differences that most of us recognize come from the basic distinctions that social scientists (especially early sociologists) work from, in which class includes notions of lifestyle and life chances. The ideas that start with Fischer are elaborated and turned into a subdiscipline with Bill Labov's work in New York City in the 1960s. Sociolinguists (for example, Peter Trudgill in Norwich) often determine a speaker's class membership through a complex scorecard involving type of home, neighborhood, income, and occupational prestige, although some recent work suggests that occupational prestige alone is enough to determine

Table 4.2.   Ratings of occupational prestige (out of 100), USA

occupation	1947 score	1963 score
Supreme Court judge	96	94
nuclear physicist	86	92
college professor	89	90
lawyer	86	89
instructor in public schools	79	82
building contractor	79	80
police officer	67	72
restaurant cook	54	55
taxi driver	49	49
bartender	44	48

Source: Adapted from Hodge et al. (1964).

social class. Table 4.2 lists the prestige scores (out of 100) associated with some occupations, based on surveys conducted in 1947 and 1963.

But this makes it sound like we're sociolinguistic robots, doomed to speak a certain way because of the class we're born into. A more complex view of the relationship between class and speech is needed to explain what actually goes on. Labov's famous department store study (2006/1966; and see "spotlight") introduced the idea of **borrowed prestige**. That is, speakers' setting and the role that they're playing can affect their use of language features associated with a particular class. Labov found that employees of fancier stores (like Saks) used fewer stigmatized forms than employees of less fancy stores (like Klein's, which no longer exists). This was true even though all the employees had roughly the same class background and worked for the same crappy pay (as you know if you've ever worked in retail).

Canadian sociolinguist Jack Chambers (1995, 2009) suggests that people often try to talk like who they *want* to be, so that we might want to identify people by their **aspirations**, not their current status. And, as Fischer had found, the speakers in Labov's study adjusted their rates of use of stigmatized forms in more formal situations, or when they were paying attention to their speech (more in chapter 8). As Labov put it, a careful pipe-fitter spoke like a casual salesman, at least in the use of linguistic variables that had social meaning in that speech community (Labov 1972b: 240). When Labov plotted rates of use of variables by social class and formality of the speech context, he found beautiful clear parallel lines, with classes stacked above each other and increasing use of prestige variants with increased formality (figure 4.1). There was one exception: a **crossover effect** with the second-highest group. When this group was speaking very formally, they used prestige variants even more often than the group above them, the people they were presumably trying to emulate. In other words, they showed **social hypercorrection**, overdoing what they saw as the linguistic requirements of the

borrowed prestige
Speakers' setting and the role they're playing can lead them to use language features associated with a particular class.

aspiration
People often try to talk like who they *want* to be.

crossover effect
In formal situations, speakers using prestige variants even more often than the group above them.

social hypercorrection
When speakers overdo what they see as the linguistic requirements of a situation (usually in the direction of formality or use of standard variants).

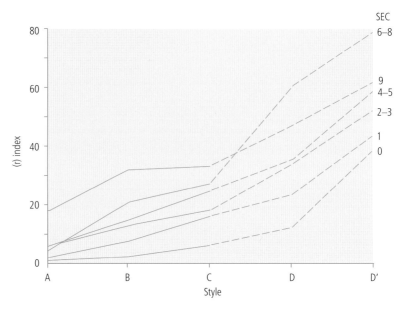

Figure 4.1.   Rates of R use, by class and formality (Labov 1972b: 114). Class stratification of a linguistic variable in process of change: (r) in *guard*, *car*, *beer*, *beard*, *board*, etc. Socio-economic class (SEC) scale: 0–1, lower class; 2–4, working class; 5–6, 7–8, lower middle class; 9, upper middle class. A, casual speech; B, careful speech; C, reading style; D, word lists; D', minimal pairs.

linguistic insecurity
The force hypothesized to drive people to use a variant that is thought to be prestigious or correct and that is not part of their own casual speech (cf. Labov 1972b).

linguistic market
The importance of standard language in the social and economic life of the speaker.

salient/salience
Usually refers to a noticeable variant – one that stands out due to physiological, social, and/or psychological factors.

stereotype
A variable that is socially marked, that is, very noticeable and often discussed.

situation. You can probably think of non-linguistic examples of this kind of "overdoing it" (the one that strikes me is the way that White rappers dress). This crossover effect among the second-highest class has shown up in studies in many different communities; it is often attributed to **linguistic insecurity** among a social group attempting to move up the class ladder. Sankoff and Laberge (1978) introduced a useful alternative explanation for at least some of these types of effects. Borrowing ideas from Bourdieu and Boltanski (1975), they suggested that we should assign speakers to social categories on the basis of where they fit into the **linguistic market** – some jobs require more standard English, even if they're not the highest-paying (for example, schoolteachers, executive secretaries, and perhaps the employees of upmarket retailers).

Terminology like *linguistic insecurity* or *hypercorrection* assumes that speakers are fairly conscious of how the things that they say are used against them, in terms of determining their social status. From the earliest research onward, though, it seems that different linguistic features involve different amounts of awareness and control (Labov tells a story about a New York City mother and daughter who were convinced that they always pronounced their Rs, and were crestfallen to hear their r-less selves on tape). Each of us has dozens of linguistic features which mark our speech (that's why socio-linguists sometimes get hired to provide information about the voices in telephone bomb threats and the like). Some features are **salient** (noticeable) and recognized within the community as having a particular social meaning. If they're very noticeable and often discussed, they may be **stereotypes**. If they're just barely noticed, but speakers control how often they use them in different styles, they're called sociolinguistic **markers**. Other features are "below the radar," but can be shown by large-scale study to be associated with particular social characteristics; these features are called sociolinguistic **indicators**. A speech community's norms affect both markers and indicators.

marker
A variable that speakers are less aware of than a stereotype, but whose use they can control in style shifting.

mobility

In a previous chapter, we suggested that nobody needs to actively mark their region unless or until they have contact with people from other regions. In the same way, perhaps people's *social* class membership has to be uncertain for them to use variable language to mark it. So we have to assume that **social mobility** plays a large role in how class and language influence each other. In fact, in societies where mobility is more difficult, the linguistic boundaries are also more rigid. We use the term **caste** to describe a social group like this, one that's very hard, if not impossible, to move out of. Most people think of caste as it relates to Hindu social structure in India. Although the influence of the Indian caste system has declined over the years, caste still matters. On Indian dating and marriage websites, the basic information you fill out about yourself to register is age, sex, religion, and caste (figure 4.2). And there are distinct language varieties or variants associated with a speaker's caste.

indicator
A variable that can show differences by age or social group and is often associated with particular characteristics but is not subject to style shifting.

social mobility
The ability to move between social classes, often determined by how defined class roles are in a particular culture.

caste
In societies where mobility is more difficult and linguistic boundaries are more rigid, social groups, or castes, tend to be fixed, for example, traditional (Hindu) Indian social structure.

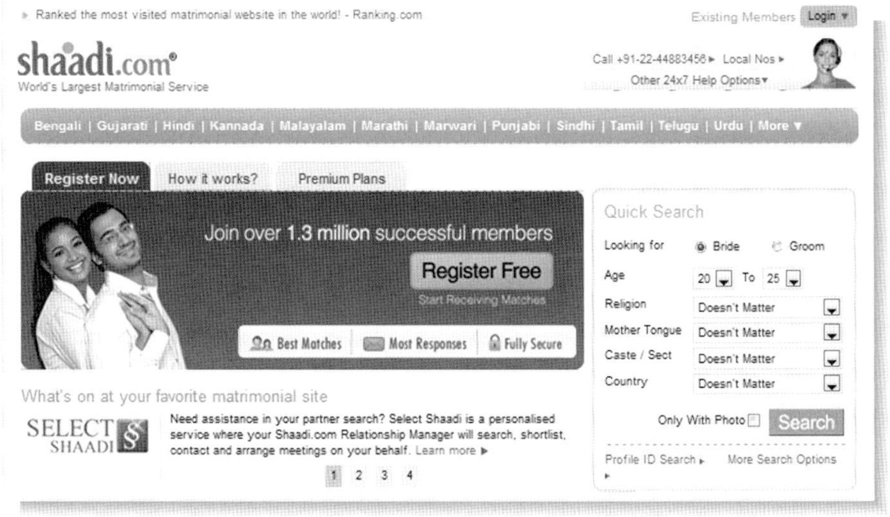

Figure 4.2. Caste remains an important consideration on matrimonial websites.

It's worth mentioning that the British class system was, in the distant past, fairly close to a caste system, with extremely limited social mobility. The slightly more fluid situation that Marx described there in the 1840s was then a fairly recent development associated with industrialization. And, in fact, increasing social mobility during that time period increased the importance of language as a way of identifying somebody's class. God forbid people of inherited wealth accidentally associated with somebody who had only recently earned their money! Luckily, one could recognize that type by their non-standard speech features.

As a result, a whole industry grew up around teaching non-standard speakers how to linguistically pass for members of the social elite. Authors competed to introduce ever more elaborate **prescriptive** rules – this is where we get things like the math analogy "two negatives make a positive" to forbid sentences like *I don't want nothing* (which had been fine until the seventeenth century; Nevalainen 2006). The result was a middle class that, again, showed social hypercorrection – at one point, in the late 1800s, forms like *ain't* and g-droppin' were used by the working classes and the nobility, but rarely by people in between. As British social mobility increased through the twentieth century, overt commentary on class differences in speech remained strong. An article from 1954 by British linguist Alan Ross identified linguistic features, especially vocabulary, that were then associated with the Upper (U) and non-Upper (non-U) classes; these ideas were popularized by the author Nancy Mitford, setting off (media-fueled) debate about class consciousness and snobbery (Table 4.3).

prescriptive
An approach to language that is focused on rules of correctness, that is, how language "should" be used. Contrasted with descriptive.

Table 4.3.   U and non-U words (from Mitford 1956).

U	non-U
they've a very nice house	they have a lovely home
graveyard	cemetery
false teeth	dentures
die	pass on
napkin	serviette
sofa	settee or couch
rich	wealthy
what?	pardon?

Note: that the non-U (i.e., non-upper-class) words involve more indirection and euphemism – they're actually more "polite" than the relatively direct language of upper-class U speakers.

In fact, the prestige or standard varieties of a language generally start off as the variety associated with a particular social or regional group, without necessarily being seen as linguistically "better." It's only as that group rises in power or status that its language acquires a glow of respectability, or correctness. Again, English is an obvious example.

When London became the permanent capital, and as early universities developed, the dialect of the Oxford–Cambridge–London triangle became the language of court documents and university lectures. This status was reinforced as a court bureaucracy developed, and again when William Caxton introduced the first printing press to England, and chose the London variety to standardize spelling. Until the status distinction fully kicked in, roughly the 1700s, it was normal that even the nobility spoke with distinct regional accents (Queen Elizabeth I supposedly called Walter Raleigh "Water," making fun of the way he pronounced his own name). And people spelled things the way they said them. In the letters from Margaret Paston (an upper-class woman of the fifteenth century) to her husband, we find spellings like *moder* for *mother*, *an* for *and*, *to a fownd* for *to have found*, and *axyd* for *asked*. If you read these words aloud, they sound very much like the casual or non-standard speech of our times.

Over a few hundred years (and a few hundred dictionaries), written English has become standardized, in the literal sense of the word – that there's a particular codified way to spell most words and punctuate most sentences, just like there are "standard" sizes for bolts or milk cartons. Things are more awkward when it comes to spoken "standard" English. In particular, whose accent wins out, and how much can we use contractions and the like? Today's spoken standard is difficult, if not impossible, to define objectively. We can agree that some forms, like *ain't*, are probably not part of the standard – at least not any more. Others, like *There's dozens of ways*, are on the boundary. Today's standard is slightly easier to pin down on social grounds. It's the language of the upper socio-economic classes, and of educated people; the language of literature or printed documents; and the variety taught in schools and used by broadcasters. In North American English, it's the accent of the American Midwest and central and western Canada; in Britain, it's the language of the south. In effect, the standard is the language of high-status people. By this definition, however, we lose any idea of "correctness" (implied by another meaning of the word *standard*, as in "living up to my standards"). We're left with a sociolect, a subset of language used by a particular social group or class. What's interesting to many sociolinguists is the *idea* of a standard: the widely held belief that some ways of speaking are not just different, but actually inherently correct. Thus, the standard gets much of its power from being seen as socially and linguistically unmarked (that is, not weird). More on this in chapter 12 on attitudes.

Of course, highly standard language *can* be socially marked, especially in less formal contexts. In fact, many second language learners find that the fairly formal version of their target language that they learn in school is inappropriate for casual conversation. The same problem besets people on the autism spectrum, who can have trouble picking up on the social meanings of language forms. They often use too many formal-type variants, and thus sound stilted or unnatural. And many of us who work in jobs with a high linguistic market value end up sounding just a little too standard even when we get home. If you've come into university from a fairly non-standard speech community, you may have been chided with comments about sounding too posh, or reminders to "keep it real."

sociolect
A subset of language used by a particular social group or class. Sometimes called *social* dialect.

unmarked
The opposite of marked, that is, a feature that does not get noticed.

As an aside: Moving on up

Social mobility doesn't just lead to collision effects like hypercorrection or social anxiety. It also means that if a group's place in the society changes, the prestige attached to features of their language can change. Kontra (1992) described a situation in Hungary, where after the communist takeover, children of laborers received government subsidies to stay in school. The result was that previously highly stigmatized working-class speech features became more and more acceptable, according to attitude survey results. A similar situation appears to be developing in Newfoundland. As religious differences have lessened, formerly Irish Catholic-associated features are changing their social value to mean "Newfoundland-y."

As an aside: Spot the "error"

Decide which of the following sentences are incorrect, according to prescriptive rules of Standard English.

Anyone who has finished their work should stay in their seat.
Whom do you want to speak to?
Who do you want to speak to?
Hopefully, it will be warm tomorrow.
There's dozens of ways to make cookies.
The professor gave the paper to Yvan and I.
Please prepare a report for Julie and myself.
Between you and I, I think this is a waste of time.
The union leader, along with all of her followers, want to talk to you.

How many "errors" did you spot? In fact, all of these sentences are wrong, according to many prescriptivists. Some constructions which are increasingly common, such as Julie and myself, result from linguistic insecurity. We know that both and I and and me are wrong in some uses, so we cop out and use and myself.

Peter Trudgill's Norwich work (1972) picked up on an interesting gendered dimension of this debate. He found, as in many other communities studied, that men used more non-standard local forms than women. For example, they pronounced words like *dew* and *tune* the same as *do* and *toon*, rather than using the southern British English pronunciations (something like *dyoo* and *tyoon*). But when he asked people which form they used, the men over-reported their use of the local form, while the women under-reported. Trudgill suggested that there were actually two kinds of prestige involved: **overt prestige** is the kind of prestige officially associated with sounding "proper," while **covert prestige** is a sort of hidden positive evaluation that speakers give to other (presumably non-standard) forms. Nowadays, we use the term *covert prestige* as the linguistic equivalent of *street credibility*, but as Miriam Meyerhoff (2006) points out, technically in the Trudgill case only the women assigned covert ("hidden") prestige to the local forms (in that they obviously valued them, because they used them – they just *said* they didn't). The men probably would have been happy to tell you what a wimp they'd sound like by saying *tyoon* and *dyoo*. Nothing covert there.

We see in the Norwich example something of the relationship between region and class/status. In each community that we study, it's more likely to be the local language features that have the lower status and are most closely associated with working-class speakers. In chapter 3, I listed a few distinct features of each region's English that were found among most speakers. But if I'd introduced features that persist among the working classes, all those national varieties might have started to look more and more different. Sociolinguistics textbooks usually visually represent the relationship between region and class with a truncated pyramid – as we move up the class scale, the forms that people use grow more similar to the forms used by people of similar status elsewhere (figure 4.3). Corporate lawyers from New York and Los Angeles may have slightly different accents, but their grammatical systems will be virtually identical. But security guards working in the same corporations in those two cities will sound much more different from each other (how different will depend on a lot of things, including their ethnicity).

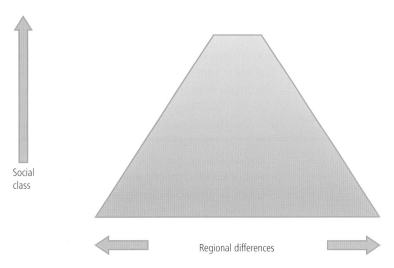

Figure 4.3.   The relationship of class and region. This is often represented as a truncated pyramid: the higher you go up the social classes, the smaller the linguistic differences from one region to the next.

This lets us think a little about what we're actually talking about when we correlate class and use of prestigious or standard forms. If (say) a northern city like Newcastle had become the capital of England, would people of past centuries have tried to sound like Londoners? Probably not. And even when people did start sounding like Londoners, it wasn't a working-class Cockney accent that they were aiming for. Linguistic prestige is directly associated with power. As Bonfiglio (2002: 23) puts it, "There is nothing in the particular language itself that determines its worth: it is the connection of the language in question to the phenomena of power that determines the value of that language and that contributes to the standardization process." (It'll be useful to keep a basic concept like the relationship to power in mind as we work our way through these chapters and think about the relationships between class and other social categories like gender, ethnicity, and region.) For all that we talk about covert prestige, in situations that involve access to power and education, it is the standard language that is expected (socially unmarked), and that is almost always linguistically unmarked. You rarely hear people correct someone for not saying *ain't*.

The links between status, language, and education have long been of interest to sociolinguists (see also chapter 14). In the early 1960s, sociologist Basil Bernstein (1961a) wrote that we could think of two kinds of English – a "restricted code," which all children use, and an "elaborated code," which only some children get, and which better prepares them for the type of language (and reasoning) used in school. Especially in his earlier work, Bernstein suggested that working-class children tended not to acquire this elaborated code. Educators tended to interpret this to mean that working-class children had linguistic deficits that would limit their cognitive development. Linguists, especially sociolinguists, didn't take well to this interpretation, and sociolinguistic work from the

overt prestige
Positive or negative assessments of variants that are in line with the dominant norms associated with sounding "proper" and that people are aware of, often coinciding with the norms of the media, educational institutions, or higher socio-economic classes.

covert prestige
A norm or target that speakers unconsciously orient to, with a sort of hidden positive evaluation that speakers give to other (presumably non-standard) forms. The linguistic equivalent of *street credibility*.

As an aside: Naming the poor

There's a longstanding tradition in English of developing names for people at the bottom of the status scale, names that distinguish between Good Poor People (who were once known as "the deserving poor" – deserving of help, not of being poor) and Bad Poor People (who aren't even *trying*). When people say *That's so trash* or *ghetto*, they're assigning volition to the poor people they're describing, presumably to legitimize putting them down (or keeping them down).

Many English-speaking societies have developed (relatively recent) terms for urban working-class people, terms such as *chav*, *bogan*, and *ned*, that are defined in remarkably similar ways (usually referring to youth, especially young White men, who adopt hip-hop style, and are presumably involved in criminality, drugs, and the production of many children). Descriptions of (or imitations of) these people often have a linguistic component, with heavy use of local stigmatized non-standard features. Over time, this may affect attitudes toward local vernacular varieties.

later 1960s directly addresses the deficit hypothesis (and, many would argue, completely refutes it). I'm not sure who listened and who didn't, though – I still meet many teachers who bring up Bernstein, while I just noticed that his name is entirely absent from at least one recent introductory sociolinguistics text.

Prestige, stigma, power, and status seem to be ideas that can translate across a range of sociolinguistic situations. Class, on the other hand, is more closely associated with somewhat mobile industrialized societies, especially urban areas. Sociolinguists need to pay attention to local concepts of social status when they try to work out how it might relate to language use. For example, John Rickford's study of the Guyanese village of Cane Walk (1979) describes a situation where hardly anybody in the community could be slotted neatly into your basic introsociology class system. Instead, the social distinction that mattered was between the Estate class, people who cut and planted sugar and tended to use deep (**basilectal**) Guyanese Creole forms, and the Non-Estate class, who had more urban contacts and used linguistic features closer to Standard English.

summing up

basilect
A term used in creole studies to refer to the most creole-like variety.

Social distinctions within communities, such as prestige and power, tend to be reflected in linguistic behavior. High-status language is often seen in a community as unmarked or "correct," while more local or working-class language is commented on and stigmatized. The language of the rich and powerful becomes desirable (at least in some situations), and speakers will adjust their language in that direction in formal situations, or to indicate their affiliation with, or aspirations toward, that class. Sometimes speakers in the middle classes will overcompensate, or hypercorrect, toward their perception of "proper" speech. The degree of change may relate to the amount of (perceived) social mobility in a society.

Where to next?

Researchers have observed that social class is not a "one size fits all" characteristic that can be investigated in all societies. But almost all societies, it seems, have notions of social prestige and stigma that are likely to affect language use, and many of the social distinctions that people make, however they label them, reflect underlying class prejudices or assumptions. Our ideas of social mobility and group membership are likely to keep changing, and presumably we'll be able to investigate how this is reflected in language changes.

Spotlight: Who is this man and why can't he find the fourth floor?

Labov, William. "The social stratification of (r) in NYC department stores." In William Labov, *The Social Stratification of English in New York City* (2nd edn.), 40–57. Cambridge: Cambridge University Press, 2006 (1st pub. 1966).

The book as a whole is a classic work, introducing many of the fully formed ideas that were to build modern sociolinguistics. Chapter 3 has one big methodological innovation: the rapid and anonymous survey. This involves the researcher asking a whole lot of people a question whose answer contains the linguistic variable under study, then quickly going off and writing down which variant each person used. In this case the variable is (r) pronunciation and the expected answer is "fourth floor" (so the study's also often called the fourth floor study). There's also a theoretical innovation, the idea of *borrowed prestige*, which I described earlier in this chapter.

Reading: Not too much difficult terminology. Just remember that (r-1) means "pronouncing the r" and (r-0) means "not pronouncing the r" and you'll be fine.

Note also the degree to which Labov foresees potential objections ("maybe all the Klein's employees were Black!") and cuts them off by re-analyzing his data to address them.

Links to other readings: The study has been replicated by Fowler (1986); if you're reading Labov in the second edition, he summarizes the Fowler study near the end of the chapter, and talks about other studies using the method. And there's a very recent re-replication by Mather (in press).

exercises

1. Compare how people online define *white trash*, *chav*, *bogan*, *ned*, and *wigger*. How many definitions overtly mention class? How many discuss language features?
2. Literature and media have long been fascinated with social mobility and change. Read or watch one of *Trading Places*, *The Prince and the Pauper*, *Keeping Up Appearances*, *The Jeffersons*, *Fresh Prince of Bel-Air*, *Outrageous Fortune*, *The Beverly Hillbillies*, *Pizza*, *The Simple Life*, *Bringing Up Father*, *My Fair Lady*, or pretty well anything by Dickens. How are class differences represented? How is language involved?
3. Identify which of the following non-standard forms you hear people use where you come from: *ain't*, *I seen it*, *I done it*, *I can't see nothing*, *him and me are going*.
4. Scolar Press reprinted a bunch of old grammar books in the 1970s. Poke around your school library and see if they have any. Have a read. Can you find any grammar rules that are different from the ones we use today? Or extreme language condemning the way some people talk?
5. Go back to table 4.2 in the chapter, which lists occupational prestige scores. Ask a bunch of people to give scores to the same jobs today, from 0 for very low prestige to 100 for very high prestige (ideally, you should present the jobs in a different order). Find the average score for each occupation. Are the rankings similar to the earlier studies (and to each other)? Did any of your respondents offer explanations for the scores they gave? What explanations can you offer for any differences?

discussion

1. At one point in this chapter, I compared social hypercorrection to dress styles. Are there any other ideas in this chapter that can be discussed using the metaphor of clothing – standard, mobility, covert prestige, identity practices, others?
2. Has your computer's automatic grammar checker ever flagged something that you are sure was completely fine?
3. Are there any concepts discussed in the chapter on place that can usefully be applied to a discussion of social status? What do *isolation*, *contact*, *migration*, or *choice* mean in this context?
4. Consider the U and non-U words listed in table 4.3 (you can find more online). Why do you think the speech of the higher classes is more direct and less euphemistic?
5. Students sometimes have trouble distinguishing between wealth and class/status, especially students who live in fairly mobile societies. Can you think of people/professions who earn a lot of money, but aren't seen as members of the upper classes? Or, conversely, people/professions that are respected, but don't pay all that well?
6. I brought up *chav* and *trash* above. Can you think of any terms that work the other way around – derogatory terms for people with money, or the ways that they behave? Do any of those terms distinguish between "new money" and old?
7. What is the relationship between education and class and language? How does this differ depending on how accessible education is in a given society?

Read Labov's *The Social Stratification of English in New York City* (1966), *Sociolinguistic Patterns* (1972b), or *Principles of Linguistic change. Vol. 2: Social Factors* (2001).

Trudgill's influential "Sex, covert prestige and linguistic change" (1972) discusses what the title says it does.

You might want to have a look at how education textbooks treat Bernstein's work on codes. How much of it is similar to what sociolinguists seem to be saying? How much is different?

Mugglestone's *"Talking Proper": The Rise of Accent as Social Symbol* (2003) traces the social meaning of accent. You can find discussions of the rise of Received Pronunciation, the "posh" British accent, in most books about the history of English.

Nancy Mitford's novel *The Pursuit of Love* (1945) is said to have been used by linguist Alan Ross as an example of upper-class speech.

See also the Scolar Press grammars and literary sources recommended in the exercises above.

Time 5

In this chapter:

- Noticing and measuring language change – how and why
- The apparent time hypothesis
- Real time studies
- Age as a social factor

How do I know I'm getting old? Young people are starting to sound funny to me. Their vowels go places that vowels never went when I was young. Occasionally, their verbs flaunt crazy *-ing* suffixes (*I'm loving it!*). Sometimes, they use words that they have to explain to me (luckily, I'm smart enough to not immediately try out this newly acquired knowledge). If I live long enough, I may hear entire sounds drop out of their repertoire, as happened to the distinction between the first sounds of *which* and *witch* in the two generations between my grandma and me. Eventually, I'll be a crabby old speaker of an obsolete dialect – I'll yell at them to get off my lawn, but they won't understand me.

apparent time

Well, actually, as I'm a sociolinguist, the above scenario wouldn't bother me at all. All spoken languages change, and variationists like me are interested in language change because of its relationship to the variation found in a community at a single point in

What Is Sociolinguistics?, First Edition. Gerard Van Herk.
© 2012 Gerard Van Herk. Published 2012 by Blackwell Publishing Ltd.

time. Think of big changes, like the Great Vowel Shift of earlier English (see box). Presumably, people in England didn't all go to bed one night pronouncing their words one way, and wake up the next morning with a completely different vowel system. At some point, either everybody used both the old and the new pronunciation (maybe for different words, or classes of words), or some people always used the old way and some always used the new, or perhaps it was a combination of these. In other words, any linguistic change that takes place over time must be reflected in variation in language use during any single time period during the change. Add to that the assumption that people's basic grammar doesn't change that much during their lifetime, which most research supports, and you get a powerful insight. Despite what earlier linguists may have thought, you *can* see language change happening in a single time period, by comparing old and young speakers. If young people use a particular form more often than old people do, that's likely to be the form that is increasing in use across the community. This idea, called the **apparent time hypothesis**, has opened up whole new areas of research.

> ### *As an aside*: The Great Vowel Shift
>
> Vowels are inherently "shifty," because they're not as closely linked to a single place of articulation in the mouth as consonants are; this helps explain why regional accents often differ in how vowels are pronounced (as we saw in chapter 3). When vowels shift far enough to affect comprehension, or spelling, people notice. A major shift (1450–1750) is known as the Great Vowel Shift (GVS). Before the shift, vowels were pronounced much as the same (written) letter would be in Italian: *name* was something like *nahm*, *beat* like *bait*, *moon* like *moan*. The GVS is one of the reasons English spelling is so hard to figure out: pronunciation has drifted so far away from what the spelling was trying to represent.

change

I acknowledge that it seems strange to suggest that studying language change should be considered particularly sociolinguistic. After all, historical linguists have studied language change, in a different theoretical and methodological framework, for two centuries. But "language change" doesn't exist in a strictly linguistic context. Languages don't just decide one day that they're going to change. The people who speak the languages change them, and the changes they make take place in a social context. When Old Norse features entered Northern British English after the invasions a thousand-plus years ago, presumably some people used more of the new features – English–Norse bilinguals maybe, or young people, or people who had more contact with Norse speakers. There must have been social evaluations attached to those features, and to the people who used them. Maybe there were hipsters who dropped a little Norse into every conversation, or young guys who were after some Viking macho cred. There were almost certainly cranky people who muttered about how the bloody Vikings were everywhere, and you could hardly recognize the language any more.

Of course, we don't want to fall into the "Flintstones Trap" of thinking that people have always behaved the way we do today, but we probably need to assume that language change has always had some social component. And, presumably, the kind of changes that are *linguistically* possible can't change all that much (I mean, people have roughly the same kinds of brains and mouths as they did in the past). So we should be able to

apparent time hypothesis
Based on the assumption that people's basic grammar changes very little during adulthood, apparent time studies compare speakers of different ages in a particular community and use this information to describe change over time. Thus, if older speakers are different from younger speakers, it is assumed that this is because change has taken place in the community.

uniformitarian principle
The idea that the general properties of language and language change have been the same throughout history and we are thus able to look at the changes going on today and assume that the same kind of forces were at play in the past.

look at the changes going on today, identify how they're happening and why, and assume the same kind of forces were at play in the past (this is known as the **uniformitarian principle**). This scheme of "using the present to explain the past" (as Labov 1974 puts it) has led to several proposed generalizations about typical patterns of linguistic change (Labov 1994, 2001).

For example, at the linguistic level, particular vowels tend to move "up" in the vowel space, as in the GVS, so that *meat* changes its pronunciation from *mate* to *meet*; other vowels tend to move down, as in the contemporary Canadian Vowel Shift, so that *bit* gets pronounced something like *bet*. At the social level, at least in the western industrialized cultures most studied, most changes start in the "interior classes," the middle classes and upper working classes, rather than in the highest or lowest classes.

Sometimes the social and the linguistic levels interact. Labov (1990: 205–15) summarizes the repeated findings of decades of studies in two and a half principles:

- Principle I: In stable sociolinguistic stratification, men use a higher frequency of non-standard forms than women.
- Principle Ia: In change from above, women favor the incoming prestige forms more than men.
- Principle II: In change from below, women are most often the innovators.

Here, *above* and *below* have both linguistic meanings (from above/below the level of consciousness – things people notice, or not) and a social meaning (from the higher or lower social classes). In effect, it means that no matter where the change comes from, women generally change sooner or faster than men.

This research, trying to figure out the particular combinations of social and linguistic behaviors in which change happens, addresses what is often known as the **embedding problem**. Another kind of obvious problem we need to address to talk about the social and linguistic forces affecting change is known as the **actuation problem**: why should change happen when it does? (See Weinreich et al. 1968; Labov et al. 1972.) As this is a sociolinguistics book, let's ignore the cases where there's a linguistic explanation for change (such as when two vowels start to sound too similar, so that one of them has to change so that listeners can tell what people are saying). What social reasons might there be for a change in language?

Broadly, we can assume that changes in the organization of a society (or the society's perception of how it is organized) may trigger language changes. Sometimes, increased *awareness* of the more prestigious local language variety through education, media, or migration might lead people to move away from traditional non-standard language features; this seems to be what's happened in Newfoundland (and many, many other places) over the last half-century (Clarke 2010a). Increasing face-to-face *contact* with

> ## As an aside: The Canadian Vowel Shift
>
> Subtler shifts in vowel pronunciations often go unnoticed, except perhaps by linguists. The Canadian Vowel Shift (CVS; Clarke et al. 1995) is a good example of this – in larger Canadian cities, young people now pronounce *bit* something like older people's pronunciation of *bet*, *bet* like *bat*, and *bat* like *baht*. The CVS's status on the edge of speaker consciousness makes it useful for linguists who want to study how young Canadians elsewhere are positioning themselves with respect to the mainstream. If you have CVS vowels, you can sound Canadian without sounding like you're *trying* to sound Canadian.

embedding problem
Determining the particular combinations of social and linguistic behaviors in which change happens

actuation problem
Determining why a particular linguistic change happens when it does.

speakers of a prestigious variety can have the same effect, as in Norwich, in England, where many football fans and tourists travel to London, where they are exposed to London English (Trudgill 1986: 54). Social aspirations may also be involved: in Northern Ireland, Milroy (1987/1980) found that there were more job opportunities in the neighborhood of Ballymacarrett than in Clonard, so Ballymacarrett language features were spreading. Sometimes, on the other hand, local culture gains social or economic value, so that local language features actually increase in use. We see this in Louisiana, where the "Cajun revival" leads to jobs in the tourist industry, where Cajun English is valued as a marker of authenticity (this chapter's "spotlight" reading, Dubois & Horvath 1999).

And sometimes, as people move in from outside the community, locals ramp up their use of local features as a form of resistance, as in Martha's Vineyard (Labov 1963), or in Yucatan Spanish (Michnowicz 2007), where locals are responding to an influx of Mexico City people (whom they associate with drugs and violence) by using more of a local pronunciation (whereby *Yucatan* sounds like *Yucatam*). Or Philadelphia, where Labov (1980: 263) describes a "renewed emphasis on local identification" among (White) Philadelphians, as African American migrants move in and compete "for their share of the jobs, housing, and political priorities in the city."

Language change, media, and influences

While I was writing this chapter, I got a phone call from a journalist who wanted a little expert advice for a story he was writing about new words in the dictionary. One thing he asked me was how we could predict which new words were likely to catch on. I told him sociolinguists could do a much better job dealing with changes in pronunciation and grammar than with individual words (partly because a lot of new words are slangy things that come out of youth or hipster subcultures, and, um, most of us aren't so young or hip), and even then, we were better at describing what kinds of things have caught on in the past than in predicting the future. "But there must be some things that help," he said. "Like, if Paris Hilton starts saying something." (Readers of the future, Paris Hilton was a woman from our time period who was famous because . . . uh . . . I don't know.)

And, in fact, there are some words (or pronunciations) that catch on just because a few influential characters use them. For example, a hundred years ago, the word *despicable* was generally stressed on the first syllable (*DESpicable*) — when people used the word at all. Ask most people nowadays, though, and they'll pronounce it *deSPICable*, thanks largely to that pronunciation being used by the cartoon character Daffy Duck. In the same way, *grimace* (formerly usually *griMACE*) is now usually pronounced *GRIM-uhs*, thanks to a McDonald's advertising character of that name. Overall, though, sociolinguistic research has found that, despite popular opinion, exposure to the language of the mass media doesn't often lead to language change. This is especially true of deeper change, at the level of grammatical structure or across-the-board pronunciation. That kind of change needs real people-to-people contact, and lots of it.

---

real time studies of language change

There are a few issues with the apparent time hypothesis that we need to address before accepting that differences between today's adolescents and their grandparents accurately represent change in progress:

age grading

When differences between age groups repeat as each generation ages, that is, when all speakers in a particular community favor a particular variant at one age and then a different variant at another.

real time study

A study that samples a speech community at two or more points in time.

dialect atlas

A collection of maps of a given area that show the distribution of various linguistic features.

panel study

A real time study that looks at the same members of a speech community at two (or more) points in time, for example, 20 years apart.

trend study

A real time study that studies different members of a speech community at different times, for example, talking to people who are 20, 40, and 60 now and then other people who are 20, 40, and 60 twenty years in the future.

- Do individuals have language systems that remain stable over the course of their lives, or do they participate in language changes that are introduced or spreading in their community?
- How do we know that the differences between, say, 20-year-olds and 60-year-olds today represent a snapshot of change, rather than just something that 20-year-olds and 60-year-olds have always done differently? In other words, how do we know we're not just looking at **age grading**, differences between age groups that just repeat as each generation ages?
- And more generally, is the little slice of change-in-progress that we think we see through this method actually part of a longer, complete change?

All three of these questions can be addressed by testing apparent time findings through **real time** studies – actually sampling a community at different points in time.

Often, this is done by finding comparable data from an earlier time, and seeing if that earlier data fits in where a line drawn from adolescents through grandparents would predict. For example, Bailey et al. (1991b) compared apparent time distribution of 14 features of Texan English (from two 1989 studies) with data collected 15 to 20 years earlier for a **dialect atlas** called the *Linguistic Atlas of the Gulf States*. In each case, after filtering out some shagginess caused by different collection methods, the real time data confirmed the apparent time conclusions. When apparent time data suggested that a feature was increasing, then its rates of use were lower in the earlier study; if it was decreasing in apparent time, then rates were higher in the earlier study; if it was stable in apparent time, rates were the same in the earlier study. It's also possible to move forward in time, in a sense, by returning years later to communities where data was originally collected, and getting new data. Real time studies like these fall into two categories: **panel studies** look at the same actual people, across time; **trend studies** match age cohorts across time, but don't use the same people (so researchers might talk to people who are 20, 40, or 60 now, then come back in 20 years to talk to other people who are 40, 60, or 80).

An interesting sociolinguistic panel study builds on a large collection of recordings of Montréal speakers interviewed in 1971 (Sankoff & Cedergren 1971). In 1984 and 1995, a subset of the original interviewees were tracked down and re-interviewed (fewer each time, because Montréalers move a lot and are hard to find). Comparisons across time periods found that not all variables behaved the same. Generally, individual speakers were able to change their vocabulary over time, as you might expect (and as you've probably observed yourself, when older people pick up on youth slang, even though you wish they wouldn't). For pronunciation features, people were generally fairly stable across time periods (supporting a necessary assumption of the apparent time hypothesis, that our language use is set early in life). If their language changed at all, it was in the direction of community change. But the amount of change differed, depending on where in the change people were. People who used either the old form or the new form almost all the time stayed like that across the decades. But if people were in between, using both forms in roughly equal proportions, then they shifted closer to the new form over time (Blondeau et al. 2002).

Language change and age grading in Panama

A well-known trend study that illustrates both confirmation of apparent time-type change *and* age grading is that by Cedergren (1988), who in the early 1980s went back to Panama City to see if a change in the local pronunciation of the *ch* sound was progressing in the way it seemed to be in her data from a 1969 study. And, in fact, it was, as you can see in figure 5.1. But she also found a spike in the rates of use among the second-oldest group in both studies, the teenagers, which suggests that age grading was also at play. This **adolescent peak**, where non-standard features are used at their highest rates by young teenagers, has since been observed in studies of other communities, and may contribute to pushing change forward – to oversimplify, it looks like the exaggerated use of non-standard forms by adolescents (to be cool or whatever) is taken by the even-younger kids as a model of normal use, then pushed even higher when that group hits adolescence and it's their turn to exaggerate (see the discussion in Tagliamonte & D'Arcy 2009).

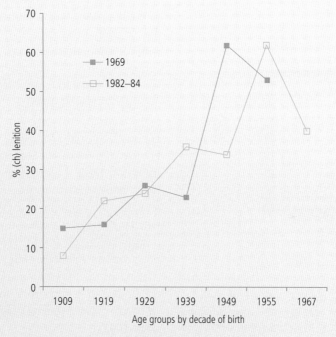

Figure 5.1. *CH*-lenition in Panama City (Cedergren 1988).

Recently, there have been several re-studies (by new researchers) of communities well known in the sociolinguistic literature. For example, Pope (2002) replicated Labov's (1963) Martha's Vineyard study, finding a similar profile – young men with strong ties to the local way of life make greater use of local speech features. However, it looks like, thanks to a combination of ongoing language change and a massive influx of people from outside, a different vowel is now being used to mark localness. When Labov was doing his research, people marked localness by centralizing the PRICE vowel

adolescent peak
The observation that some variants (especially incoming variants) are actually most used by adolescents, not by the youngest group.

As an aside: Rule Britennia – royal vowel changes over time

In a panel study (with a one-person panel) that got a lot of attention, Harrington et al. (2000b, 2005) took acoustic measurements of Queen Elizabeth's vowels in samples of her annual Christmas message across four decades, and found that between the 1950s and the 1970s, her vowels changed in ways that parallel community changes from the same time period. In particular, her pronunciation of the KIT, DRESS, and TRAP vowels moved farther apart. The result is that her vowels sound less "snooty" – less like what people imitate when they make fun of the queen!

(pronouncing it something like *pruhyce*). For current generations, centralization of the MOUTH vowel (which is increasing) has taken over from PRICE-centralization (which is decreasing).

These findings, taken together, offer fairly strong support for the apparent time hypothesis, without denying that age grading can occur. Of course, if we have the right data, we can also do real time studies on their own, just to look at how change works (this is getting easier over time, as the number of years covered by recording technology increases). For example, a trend study of Dutch radio broadcasts shows something similar to the Montréal study – an incoming feature (pronouncing /z/ and /v/ as /s/ and /f/) is more common with younger announcers, as you'd expect. But it's also more common with older announcers now than with announcers of their generation recorded in an earlier time period (Van de Velde et al. 1996).

We can also use real time studies to show stability. For example, older recordings of speakers of Québec French (Poplack & St-Amand 2007) and African American English (AAE; Bailey et al. 1991a) show that many non-standard features have a long history (counteracting the common assumption among people who hate language change that anything non-standard must be new and result from the slackness of today's youth). Analysis of older written language shows the same thing. For example, I've found the same linguistic constraints that govern use of unmarked past tense verbs (e.g., *come* instead of *came*) in AAE today in letters from the mid-1800s (Van Herk 2011), and the still-used term *mother wit*, meaning "common sense," in a letter from 1796 (Van Herk & Poplack 2003).

There are also more and more studies working solely with written data, to look at changes that took place centuries ago. This kind of research has been going on for a while – there's actually a big quantitative study of changes in question formation in Shakespearean-era English, undertaken by Ellegård in 1953. The more recent studies are likely to have a stronger sociolinguistic component. For example, Nevalainen (2006) shows that the decline of negative concord (double negation, as in *I never saw nobody*) in Standard English was led by men, especially in legal documents.

the s-shaped curve of language change

An important paper by Kroch (1989) took the data from Ellegård's 1953 study and re-analyzed it to show that language change seems to happen in a particular way. New forms start off slowly, then at some point pick up speed, being used by more and more people in more and more contexts, until eventually they become the main way of doing things, with the old form slowly petering out. If you plot this change on a frequency graph, it comes out looking like an S, and this pattern of change, since replicated in a ton of studies, is known as the *S-shaped curve* (figure 5.2). This makes sense, if you think about it in terms of how we come into contact with new words or ideas. It's like transmission of a disease. In the beginning, hardly anybody's using the new form, so they don't get the chance to transmit it to many people. Then, at some point, the new form becomes common enough that new-form-users are in frequent contact with old-form-users, and the form spreads quickly. At the end, the old form just hangs on at low rates of use.

This last bit isn't entirely what you'd expect, and in fact Raymond Hickey (2003) has wondered why changes don't just rush to completion at this point, as the new form is

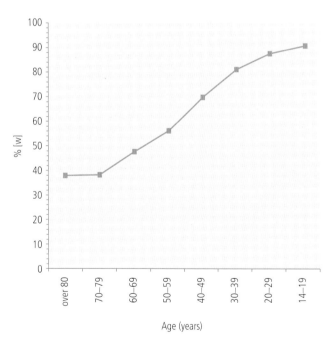

Figure 5.2. Percentage of central Canadian speakers with [w] in WH words, by age (from Chambers 2002).

available to everyone. Some fairly recent papers suggest a possible answer: once the old form "loses its job," so to speak, it sometimes gets a new, smaller job. For example, in Canadian French, the standard *ne* form of negation (saying *Je ne sais pas* instead of *J'sais pas*) has almost disappeared from casual spoken language – it's been used less than 1 percent of the time for 150 years. But it's still useful when speakers want to sound formal, such as when they discuss religion or education (Poplack & St-Amand 2007). And in urban areas of Newfoundland, the *-s* suffix on verbs (*I knows that*) has almost disappeared, but is still used with a handful of verbs, apparently for identity maintenance purposes (Van Herk et al. 2008).

subtle sound change: vowel shifts

Changes are easy to notice when they involve words, or whole grammatical structures, or an entire sound – two formerly separate sounds merge (as with *which* and *witch*), or an alternative pronunciation dies out, or is born. A lot of sound change is subtler than that, though, especially when we look at vowels. Vowels may shift their pronunciation relative to other vowels, sometimes so slightly that the change is only evident through acoustic analysis. Recording and measurement technology lets us track major changes that are happening in North American vowel pronunciations. One dramatic shift, affecting 30 to 40 million speakers in the US Midwest, is known as the Northern Cities Shift (NCS). Younger speakers in cities between Milwaukee and Rochester (NY) are involved

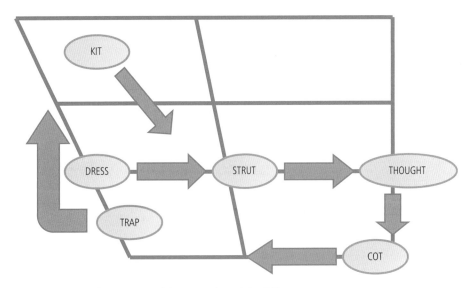

Figure 5.3. Vowel movements of the US Northern Cities Shift.

in a complex vowel shift, illustrated in figure 5.3. Their pronunciation of *hot*, for example, sounds to non-NCS people like *hat*, while their *Ann* sounds like *Ian*.

The NCS shows an interesting interaction between time and place. The sound shift shows change over time, of course, but the places where it's happening are similar to what dialectologists know as the Northern dialect area, as determined by earlier research on word choices. The boundaries of this area reflect earlier North American settlement patterns, but not contemporary population movements (such as people migrating to find work). In other words, it's unlikely that the NCS was brought into the area by people moving in. Rather, it seems that the earlier dialect of the area contained the seeds of the current change, and just needed something to set it off.

On the other hand, regional boundaries can't explain everything about the NCS. The shift isn't found across the entire Northern dialect area, and is absent or slowed in rural areas and among African Americans. And, even though it seems to be led by women, it doesn't seem to carry any particular prestige, if speakers notice it at all. But just because the shift is below the level of consciousness for people who use it, it doesn't mean that it's the same for people *outside* the community. Non-NCS people really hear the NCS: when I imitated NCS-style vowel shifting for a well-travelled musician friend, he immediately said, "Oh! Like in Michigan!"

As an aside: Variation without change

Near the beginning of the chapter, I talked about how change over time implied variation in any one time period. The reverse doesn't have to be true, though. Sometimes we find variation without change, usually known as **stable variation**. A good example in English is g-droppin', which people have been doing for at least a century without one of the variants (*jumping* vs. *jumpin'*) winning out over time.

Stable variation can be destabilized, though, if a community's social situation changes. For example, if many people from another area move into the community, the locals might become more aware of which features distinguish their speech. They might increase use of those features to show their local-ness, or decrease them to fit in with (or suck up to) the newcomers. That seems to be what happened in Placentia, in Newfoundland: when a naval base was built there during World War II, American military personnel would correct the locals' high rates of g-droppin'. Over a generation, the rates dropped dramatically, especially for women (who often dated or married those Americans). Since the base wound down a generation ago, local people have returned to their old g-droppin' ways (Power 2011).

---

age: change across the lifespan

Let's assume we're now all comfortable with the idea that age differences in language can tell us something about change. But that doesn't mean that today's baby boomers are simply walking archives of a Beatles-era adolescent linguistic system. Age exists as a meaningful social category, just like class or ethnicity or gender. And variable language features serve a social function in the here and now, separate from their origins and eventual destinations, even if they're undergoing change – or maybe especially if they're undergoing change. In other words, people can decide that a particular language feature is "old people talk" or "ditzy young people talk," without really thinking about whether it'll have the same social meaning in 40 years. In this section, we'll look at how age and the social meaning of language work together, working our way through the lifespan.

stable variation
Variation without change; when multiple variants survive for a long period, without one replacing the other.

acquiring sociolinguistic competence

Linguists know quite a lot about how children acquire the basic tools of language, and at what age, but we're a little less certain about how and when they acquire sociolinguistic competence, the ability to use language according to community norms. One problem is that it's hard to get enough child language data to analyze using our normal techniques. One study found that it takes eight to fourteen hours of interviews with kids to get the same amount of data as in an hour or two with adults (Roberts 1996). Another problem is that it's hard to separate social variation from regular developmental issues. (Are children mirroring local variation in pronunciation of a particular sound? Or are they just still in the middle of learning the sound?) Also, many child acquisition researchers focus on "acquisition" of a linguistic feature (in the sense of children hitting a certain percentage threshold of "correct" adult-like use), rather than on how the variation they see is actually working.

But generally, there seems to be an order of sociolinguistic acquisition among children.

- First, kids acquire the variation that's available in the surrounding language (as early as age 3). If the community has two ways to pronounce a particular sound, kids will use them both.

style shifting
An individual's speech changes according to differences in interlocutor(s), social context, personal goals, or external factors.

- Next, they pick up on **style shifting** – that is, they understand that people change their speech depending on what they're doing and who they're talking to. For example, 4-year-olds use simplified speech when talking to 2-year-olds, but not to adults (Steinberg et al. 2001: 38). Youssef (1993) demonstrates that in Trinidad, children have to differentiate between Standard English and Trinidadian Creole from an early age, and they do so. Andersen (1992) gave children (aged 4 to 6) puppets with roles (father, mother, child, doctor, patient, foreigner) and encouraged them to play out those roles. And they could do it! For example, they never used *well* as a discourse marker (as in, *Well, I guess it's time to go*) except when pretending to be adults.

linguistic constraint
A linguistic factor that governs the use of a particular variant.

- Finally, kids pick up the **linguistic constraints** on variation. Kovac and Adamson (1981) found that kids with AAE as a home language deleted the copula (the "be" verb, as in *he gonna go* vs. *he's gonna go*) by age 3, but only got all the adult-like constraints on when to use it at age 7. A small study by Labov (1989) in Philadelphia showed that children figured out the stylistic constraints on g-droppin' (it's casual) before they got the linguistic ones (it's more common with verbs like *runnin'* than with pronouns like *something*). They got most constraints (of both types) by age 7, but the different effects of particular verb types took them even longer to figure out.

There's a fair bit of evidence suggesting that there is a sensitive age period for picking up sociolinguistic competence in a speech community, in the same way that there seems to be a sensitive age period for learning language at all (Lenneberg 1967). This can be seen in studies of children who move – the older they are, the more trouble they have acquiring the variable language system of their new homes (Payne 1980; Chambers 1992; Kerswill 1996). For some pronunciations constrained by word class rules (such as in varieties where TRAP and BATH vowels are pronounced differently), it seems that the rules have to be learned by age 3 to be fully acquired. If you've ever met people who moved to or from England during their early teens, you may have noticed that their A sounds are all over the place.

As children get older, they tend to focus on people their own age or slightly older as their speech models, rather than adults and other family members (Labov 1972b; Eckert 2000). This might happen sooner in some speech communities, especially in the developing world, where it's often older siblings, rather than parents, who are largely responsible for raising younger children. Non-standard feature usage seems to peak in adolescence (even for features that are not undergoing change; Romaine 1984; Holmes 1992: 184). Rampton (1995) discusses adolescence as a time when people experiment with language features from other cultures (and see chapter 6).

As adolescents move into the world of work, we often see a dip in their use of non-standard features. This seems to result from their moving into a **linguistic market** (*marché linguistique*; Sankoff & Laberge 1978) in which control of standard language has real social and economic benefits. The degree of shift obviously varies with where people fit into the market. Middle-class women in particular seem to show a big drop in use of non-standard features in their middle years (Holmes et al. 1991).

Older speakers have until recently not received much sociolinguistic attention. If researchers look at them at all, it tends to be as repositories of traditional speech features (an apparent time thing), rather than as sociolinguistic actors. (An exception is recent work by Mary Rose (2006), who looks at a seniors' center from an ethnographic perspective.) Part of this is presumably practical – most research assistants are graduate students, who tend to be young, and so if they exploit their social networks to find people to talk to, they're likely to end up with a lot of people in their own age group. Coupland et al. (1991: 13) have come down hard on linguists' tendency to ignore the elderly (except in terms of language pathologies, as with Alzheimer's-related speech issues), saying that it reflects an "ageist ideological slant." They've done some interesting work on how people talk *to* the elderly, describing the speaking-to-old-people register as "secondary baby talk" because it shares features with speech directed at children. As the elderly make up an increasing share of the population of industrialized nations, we may find that research on their language also increases.

> ### As an aside: Those darn kids!
>
> Recent research in Japan has looked at *kogyaru kotoba*, "high-school girl language" (Coulmas 2005: 58–9). Slangy, full of abbreviations, and rapidly changing, it seems to behave like many other adolescent varieties. The fact that its culture has given it a name says something about how socially significant it is seen to be, disliked because it seems to show contempt for traditional notions of propriety, such as the avoidance of **honorifics** like *-san*, ways of marking respect. Given that in traditional Japanese culture women are supposed to defer to men and youth are supposed to defer to older people, it's no surprise that sociolinguistic changes among girls should attract a lot of attention (and criticism). (See also chapter 7 on language and gender.)

honorific
A form of address expressing respect and esteem.

linguistic market
The importance of standard language in the social and economic life of the speaker.

summing up

Time is relevant to sociolinguists in two main ways. First, variationists study language change over time, usually within its social context. By comparing the language of older and younger speakers in a community (that is, looking at language in *apparent time*), we can observe change as it happens. However, age differences might sometimes simply reflect differences in the ways that old and young people have always spoken in a community (*age grading*). To verify our findings, we need *real time* studies, where we sample the same community at two (or more) different time periods. Second, we can study age as a social factor, by looking at how young people acquire sociolinguistic competence in the norms of their community, how language changes over the lifespan, and how speakers use language to reflect the norms associated with their age cohort.

Where to next?

While it's unlikely that apparent time studies will disappear – they tell us so much, and not every community or language has a long recorded history – it's becoming easier and easier to compare language use across real time. Recording technology has been around long enough for us to compare the real language of multiple generations – for example, researchers have unearthed recordings from the 1930s and 1940s of African Americans (Bailey et al. 1991a) and Québeckers (Poplack & St-Amand 2007) born as early as the 1850s, allowing for a century and a half of real time comparisons. And historical researchers continue to track down written documents that give us a glimpse into the vernacular language of earlier times. Even early sociolinguistic studies are now entering middle age, so that we can look at multiple generations of people recorded under similar circumstances.

Spotlight: Ragin' Cajuns

Dubois, Sylvie, and Barbara Horvath. "When the music changes, you change too: Gender and language change in Cajun English." *Language Variation and Change* 11, no. 3 (1999): 287–313.

It hasn't always been cool to be Cajun. In this paper, Dubois and Horvath look at how rapid social change in Cajun country (southeastern Louisiana) has elevated the status of local people and culture, at just the point where French is disappearing as the community's language. As a result, Cajun English is becoming the way to "be" Cajun, linguistically. In the past, the dialect was the result of English being spoken by people who used French as their primary language (see chapter 11 on language contact). That was followed by a generation that moved toward English to find jobs, especially in the oil industry. The Cajun Renaissance led to positive associations for Cajun-ness – the dialect became "socially charged" (p. 291). But Cajun-ness is more useful for men than women, so they're the ones adopting (or re-adopting) Cajun-associated linguistic features.

Help with reading: The paper spends a while at the beginning setting up the theoretical background, the ideas from (variationist) sociolinguistics that are going to figure in the later discussion. Then there's a description of a pile of linguistic features of Cajun English. You can follow the argument without understanding the linguistic details, but they do help to give you the flavor of the variety: (th) and (dh) are the pronunciation of *thin* and *this* as *tin* and *dis*; (ay) monophthongization is pronouncing PRICE something like *prass*; nasalization is what you think it is; and unaspirated (p, t, k) make *pan*, *tan*, and *can* sound a bit like *ban*, *dan*, and *gan*. The paper continues with a recent history of the community, and ties the changes to identity work among young people.

Links to other readings: Dubois has more writings on Cajun English, as does Megan Melançon (e.g., Dubois et al. 1995; Dubois & Horvath 1998). The "post-insular" situation described here is not all that different from what Labov described for Martha's Vineyard back in 1963, or what we're finding in Newfoundland today. People with a strong local variety often seem to respond to fancy-talking arrivals from outside by first starting to sound like them, then later reclaiming their traditional ways of speaking. You might also want to check out Miriam Meyerhoff and Nancy Niedzielski's 2003 article, "The globalisation of vernacular variation."

---

exercises

1. An entertaining Hallowe'en pastime (if you're nerdy) is to compile a list of *zombie language* features: words or grammatical features that you can still find in dictionaries, grammar books, or very standard language varieties, but that hardly anybody uses (thus the name – they're dead, but won't go away, just like real zombies). In Canada, these would include *whilst, shall, amongst,* and *should* used for *would* in sentences like *I should be careful if I were you.* What zombie language features can you think of? (If you know people who are British and American, see if any of the American zombie features are still part of everyday speech for the British folks.)

2. Write down as many slang terms as possible that you think have come into English in the last 15 years or so. Now, write down some that you think have been around for a long time. Look your words up in a source that gives year of origin (dictionary, website), and/or ask somebody older than you if they know the term (and can remember when they first started hearing it). Any surprises?

3. Look at your list from exercise 2 and check off the terms that mean *good/cool, bad/uncool, drunk/ stoned, vomit, urinate, have sex, overreact, kill,* or *marijuana*. Do these account for most of your list? Why do you think there are so many youth slang terms for these things? Is there another category that accounts for many of the remaining terms on your list?

4. As you go through your day, note any things that you hear said by people of one age group that you think would sound very odd coming from people of another age group. Write them down.

5. "Age-inappropriate" language and behavior are often used for comedic effect in film or television. Note any examples that you run across (or can think of). Which direction does the humor usually go – are old people trying to sound young considered funnier than young people trying to sound old, or vice versa? Why do you think this is so?

6. Ask people in their thirties or older (including, ideally, your parents) if they can remember the first time they caught themselves sounding like their parents. Have them describe the situation and how they reacted to it.

discussion

1. Do you know the meaning of *glasnost, telex, macramé, seltzer, International Reply Coupon, running board, Mackinaw, dungarees, jazzbo*? Have you ever heard anybody use any of these words? If you *have* seen or heard them used, who used them? If you haven't, why do you think they have disappeared from use?
2. When you were younger, were there one or two people that you knew who always seemed to be the ones who knew the latest slang (or the latest everything, like clothing or music)? Why them? How did they get to be so cool? (As in, why did they know about stuff first, and why did the stuff they did catch on with other people?)
3. Can you tell whether people you know are talking to elderly relatives or friends on the phone, by a change in the way they talk? What in particular is different? Can you imitate it?
4. Do you know people who talk to children in exactly the same style and tone as they talk to adults? Do you know people who use crazy exaggerated baby talk? How do kids seem to react to either of those approaches?
5. Are there things you used to say when you were in high school that you've completely abandoned since? Maybe things that you're only reminded of when you reminisce with former schoolmates? How do those reminiscing conversations go (i.e., is it "Oh my God, we were such morons")?

other resources

Books on the history of English will tell you more about how the language has changed (not necessarily from a sociolinguistic perspective), and give you examples of earlier stages of the language.

The three volumes of Labov's *Principles of Linguistic Change* (1994, 2001, 2010) lay out the core variationist approach to language change.

Tagliamonte and D'Arcy's "Peaks beyond phonology" (2009) is a good example of how we use ideas like apparent time and age grading, with a nice bit on the adolescent peak and gender.

Chapter 4 of Chambers' *Sociolinguistic Theory* (1995, 2009) lays out the relationship between age and change in detail, then chapter 5 riffs on possible explanations for language change.

Online slang dictionaries come and go – search "slang dictionary" and see what you find, but don't assume you can trust the linguistics of what you read there.

6 Ethnicity

Many chapters back, I introduced the idea that regional language varieties tend to get their distinct characteristics through isolation (we sound like the people around us, and not like the people we never interact with). Those regional varieties then acquire their social meanings when people from different places come into contact. The same description could be applied to ethnic varieties of language.

ethnic language varieties

Through immigration, colonization, war, travel, and other social forces, people from different cultural backgrounds end up in the same place. Often, each group's language will change over generations: at first, they may speak their native language, then the language of their new home, but with many features of their original language (see also chapter 11), then a variety of the new language that in some way marks them as distinct from other speakers of that language, especially if there are enough people from the same background around. This new variety, if it retains its associations with the original ethnic group, is often called an ethnolect.

ethnolect
An ethnic variety of a language or dialect.

What Is Sociolinguistics?, First Edition. Gerard Van Herk.
© 2012 Gerard Van Herk. Published 2012 by Blackwell Publishing Ltd.

Societies choose which ethnic distinctions are important to them, and both the distinctions that matter and the boundaries between groups differ from one society to the next. In the USA, the ethnic distinction that has historically been most relevant has been between Black and White, a result of the country's slave past, and this is reflected in sociolinguistic fact – African American English (AAE) is the most salient and most discussed (and most researched) ethnic variety of English. In recent years, the influx of Spanish-speaking immigrants has increased American public discourse about Hispanic or Latino English. In other countries, other ethnic distinctions are central to public discourse – English/French in Canada, Protestant/Catholic in Ireland, Flemish/Walloon in Belgium – especially if the groups in question have been living there for long periods of time.

In each case, speakers may be more familiar with one language or language variety, but the choices they make about how to use language let them position themselves with respect to other people, and let them build their (ethnic) identity. A single linguistic choice can mark you as a member of (or let you affiliate with) a particular community (remember shibboleths?). *Aks* for *ask* makes you African American in the USA, *haitch* for the eighth letter of the alphabet makes you Catholic (or Catholic-educated) in Newfoundland, saying *eh?* a lot marks you as Maori in New Zealand. In practice, of course, sociolinguistically competent people can draw from a large repertoire of linguistic resources to perform an ethnic identity. For example, Fought (2006: 21–3) lists ways that Latino American community members can construct ethnic identity: their heritage language (Spanish), code-switching (see chapters 10 and 11), pronunciation, grammar, stress patterns, discourse features, or even features from another language variety (such as AAE).

As an aside: Ethnic hypercorrection – not sounding like your parents

The children of immigrants often work hard to fit into their new communities, and may have derogatory terms for people who sound like they just arrived from the old country (in Canada one term is *fresh* or *freshers*, as in "fresh off the plane"). One of the ways people try to fit in is through language choices, with some interesting results.

In New York, Labov (1966, 2001) found that some vowel patterns were stronger among particular ethnic sub-groups. Second- and third-generation Jews had CLOTH vowels that were closer to GOAT (ask people to imitate New Yorkers saying "coffee talk" and you'll know what I mean). Second- and third-generation Italians had TRAP vowels that were closer to DRESS. Those vowels are the opposite of what you'd get due to influence from Yiddish and Italian. In other words, these speakers were trying so hard not to sound like freshers that they went further in the opposite direction than other New Yorkers, a process Labov calls **ethnic hypercorrection**.

ethnic hypercorrection
When people use a feature associated with their ethnic group even less often than non-members of the group.

enclaves
A distinctly bounded geographic area in which many residents share an ethnicity or other social characteristic.

Of course, at the same time that speakers perform ethnicity, they're also performing other aspects of their identities, including gender, class, and region. Sometimes, this seems to involve a sort of pick-and-mix process: Childs and Mallinson (2004) show how African Americans in rural western North Carolina use a lot of local pronunciation features that they share with their White neighbors, but then set themselves off by using vocabulary from wider AAE. Hoffman and Walker (2010) find second-generation Italian Canadians in Toronto participating in a vowel shift that lets them sound kind of Italian and kind of young urban Canadian at the same time.

Hoffman and Walker also find that the amount of ethnically identified language people use is greater if they live in ethnic **enclaves**, places where many residents share an ethnicity and where they can often live much of their lives in limited contact with people from other backgrounds (figure 6.1). We can see that ethnic neighborhoods have

Figure 6.1.   Toronto's Chinatown. Such ethnic enclaves encourage the retention of ethnically identified language features. Source: Street signs in Chinatown, Toronto, Canada. © Rolf Hicker Photography / Alamy.

a social reality to people in that they are given names. Novelist Wayson Choy (1995) points out that the Chinese term for Vancouver's Chinatown translates literally as "China People Street" – in this case, when the dominant group names the neighborhood ("Chinatown"), it's literally the people who are left out. Note also that immigrant or in-migrant groups who are able to assimilate quickly into a target culture don't have named neighborhoods. There's nowhere in Canada where you can go hang out in Little Holland or Scotstown, but in Barbados, there *is* an area nicknamed Scotland, tradition-ally the home of poor Whites. And Toronto *does* have named neighborhoods associated with ethnic groups who are now fairly assimilated (Corktown for Irish, Cabbagetown for eastern Europeans).

Who's ethnic?

Ethnic boundaries are determined both internally (by a group) and externally (by other groups), and what counts as an ethnic divide can vary according to place, time, and social situation. King and Clarke (2002) look at the derogatory term *Newfie* through considering Newfoundlanders as a distinct ethnic group, applying the definition from Giles and Coupland (1991: 106): "those individuals who say they belong to ethnic group A rather than ethnic group B, are willing to be treated as A rather than B, allow their behaviour to be interpreted and judged as A's and not B's, and have shared systems of symbols and meanings, as in norms and rules for conduct, normatively associated with community A." We could also note the degree to which Irish-origin Americans have become bleached of ethnic markedness over the generations, described in Ignatiev's (1995) *How the Irish Became White*.

What "counts" as ethnicity (or race) also varies across lan-guages and communities. A recent blog (Fish 2010) contrasts how in the USA Latinos of all backgrounds are sometimes considered a single race, while French people (of varied backgrounds) are not. But in French, the term *race française* ("French race") was wide-spread a century ago. (An internet search for the term today turns up mostly links to neo-Nazis and the Tour de France.)

as more highly accented than that of White speakers (Rubin 1992; Atagi 2003). And White schoolteachers rated the language of non-White children as less standard (Williams 1983). The catch in all three studies is that respondents were actually hearing the same recordings, accompanied by different photos or descriptions – in the words of Fought (2006), they "halluci-nated" the accents, making assumptions based on the appearance of the supposed speakers. You can imagine the very real consequences of these assumptions – non-White students getting lower grades, or being streamed into lower-level classes, or non-White teaching assistants and professors getting worse evaluations from students.

crossing: using the language of others

Given the markedness of Whiteness within non-White cultural communities, it's no surprise that there are negative sanctions for community members who are seen as "acting White" (sociolinguistically or otherwise). Use of White-identified language (including the standard), or non-use of community-identified language, is seen as selling out or stuck up, perhaps an attempt by the speaker to deny community membership (Urciuoli 1996; Fought 2003). Socially mobile members of these communities employ a range of strategies to negotiate this divide. Middle-class African Americans might use standard grammar, but retain AAE pronunciations or discourse strategies (Spears 1998). Children and grandchildren of immigrants might salt their language with words from the old country, even if they no longer speak the language fluently. In these cases, the conscious choice to use community language is a way of expressing solidarity and demonstrating local sociolinguistic competence.

What about switching in the other direction, when speakers of a mainstream (in this case, White) variety adopt the language features of a marked ethnic variety? This behavior can be highly marked, for several reasons. First, thanks to the power relationships between these varieties, this kind of switching is less frequent. And second, the strong community-building connotations of the marked ethnic varieties makes their adoption (or co-opting) threatening for the communities involved. Still, the positive connotations that these varieties might buy a speaker (urban-ness, hip-ness, masculinity) make them appealing, as we can see by the constant adoption of AAE words into mainstream American English over the decades (and, usually, the subsequent rejection of the same words by urban AAE speakers). So young White Britons adopt Punjabi words (Rampton 1995), and young White American hip-hop fans adopt AAE words, grammar, and pronunciations (Cutler 1999). This process is usually called **crossing** (Rampton 1995). Notice that there isn't really a similar term for when speakers of marked ethnic varieties (like AAE or Punjabi British English) adopt White-identified features. This demonstrates how unmarked that behavior is (in other words, people who speak non-Standard non-White varieties are *expected* to pick up the language of power, and so nobody comments on it, or names it). There are, of course, names for this *within* particular non-White communities, names like "sounding White."

Of course, there's also the possibility of what we could call "sideways crossing," when speakers of one marked variety adopt features of another (as when young Somali Canadians or Latino Americans pick up AAE features). Some writers (e.g.,

crossing
When speakers use language features or linguistic styles associated with another ethnic group.

Adams 2000) suggest that we're moving toward a world in which our identities are much more fluid and complex, less restricted by the traits we're born with and more open to conscious blending and hybridization. If so, we might expect richer sociolinguistic performances of identity, or at least performances with more points of reference to choose from. It'll be up to sociolinguists to develop theoretical and methodological tools to keep up with what people are doing with language. Given how invested we are in the central role that language plays in culture (and maybe vice versa), this might take a little work.

summing up

Sociolinguists tend to study the relationship between language and ethnicity in a few ways. They might consider ethnicity as a social characteristic (like gender or class) that affects the language that people use, leading to ethnolects. They might look at how ethnic features can (or can't) be used by different groups. Or they might consider the (linguistic) ways that ethnic groups can be identified and described. In each case, implicit in the analysis is an understanding of the power relationships between the ethnic groups involved.

Where to next?

The recent shift in sociolinguists' focus toward discussing identity performance is almost as strong in the study of ethnic differences as it is in gender studies. It's a safe bet that the next decade of research will see an expansion of this area, especially as it relates to the expression of multiple or hybrid identities. Gender and ethnicity researchers are already starting to use each others' terms (especially *crossing*, *dragging*, and *passing*).

Spotlight: Wigga figga

Cutler, Cecilia A. "Yorkville Crossing: White teens, hip hop and African American English." *Journal of Sociolinguistics* 3/4 (1999): 428–42.

"Dis is gonna sound mad weird, yo," says Mike, the well-off White teenager who's the subject of Cutler's case study of ethnic crossing. Cutler describes a now well-known phenomenon, the adoption of AAE features by White hip-hop-identified youth. The paper introduces Mike and his personal history, identifies which AAE features he does and doesn't use, and describes the paths by which features migrate across ethnicity and class. Then there's a longer section, in which Cutler examines how Mike talks about race and identity and identification.

Reading the paper: The process of crossing that Cutler describes will presumably be familiar to most readers (you may know terms for this kind of crossing, such as *wigga*). Given that, the academic language isn't much of a barrier to reading. There are quite a few linguistic terms in the paper. As usual, you don't have to know them to follow the argument, but knowing them will help you get a sense of what Mike sounds like. AAE features that Cutler says Mike *doesn't* have are third singular *-s* absence (*he go*), habitual be (*she be complaining*), and widespread copula deletion (*she gonna go*). The "schwa *the*" that Cutler mentions is saying *thuh apple* instead of *thee apple*. Mike's r-less even in "linking r," which is R between vowels. In other words, as well as *huh dog* for *her dog*, which many New Yorkers say, he also says *huh age* for *her age*. "TH stopping" is *duh* for *the*. "Prosodic features" are things like pitch, stress, and vowel length, the rhythm and melody of speech. "Lexis" is vocabulary.

More: For a short and accessible version of this topic, check out Cutler's piece on crossing on the website for PBS's *Do You Speak American?* at http://www.pbs.org/speak/speech/prestige/crossing (accessed August 18, 2011). For more detail, at a pretty high discourse level, there's Rampton's book *Crossing* (1995).

1. Look up the words *quadroon* and *octoroon* in a dictionary. How are they defined? Were you familiar with the terms before looking them up?
2. If you have a thick skin: use a search engine to find jokes about people from two or more different ethnic groups. Are the jokes similar, or different? Do you get different numbers of "hits" for the different searches? What (if anything) does this tell you about the markedness of the particular ethnic groups – or about the degree to which the joke tellers think it's OK to tell jokes about that group?
3. Ask some White people and some Black people what their ethnicity is. If your respondents match those studied by Bucholtz (2011), the Black people will say "Black" and the White people (especially the young ones) will name a nationality (e.g., Polish). Why do you think this is? If your respondents *don't* match Bucholtz's, why do you think you got a different result?

1. If you live somewhere where the term "ethnicity" is usually associated with racial differences, does it strike you as odd when the term is used for, say, French and English groups in Canada?
2. How would you describe your ethnicity? What other terms do you know that are used to describe the ethnic group(s) that you belong to? What ethnonyms (if any) have been used to describe you? Are there terms that in-group members can use that out-group members can't? (This discussion will go better if you and your classmates are a happy, supportive group. Please tell people in your group if you don't like the way the discussion is going.)
3. Can you recognize members of your (or others') ethnic groups by voice alone, for example, on the telephone? Can you identify particular cues that you pick up on, or is it just a "feeling"?
4. Are there words or expressions that you use that you didn't at first realize weren't used by members of all ethnic groups? What are they?
5. Have you ever been in a situation where somebody (maybe you!) used a word or expression that "belonged" to another group? What happened?
6. Can you think of any portrayals of crossing from films or television? Was it portrayed in a positive or negative light? How do you think the crossing was supposed to be interpreted (funny, ingratiating, unpleasant, incompetent, etc.)?
7. Chapter 8, on style, talks about accommodation (moving toward the speech of your interlocutor) as something that lets you move closer to that person socially. How does crossing relate to that idea?
8. Do people at your university complain that they can't understand foreign-accented teaching assistants? Are there particular ethnic groups that get criticized the most? Why do you think this is?
9. Have you, or anybody you know, changed your name to match that of another linguistic or ethnic group (for example, from Jiang to Henry, or vice versa)? If so, why? And how did you decide what name to choose? If not, why not?

accommodation
Changing your speech style to sound more like the people you are speaking with.

other resources

There's good fairly recent writing on language and ethnicity. You might want to start with Carmen Fought's *Language and Ethnicity: Key Topics in Sociolinguistics* (2006). For crossing, Ben Rampton's *Crossing: Language and Ethnicity among Adolescents* (1995) is rough going in the theory sections, but the frequent examples and comments from speakers keep it moving along. For Whiteness and more, try Mary Bucholtz's *White Kids: Language, Race, and Styles of Youth Identity* (2011).

7 Gender and Identity

So far, this book has been operating on the assumption that you talk like who you talk to. That idea worked well for region, but a little less well for age and social class and ethnicity. In those chapters, we started considering the possibility that people were making some choices, conscious or not, about their language use, in order to position themselves with respect to others. In other words, we started to assume speaker agency.

Now that we're ready to discuss language and gender, speaker agency will become even more relevant, as "you talk like who you talk to" doesn't work as well. Presumably most of us speak pretty often to people of a different sex – often enough to talk like them, if we chose to. Yet we still sound different from them. Sure, part of this difference is biological – men tend to have longer and thicker vocal cords than women, and thus have lower-pitched voices. But, in fact, the actual pitch difference between men's and women's speech is usually larger than it would be if it was due to vocal cord length and thickness alone. Why would this happen? It seems that we men are taking a real pitch difference, then exaggerating it to make sure that people know we're men, taking our

speaker agency
The ability of speakers to control what they do and to make conscious choices.

What Is Sociolinguistics?, First Edition. Gerard Van Herk.
© 2012 Gerard Van Herk. Published 2012 by Blackwell Publishing Ltd.

As an aside: Gender vs. sex

Contemporary English speakers often use the word *gender* to mean biological sex, maybe because we've decided to use the word *sex* to mean intercourse. This tendency has spread so far that it's found even in places where there's no possibility of socially constructed identity being an issue. For example, some scholarly articles in biology journals refer to the "gender" of nesting birds!

gender
A socially constructed identity, rather than a biological category.

grammatical gender
In some languages, such as French and German, a way of classifying nouns, usually as feminine, masculine, or neuter.

big Barry White voice man-selves through the world. And that's just for pitch. Think of all the other gender-associated language features out there. Stereotypically or not, who's more likely to say *cute*? Or *Oh my God*? *Fabulous*? To compliment others? To swear? And what are the social penalties (in terms of listener perception) for using the "wrong" gender-associated form? Surely none of this is due to our chromosome count.

So let's say it's not too controversial that language differences linked to gender are not just something we have, but rather something we *do*, or have done to us (Wodak 1997). That fits nicely into gender and feminist research more broadly, which assumes that most things about gender are things we do – as Simone de Beauvoir put it back in 1949: "One is not born, but rather becomes, a woman." This suggests a definition: in the non-grammar-book sense, **gender** refers to a socially constructed identity, rather than a biological category. And, of course, there's also **grammatical gender**, which in many languages requires tables and turnips and everything else to be linguistically marked as feminine or masculine (or neuter). Later in the chapter, we'll see how grammatical gender might also play a role in the construction or maintenance of social gender. In this chapter I try to keep the terms separate, using *gender* when I mean something socially constructed and *sex* when I mean something biological.

gender and interaction

Research in the field of language and gender really took off thanks to work by Robin Lakoff (1972, 1973, 1975). In fact, a major textbook on language and gender (Eckert & McConnell-Ginet 2003) makes a point by introducing Lakoff's work in the very first sentence! Lakoff's 1973 article, which later became a book, *Language and Woman's Place* (*LWP*), got people talking, and doing research to investigate her claims. The major premises in *LWP* were:

1. There is a thing called women's language.
2. Women's language is characterized by an identifiable group of linguistic features. These include:
   (a) hedges (*sort of*)
   (b) fillers (*well, you know*)
   (c) tag questions (*It's nice, isn't it?*)
   (d) rising intonation even in non-question sentences (sometimes called "uptalk")
   (e) "empty" adjectives (*divine, cute*)

    (f)   precise color terms (*chartreuse*)

    (g)   intensifiers like *so* (*It was soooo good!*)

    (h)   increased use of standard language forms

    (i)   super-polite forms (such as indirect requests and euphemisms like *Oh, fudge!*)

    (j)   avoidance of strong swear words

    (k)   avoidance of interruptions.

3.   These features, along with other aspects of women's language, reflect women's generally subordinate role in society's power structure. Hedges and tag questions signal lack of confidence; intensifiers supply extra reassurance of an utterance's truth or value; and not swearing reduces the means available to express something strongly. And, of course, if you don't interrupt, you may not be allowed to decide what the conversation is going to be about.

4.   Women's place in society is also indicated by how we use language to talk *about* women and men (e.g., men *pass out*, but women *faint*).

Research motivated by Lakoff's work looked at whether the gender differences that she discussed could be measured, and, if confirmed, what they told us about language and society. One common approach was to measure the frequency of the forms listed from (a) to (k) above, to see whether women actually used them more. Results were mixed, with some findings supporting Lakoff's claims, some not, and some suggesting that things are (or should be) messier than the way she presented them. For example, Dubois and Crouch (1975) found that at the academic meeting that they studied, men actually used *more* tag questions than women, but Fasold (1990) points out that some of the tag questions they describe seem to mark antagonistic sparring, rather than uncertainty (such as *You would miss it, wouldn't you?*). James and Clarke (1993) looked at 54 studies (!) of interruption – in particular, whether men use interruption to control interactions. Most of the studies that they looked at found no significant gender differences, but they did find a small amount of evidence that "females may use interruptions of the cooperative and rapport-building type to a greater extent than do males, at least in some circumstances" (p. 268). So to some degree, the issue is not how often you do something, but what you do to the conversation by doing it.

James and Clarke's observation, like Fasold's point about tag questions, reminds us that there isn't a single thing called "interruption" that always does the same work in interactions. Compare the following invented (and, I hope, exaggerated) conversational exchanges.

(1)

Pat: So they told me it would take a week to deliver it.

Sam: (silence)

Pat: Uh . . . so I picked up the phone and called their boss.

Sam: (silence)

Pat: I said they were stalling me, and –

Sam: Are we out of beer?

(2)

Pat: So they told me it would take a week to deliver it.
Sam: Uh-huh.
Pat: So I picked up the phone and called their boss.
Sam: Mm.
Pat: I said they were stalling me, and –
Sam: You didn't!

In conversation (1), Sam is using silence and interruptions to control the conversation, through non-support. Zimmerman and West (1975) found that men were more likely than women to use silence and interruptions in this way. West and Zimmerman (1983) developed the notion of *deep interruption* to describe conversation stoppers like these. They defined deep interruptions in discourse terms, as starting two or more syllables before or after the last syllable of a place where you'd expect to switch speakers. In 10 same-sex conversations, there were only 7 such interruptions. In 11 cross-sex two-speaker conversations, there were 48 deep interruptions, 46 of them by men.

Compare that to conversation (2), where Sam is using minimal responses like *uh-huh* to encourage Pat to keep the conversation going. Although technically these are "interruptions," in that Sam speaks while Pat isn't finished, it's clear that this is co-operative behavior. Fishman's (1980, 1983) analysis of (cross-sex) couples recorded in their homes found that women did most of this kind of support work – what Fishman (1980) called "interactional shitwork." The men in Fishman's studies used minimal responses, slowly, to resist contributing to conversations that women initiated. (I'm reminded of a comedy routine by Chris Rock, where he underlines how low the conversational bar is for men by suggesting that even two or three repeated phrases would be enough to improve their perceived contribution.) To overcome this resistance, women employed other strategies to elicit a response – especially questions, which they used more than twice as often as men, who just threw out statements. James and Drakich (1993) found that across multiple studies, it was women who were expected to do the work required to keep conversation going. But despite the unsophisticated nature of men's contributions (discourse-wise), their topics of conversation were far more likely to be followed up on.

In fact, that seems to be more or less the point of men's conversations. In an experimental study, Leet-Pellegrini (1980) gave some participants background information about a topic, then invited people to converse. Male "experts" took control of conversations more often than female experts in cross-sex conversational pairs, and more than either partner in same-sex pairs where neither was an expert. Leet-Pellegrini interpreted this and other findings to mean that men used their expertise for control (with other men resisting), while women used it to inform: "Whereas the name of the man's game appears to be 'Have I won?' the name of the woman's game is 'Have I been sufficiently helpful?'" (Leet-Pellegrini 1980: 103). Pilkington (1992) looked at same-sex groups of men and women during break time in a bakery, and found that men's conversation was competitive, while women's was supportive. In both cases, though, the conversation served the same purpose: to build solidarity. Freed and Greenwood (1996) found that men and women actually used features like *you know* and questions equally in conversations between same-sex pairs of friends. They suggest that the linguistic task or the speaking situation has more effect than the gender of the speaker in determining the style of speaking.

These research projects don't all come to identical conclusions, but taken together, they suggest that it is in cross-gender interaction that we can expect to see the strongest gender effects. Holmes (1992: 329) proposes that perhaps the norms for women's talk are small group interactions in private contexts (whose goal is to maintain solidarity), while men's talk is normed to "public referentially-oriented interaction" (where speakers compete for the floor). It is when these norms come into conflict that we see a clash of conversational cultures.

difference and dominance

In fact, there is a well-known research tradition, most closely associated with Deborah Tannen, that suggests that gender differences in language do reflect different cultures of conversation (a **difference model**), rather than differences in access to power (a **dominance model**). Tannen claims that women are more likely to use language to build and maintain relationships (a **rapport style**), while men are more likely to use language to communicate factual information (a **report style**). Tannen's work has become well known, especially through best-sellers like *You Just Don't Understand* (1990) and books by others that popularize her ideas for the self-help market (such as John Gray's 1992 book *Men Are from Mars, Women Are from Venus*). Given that the (perceived) market for the Gray book is women who are going to "fix" themselves, it is tempting to interpret the rapport/report perspective as bleaching issues of inequality from the debate. But Tannen has been clear in pointing out that her approach doesn't deny the existence of male dominance. She cites Lange's (1988) study of teenage speech, which found that boys tended to talk in the same way whether they were with other boys or there were girls present. As a result, says Tannen, mixed gender conversations tend to be more like men's conversations, which puts women at a conversational disadvantage, as they have had less practice with men's conversation (1990: 237). This is not so different from the findings about the co-operative principle described above. The question, of course, is why it should be the job of women to do the shifting in such a situation, and the answer seems to be that men have more power and status and thus don't feel that they have to switch, which brings us back around to the power imbalance.

And whether we're talking about difference or dominance, we want to keep in mind that most of this research has been done on the speech of middle-class speakers in industrialized societies, and mainly on English. Critics who suggest that we should limit the claims we make on the basis of such research often support their point by referring to Keenan's (1974) study of gendered language use in a village in Madagascar. In the community Keenan studied, it was men, rather than women, who used indirect speech and a formal speech style (called *kabary*). For example, instead of directly saying *Manasa ny lamba amin 'ny savony* ('wash the clothes with soap'), they might say *Sasao ny lamba amin 'ny savony* ('have the clothes washed with soap') or even *Anasao lamba ny savony*

difference model
The idea that gender differences in language reflect different cultures of conversation (cf. Tannen 1990).

dominance model
The idea that gender differences in language reflect differences in access to power (cf. Tannen 1990; Lakoff 1972).

rapport style
Using language to build and maintain relationships.

report style
Using language to communicate factual information.

('the soap is to be used to wash clothes'; Keenan 1974: 132–3). Still, despite women's directness of speech in this community, they were politically subordinate, and in this case it was *indirectness* that was prized by the culture. This suggests that indirectness doesn't automatically indicate lack of power (although it appears to do exactly that in many of the studies mentioned earlier). Keenan's findings also reinforce the idea, which by this point should come as little surprise to us, that communities assign higher status to the linguistic and stylistic variants of the dominant subgroup, whatever those variants might be.

how languages encode gender

"Somebody called for you, but they wouldn't leave a message."

Although many of us are now comfortable with "they" (in the sense of "she or he") in the above sentence, for many people it's still kind of weird in this context. Surely the person who answered the phone could at least tell if the speaker was a she or a he? Even if that was the only thing she (or he) noticed? In fact, some researchers argue that biological sex is the very first thing we notice about somebody (Gross 1992). This suggests that we're strongly conditioned to categorize people by sex. And as you see in the "somebody called" example, the English pronoun system actually forces us to do that kind of categorizing. Sex is the *only* personal trait that English speakers have decided is important enough to keep in our pronoun system. (Try calling somebody's baby *it* and see what happens.)

In many languages, including French, *everything* is either masculine or feminine (or, in some languages, neuter). This is true not just for inanimate objects like *la porte* (the door, feminine) or *le beignet* (the doughnut, masculine), but also for living things, so that speakers are constantly required to assign a gender/sex to referents (the things the speakers are referring to): *étudiant*, *chat* (male student, male cat), *étudiante*, *chatte* (female student, female cat), and so on. These distinctions are marked not just on the thing, but also on the other words in the discourse that refer to that thing. So when I say *je suis paresseux* ('I am lazy'), the form of the adjective also tells you I'm male (if I were female, I would be expected to say *je suis paresseuse*). And if we're following the rules in traditional grammar books, when we talk about how lazy we all are, we have to say *nous sommes paresseux* ('we are lazy'), with the masculine form, even if almost all of the "we" in question are female. Note that I'm not trying to argue here that marking grammatical gender in this way forces us to consciously prioritize males over females whenever we speak. If that were completely true, as Wardhaugh (2006: 320) wryly notes, we'd expect to find reduced sexism in non-gender-marking-language societies like China. But sex/gender marking does have the effect of foregrounding the maleness of any collection of people and of constantly leading us to re-inscribe (i.e., to repeat or "re-write" a way of being over and over, so that it becomes harder to change) our gender/sex and that of others.

When people write in French nowadays, they may try to avoid implying that only one gender is involved by using either/or forms, such as *étudiants et étudiantes* or *étudiant(e)s*. This falls into a gray area between grammatical gender and social practice, as can be seen by its uneven application. In Québec, for example, the student associations at the microbiology school and smaller-city universities are called the *Association des étudiants et étudiantes* (both forms, male first); in education and at big-city universities they're called the *Association des étudiantes et étudiants* (both forms, female first); and at the polytechnic and public administration schools they're called the *Association des étudiants* (male form only). An English-language equivalent would be the move toward generic *they* (or in formal speech, *he or she*), rather than the formerly prescribed *he*, in sentences like *If a botanist wants to succeed, [he/she/they] should do [his/her/their] work*. Defenders of generic *he* (or of *mankind* or *the Age of Man*) may argue that forms like this are interpreted as gender-neutral, but experiments with generic *he* (such as MacKay & Fulkerson 1979) suggest that the forms coerce male interpretations in listener's minds.

There are other cases where, especially in the past, the male form has been seen as the default (*fireman*, *mailman*, now often replaced by gender-neutral *firefighter* or *letter carrier*). Or the female form has been a sort of "little sister" version of the male form, as in *actor/actress* (now more and more often *actor* for both genders). And, of course, there are some words where a supposed female equivalent word has grown to index something different (and always worse): *governor/governess*, *master/mistress*, *bachelor/spinster*. These are the kind of language and gender things that people are now more aware of, thanks to years of research and advocacy. This change in awareness seems to have led to changes in use: forms like generic *he* declined drastically in use in the media from the 1970s onward (Holmes 1992: 329). And *governess*, *mistress*, and *spinster* sound almost Victorian now. (Although I'm not sure *bachelorette*, another "little sister" word, is much of an improvement.) Of course, this is not to say that the gendered naming of things has stopped being an issue, as we can see by recent debates over the definition of the word *marriage*.

When talking about gender-associated language, it's useful to consider a distinction introduced by Ochs (1992) between **direct** and **indirect indexing**. A word like *brother* or *he* directly indexes maleness, so that you can't really say *My brother was sick but she's getting better*. Most of the gender differences we see in language, though, are tendencies, rather than absolutes. For example, Japanese men tend to use the particle *ze* at the end of sentences, while women tend to use *wa*. Ochs argues that *ze* actually (directly) indexes assertiveness, and *wa* indexes hesitancy. The links to gender are indirect, and based on which of those traits Japanese society expects men and women to display. If it's easier (or more permissible) for men to be assertive, then they'll end up using more *ze*. The large number of social indexers like these makes Japanese fun for sociolinguists to study, but also lets speakers of the language make all kinds of social statements through language. Consider the first person pronouns, words meaning *I*, a few of which are laid out in table 7.1.

Reynolds (1998: 320) points out that junior high school girls, especially in Tokyo, have started using *boku*, as well as other male-associated markers: "Girls who were interviewed in a TV program explain that they cannot compete with boys in classes, in games or in fights with *watasi*." It is probably no accident that this innovation comes from junior high, a time of life that foregrounds identity and gender.

direct indexing
A linguistic feature directly indexes something with social meaning when it is categorical and exclusive, for example, using *he* to refer to a man.

indirect indexing
A linguistic feature indirectly indexes something with social meaning when it is not categorically associated with that meaning, but rather is linked to another meaning that is itself linked to that social meaning.

Table 7.1. First person pronouns in Japanese (a sample).

form	used by	social meaning
watasi	males and females	formal
atasi	females	informal, cute
atai	females	very informal, slang
speaker's name	children, some females	cute
boku	males, rarely females	informal, casual deference
ore, oresama, onore	males, rarely females	informal, macho, familiar, sometimes rude/aggressive

Sources: Takahara (1991); www.jref.com (accessed August 18, 2011).

As an aside: Ska pronouns

Some of you may be familiar with a Japanese ska group called Oreskaband. The band was formed by a group of girls while still in middle school in the port city of Sakai. Their name, which means *I/we are a ska band*, deliberately uses the male/ macho pronoun form *ore*, and the band performs in boys' school uniforms. By rejecting "girl" language and dress, they reject expectations of "girl" behavior. Their pronoun choice makes them, literally, "rude boys."

What makes these choices so powerful is that although the indexers are indirect, they are still highly gendered. In some cultures, the link between language use and gender is even tighter, to the point that some observers have claimed that men and women actually speak different languages or dialects. These include the Australian aboriginal language Yanyuwa (Bradley 1998), where men use one whole set of prefixes on nouns, verbs, and pronouns, while women and children use another set. Yanyuwa-speaking boys are expected to shift to the men's dialect when they are initiated into manhood. There are also some languages where male and female speakers pronounce particular sounds differently: in Gros Ventre, an American aboriginal language, men say *[dj]* in every word in which women say *[kj]*, and in Koasati, another American aboriginal language, men put an *-s* on the end of verbs, while women don't (Haas 1944; Wardhaugh 2006). One interesting difference is that when Koasati men quote women, they switch to the female forms (and vice versa for women quoting men), but Gros Ventre speakers don't make this switch. There are also languages with different forms depending on who you're talking to: for example, in the Indian (Dravidian) language Kurux, one verb form is used for women talking to women, and another for women talking to men and for men talking to anybody (Ekka 1972; Fasold 1990: 91). While this might reflect status differences, it might just be yet another case of women shifting more (or better) than men.

---

gender and language change

In chapter 5, we saw that gender is implicated in language change. Labov's (1974, 1990) principles I and II suggested that women use more of the standard variant in situations where language variation is stable, and use more of the incoming variant in situations of change. By thinking about the relationship between gender and class, power, place, prestige, and identity, we can find some interesting ways to add complexity to this observation.

First off, why is principle I true? Why would women use standard variants more often than men? Several authors (Trudgill 1972, 1983; Key 1975; Eckert 2000) argue that women use linguistic style shifting to position themselves with respect to social groups because, well, that's what they have to work with (I'm paraphrasing here). Men have better access to some ways of marking their social status (e.g., jobs), so women are encouraged to be more aware of other ways of doing that, including language (Chambers 1995, 2009). This argument actually works the same way whether women are shifting toward the standard or away from it (and "away" is closer to what Eckert explores in the article in question). Basically, the argument goes, language is what women use to do things, socially.

It may also be that there are no social or economic advantages for women in sounding local (which in many studies is set up as the opposite of using standard language). In rural Newfoundland, for example, there are still high-paying or steady jobs in forestry, fishing, and mining available for men, but the traditional female equivalents (like fish processing) are disappearing. Pretty well all the good jobs for women require higher education and Standard English, and so it's no surprise that we find women using more standard language in the rural communities that we study. Nichols (1983) describes a similar situation among Gullah speakers in coastal South Carolina. Fasold (1990: 96) takes this a step further by speculating that "By sounding *less* local, female speakers might be subtly and subliminally protesting traditional community norms which place them in a subordinate position to men in favor of a more egalitarian social order in which women are treated more nearly equal to men." Either way, the argument is that women favor standard forms because the standard is more closely associated with increased status or opportunities for women than it is for men.

What about principle II? How can both parts be true? Women lead changes above the level of awareness, which tend to be toward higher-prestige forms. But they also lead changes below the level of awareness (like vowel shifts), which are not necessarily toward higher-prestige forms. This is sometimes known as the **gender paradox** (Labov 1990). Now, you could argue that basically, women lead all successful change, because their role as primary caregivers for children means that the innovations that they adopt are passed on to the next generation (this argument seems to go way back – Gauchat 1905; Brun 1946). But that's an argument about transmission across generations, not about adopting a change in the first place. You could also repeat the argument from the previous paragraph that women use language to do things, and thus notice and adopt incoming variants sooner. Then, once women get a little ahead in rates of use, the new variant becomes associated with them, and men retreat or resist (Kroch 1978), so that the gap between genders grows (this is summarized well in Tagliamonte and D'Arcy (2009)). Interpreting the gender gap as men resisting change (rather than women adopting it) is appealing for those of us who work in changing rural communities, where we often see young men keeping or reviving traditional forms. And some of the male-led changes described in earlier sociolinguistic literature seem to be of this revival/resistance type, notably the Martha's Vineyard study, where a traditional pronunciation was most popular with young men who had left and returned, and didn't want to have anything to do with the influx of outsiders to the community (Labov 1963).

Or you could argue that "women" and "men" are big, catch-all categories that flatten out a whole lot of things that people do with language and identity (Eckert & McConnell-Ginet 1992, 1999; Ochs 1992; Meyerhoff 2006). Maybe the women who lead one change are not the same ones who lead another change. A lot of our uncertainty about this actually may result from the way we variationists do things. For one thing, we usually study variables one at a time, so it's hard to see how they relate to each other, or whether the same speakers behave the same way from one variable to the next. For another, our studies usually divide people into two groups on the basis of biological sex. As a result, we miss out on the reality that male/femaleness is gradient rather than absolute. In fact, studies that use even really simple gradient measures, such as asking people how female or male they consider themselves (Boberg 2006), seem to better model the frequency of use of gender-identified language features than just splitting respondents into males and females. More crucially, we miss out on the fact that a study participant identified as a woman might also be a parent, a communist, a guitarist, an Aspie, and a participant in a whole pile of social networks and communities of practice, and that all those things

gender paradox

Emerging from Labov's (2001) principles I, Ia, and II, the idea that women are more likely to use standard forms and lead in changes from above, but are also leaders in changes from below, which are not necessarily toward higher-prestige forms.

interact and contribute to language choices, and because of that those interactions themselves become something worth studying (Meyerhoff 2006: 222).

_____ class

What about the relationship between gender and class? We know that forms associated with higher socio-economic status speakers tend to have more prestige (chapter 4), or are seen as more standard, and that women tend to use more standard forms. So it's no surprise that the linguistic behaviors of men and of the working classes tend to be similar. Our work in Newfoundland shows that, in effect, middle-class urban and/or university-affiliated men ("townies") pattern with women (or women pattern with middle-class or university-affiliated speakers), replicating the findings of a huge number of quantitative studies. There's a longstanding debate in the field about whether gender trumps class or vice versa (see Horvath 1985; Milroy 1987/1980). But do people actually see _middle-class_ and _female_ as being similar, sociolinguistically? It seems the answer is yes (sort of). You'll remember (from chapter 4) that the men in Trudgill's (1972) discussion of covert prestige didn't just behave more like working-class speakers; they actually _aimed_ for a working-class and local norm. And it seems that class differences in sociolinguistic gender expectations develop from an early age. Edwards (1979) reports on the results of an interesting study in this regard. People in Dublin were played recordings of boys and girls who were too young to have yet developed physiological speech differences (like pitch differences) and asked to guess the sex of the speaker. When listeners got it wrong, it tended to be by identifying middle-class boys as girls and working-class girls as boys. Lakoff (2004) describes "women's language" as also being the preserve of homosexuals and academics, all groups who are "marginalized or excluded from institutional varieties of male power" (Meyerhoff 2006: 232). Note Newfoundland singer Colleen Power's wry quotation of the expression, "If you can't get a man, get a townie" in the title of a 2008 track. This is not to say that women are excluded from claiming local (vernacular) identity through language. Cheshire (1982, for Reading, UK) and Schatz (1986, for Amsterdam) found that both male and female speakers used local stigmatized forms, but that they chose different ones. On Ocracoke Island in coastal North Carolina, Schilling-Estes (1998) described one community of practice, poker-playing middle-aged men, who made heavy use of one local speech feature (the PRICE diphthong raised to something like "pruhyce"); women and gay men of the same age range used a different local feature (the MOUTH diphthong fronted to something like "mehwth") as a way to be local without being macho.

One last question here: does the correlation between standard language and women's speech hold true everywhere? The answer seems to be no (sort of). Sometimes the correlation is weak, or found only with particular features or levels of formality. And it may not hold in some non-western societies. A frequently invoked counterexample is the case of Arabic, where multiple studies (e.g., Bakir 1986; Haeri 2003) show men using more of the standard Classical Arabic forms, while women use more local forms. This is usually attributed to women in the countries studied having less access to formal education, or, when they do have access to education, less access to the jobs that require Classical Arabic. I'm not sure that we want to assume that this situation is completely different from the typical sociolinguistic finding, though. Several authors (Al-Wer 1997; Haeri 1997) point out that the sociolinguistically relevant comparison variety should be the local urban high-prestige dialect, not Classical Arabic. When we look at data from that perspective, as in work by Assiri (2008, in Saudi Arabia) and Omari (2009, in Jordan), we get something much closer to the typical correlations. Women (and educated and urbanized men) use more prestige forms than less-educated locally affiliated men, and men seem to avoid highly salient forms that are associated with women's speech. Al-Wer points out that the relevant social characteristic is *education*, not because it exposes women to Classical Arabic, but because "in most cases, college and university education involves leaving one's home town and interacting with speakers from different linguistic backgrounds" (Al-Wer 1997: 259). In other words, it's all about practices. A similar result (with greater access to education, women move away from local vernacular forms) is reported for Bengali (Bodine 1975; Gupta Fraser p.c.). On the other hand, it seems like women in Mombasa, Kenya, are the ones "preserving the more obvious markers" of local vernacular Swahili (Russell 1982: 140), even though they have exposure to the standard variety.

identity, performance, and practice

agentive
A word borrowed from traditional grammar that, in this field, suggests that there's an active doer or chooser at work. In this framework, people actively perform aspects of their identity.

At the beginning of the chapter, I talked about gender as something you do. In this section, I'd like to expand on that, as recent sociolinguistic work on gender has moved heavily toward considering speakers' **agentive** behavior – *agentive* being a word borrowed from traditional grammar that (in this usage at least) suggests that there's an active doer or chooser at work. From this viewpoint, each person's sense of our gender identity at any time results from a combination of our own background and experiences and the way we relate to social expectations (by either challenging them or conforming to them). An approach like this can usefully be applied to pretty well any aspect of our identity, but it's especially useful for gender for a few reasons. One is that social expectations relating to gender are so powerful, and so often reiterated (people write *It's a boy!* or *It's a girl!* on birth announcements, and it's the expected answer by new parents to the question *What is it?*). A second reason is that gender and other aspects of identity are so heavily implicated in each other. What (people think) it means to be a communist or a parent or a guitarist is different for women and men, and (people think) being a woman or a man involves different amounts or types of communism and parenting and guitar playing. A third reason is that researchers working from this perspective often move into sociolinguistics from other disciplines, such as anthropology, where gender has long been studied as a practice or performance. Related to this is a research tradition of looking closely at short stretches of language practice for clues to what counts as doing gender, rather than conglomerating large amounts of data into something easier to count and measure.

performative
Typically used in discussion of gender, the idea that actions and speech acquire constitutive force and are used to create a particular gender identity.

One influence on work in this area is the philosopher Judith Butler, who in *Gender Trouble* (1990) proposes that gender is "**performatively** constituted by the very 'expressions' that are said to be its results" (Butler 1990: 25). This is a more radical idea of gender than just saying that it's something that we do, or that we learn to do, or that we "reveal" through doing it. Rather, Butler suggests that we learn to do gender by doing it, and by judging the response to our performances (although we're not completely free to perform whatever gender identity we want – things happen within a "rigid regulatory frame" (p. 33)). From this perspective, there's no such thing as (say) "masculinity" except as it exists in the acting out of masculinity. The act, and all previous acts, and responses to those acts, are what create or reinforce the idea that masculinity exists. To put it strongly, *the act is all there is*. And given our reduced opportunities these days to spear woolly mammoths or dance the gavotte, this act of gender often takes the form of talk, or response to talk. Meyerhoff (2006: 206) puts it well: "A speaker uses one variant more than another, not because he *is* male but because in speaking like that he is *constituting* himself as an exemplar of maleness, and constituting that variant as an emblem of masculinity." We can see how talk builds gender by comparing talk in different situations, with different audiences.

For example, participants in a conversation have to relate to social expectations of gender behavior in homosocial contexts, situations involving same-sex groups or relationships that are (presumed to be) non-sexual: fraternities, prisons, the military, police, and religious orders. Kiesling (2005) looks at how fraternity brothers balance "competing scripts of male solidarity and heterosexuality" through, for example, ritual insults or conversations about shared non-personal interests such as sports. (See also this chapter's "spotlight" about Kiesling's work on the "cool stance" implied by men's use of *dude*.) In this group, the content of the discourse is often competitive, which seems to permit (or masculinize) the use of collaborative, stereotypically female ways of sharing the conversational floor. Kiesling uses this observation to warn us that simply identifying gender-associated little bits of language isn't enough to explain what's actually going on. Cameron (1997) looks at how a group of fraternity brothers use language to deal with "the perceived danger that so often accompanies Western male homosociality: homosexuality" (p. 281) by discussing a classmate (not part of the frat) who they describe as "gay" by mentioning, among other things, his shorty shorts. In effect, they're gossiping about clothes, but in this instance gossip (or its content) works to reinforce the idea that non-masculine stuff is what *other* people do. Thus, the members of the group collaboratively build solidarity (in a socially sanctioned way) by building a model of a less masculine other guy.

There are, of course, plenty of homosocial male contexts in which you have to look pretty hard for any signs of collaboration. Let me talk to a subset of readers for a minute – women who date men (the rest of you can skip to the next paragraph). You may at some point have dated a man who behaved and spoke like a normal human being when he was with you, but like a bit of a jerk with his male friendship group, especially if he didn't know you were there: swearing, trying to top everybody's stories, talking over others, or putting people down. Although everybody in the group behaved like that, they all probably seemed to get along pretty well. If you've been in that situation, did you talk about it later (with the man, not just with your non-straight-male friends)? Did the conversation turn to a discussion of authenticity? As in, which version of the man involved was the "real" one? I think most language and gender scholars would suggest that there isn't a "real" version, but rather that both involved different performances of heterosexual

homosocial
A term used to refer to situations involving same-sex groups or relationships that are (presumed to be) non-sexual, such as fraternities, prisons, and religious orders.

masculinity (although the men in the fraternity may have claimed that the fraternity version of themselves was more real – or at least claimed that to their frat brothers). So why did the "with my boys" man need to perform such an extreme version? Or maybe more to the point, how could the "with you" man get away with such an under-performance? The answer, according to Cameron (1997), is you. Your closeness confirmed his "straight cred," so that he had to do less masculinity-building work with his language.

language and sexuality (or something)

There are a few ways to use sociolinguistic research to say something interesting about dominant gender ideologies. One way is simply to look at aspects of society that have previously been taken as so natural that they're ignored (and many researchers would argue that these aspects of society actually get most of their power from being ignored, or from getting vanilla labels like *common sense* or *ordinary*). This is the approach taken by the work on heterosexual masculinity by Cameron and Kiesling, described above. (It's also a tactic successfully used by observational comedians – by discussing and pulling apart something apparently ordinary, they lead us to see how strange or artificial it really is.)

Another way is to define something by looking at its edges, at people and practices that don't match the dominant model. For gender, a good example of that approach is recent research on language and sexuality. Cameron and Kulick (2003) suggest that language and sexuality research is actually fairly constrained. The research literature doesn't interpret "sexuality" broadly: "It does not refer to fantasies, fears, repressions or desires. It means 'sexual identity' . . . the focus is on how language is employed by speakers to signal their identity as homosexuals" (p. 78). Of all the ways of being sexual, only homosexuality has a long history of being described as having specifically linguistic correlates, even as research on gay speech has moved through different stages – from pathologizing ("gayness as illness") to anti-pathologizing ("gayness as not illness") to community-based ("the gay speech community") to performance-based ("doing being gay").

Within those restrictions, though, recent work on gay and lesbian language use has helped illuminate a whole range of gender and identity questions for sociolinguists, while also revealing ways that smaller-scale, more ethnographic work can help us understand what's going on. For example, Podesva (2004) showed the complex identity work that people can do with a single linguistic feature, in this case the use of fully released word-final [t] (which makes the [t] in a word like *get* very noticeable). Podesva showed how Heath, a gay male medical student, takes the feature (which generally seems to index *articulateness*) and increases it, using more and longer released [t] with friends when performing a diva-type identity. Podesva argues that Heath has taken the *articulate* connotations of the form and ramped them up into something like *prissy*, which works for his diva thing. In other words, exaggerating the linguistic feature exaggerates the sociolinguistic meaning.

A major way in which research on gender performance helps us to understand what's going on elsewhere (and vice versa) is to consider some of the different ways in which people actively perform gender (and here I mean perform quite literally). Hall (1995) looked at the language use of telephone sex line workers in California. These "fantasy makers" were skilled at using language alone to portray themselves as their (straight male) clients wanted them to be, to construct heterosexual femininity through the kind of "women's language" features that Lakoff described. It was crucial to the phone workers' success that callers believed they were actually talking to (say) a young straight female of whichever ethnicity they wanted, even though the actual worker might not be young, or straight, or of the same ethnicity, or, in one case, even female. (For a nice discussion of heterosexual male investment in the authenticity of the female sexual experience, and how it relates to our linguistic construction of manhood, see Cameron and Kulick's (2003: 15–18) discussion of Meg Ryan's faked-orgasm-in-the-restaurant scene in *When Harry Met Sally*.) This kind of performance, where the goal is to be accepted as authentic (or, more accurately, to have your audience not even *think* about your authenticity, or the possibility that you're performing), is sometimes called passing, using a term borrowed from the African American community (in which light-skinned people of color may or may not be able to "pass for White"). Passing is also generally seen as the goal of language changes adopted by transsexual people.

Compare that to drag performances, in which awareness of the performance is central to the whole idea. Barrett (1995, 1998) showed how African American drag performers were able to use both African American and "White woman" speech features – and, crucially, their audience's awareness of what those features meant – to be funny, or clever, or dismissive. Through the long history of drag in comedy theater and film, the humor comes from the audience's knowledge that what they're seeing is a perform-ance. So we can extend the term dragging to refer to any kind of identity performance in which awareness that it is a performance is important. For example, in our recent research (Van Herk et al. 2008), we see local drag performers adopting and extending a feature of traditional Newfoundland English that has recently become associated with young urban women: the use of *-s* on the end of some verbs (*I loves it, I knows*). Clearly, they're playing with the form. They're dragging. But, we argue, so are the young urban women, who have taken the old uses of the form, changed the linguistic rules, and made it into a playful, ironic identity marker.

Another option, of course, is to not play along at all. Bucholtz (1998) looks at a group of nerd girls and shows how their non-participation in a youth-led California sound change (the fronting of /u/ – sometimes represented in writing by spelling *cool* as *kewl*) is part of a broader attempt to move away from their school's mainstream norms for femininity, away from participation in what Eckert (1994) refers to as the heterosexual marketplace, the (media-driven) institutionalization of heterosexuality and traditional gender roles. Bucholtz's detailed discourse analysis reveals other ways in which these girls set up their own linguistic norms. Although this work is based on analysis of local practice, Bucholtz's claim (that *nerd* is something you do) is supported by a very differ-ent research approach. When my students and I (Van Herk & the Ottawa Intensifier Project 2006) did a traditional quantitative analysis of intensifier use (*so cool, very cool*, etc.) in online communities, we found that nerds and geeks avoided the most highly gendered forms even more than their parents' generation did. This suggests that nerds aren't just left behind by the language choices of self-perceived cool youth groups (if that was the case, their rates of use would be somewhat neutral, near the community norms of their parents). Instead, nerds actively move *away* from how those groups

passing
From discourse on ethnicity, when people adopt (linguistic and other) behaviors from another group in order to be taken as authentic members of that group.

dragging
From gender studies, when people use features that both they and their audience know are associated with another group (e.g., the other gender).

heterosexual marketplace
The (media-driven) institutionaliza-tion of heterosexuality and traditional gender (cf. Eckert 1996).

discourse analysis
An examination of the structure of a conversation, looking for linguistic regularities.

linguistically construct gender. In doing that, they are aligned with other groups on the margins of socially dominant views of gender, such as the pronoun-shifting young Japanese women I mentioned earlier.

Why is this chapter so long?

That's a question you may have asked yourself while reading, and one I definitely asked myself more than once while writing. I can think of three main reasons that gender gets its own chapter and that it's longer than some of the others.

The first reason is that the other social characteristics that sociolinguists investigate are somewhat less generalizable. Although we can identify something that we call social status in most groups of people (except, maybe, in very small communities), status in different places is socially organized and significant in very different ways (such as class, caste, education), and often seems to affect our linguistic performance indirectly (for example, through other salient identities like *jock* or *burnout*). Likewise, the role of ethnicity can vary widely from one context to another. Gender, on the other hand, seems to be a big deal everywhere.

A second reason is that sociolinguistics programs (and universities generally) are full of people from the groups that Lakoff says are on the wrong end of institutional varieties of male power. We're girls, gays, and geeks. We're lots of other things, too, but it makes sense that gender issues would interest many of us. (Most university campuses are less well populated by people on the wrong end of other power imbalances, such as class or ethnicity.)

The third reason that I've written so much here is that I think that gender is where the buzz is in sociolinguistics right now. People who do research on language and gender, or language and sexuality, are actively bringing in ideas and methods from other disciplines. Maybe because of that, they're also the researchers most likely to focus on identity and performance, and on the idea that speakers are actively doing things with language. Note that this chapter is called gender *and identity*. So, in effect, I'm trying to fit two big ideas into a single chapter here. And that takes room.

summing up

In the same way that gender is seen as something that is performed, rather than inherent, gender differences in language are also seen as performed, reinforcing our sense of both gender and gendered language through performances and the feedback they receive. Scholars continue to debate how large the linguistic differences between genders are, and whether they reflect gendered differences in access to power or differences in the culture of talk. Recent work looks at people on the margins of mainstream gender assumptions and performances to clarify how those assumptions and performances work.

Where to next?

discourse
An extended language interaction, that is, longer than a sentence. Also, the study of such interaction.

Language and gender research has moved squarely into considering individual acts of gendered language – that is, the focus of study has moved toward small-scale ethnographic or **discourse**-type studies, rather than counting how often people of each gender use a particular linguistic form. However, the powerful effects of gender found in quantitative studies of change and variation suggest that these small-scale behaviors reflect larger social patterns. It'll be interesting to see the degree to which researchers at different "sizes" of study are able to adapt each other's ideas to push the field into new territory.

Spotlight: Dude, where's my solidarity?

Kiesling, Scott F. "Dude." *American Speech* 79, no. 3 (2004): 281–305.

Not many sociolinguists can claim that their research was turned into a beer marketing campaign, but that seems to have been the case for Scott Kiesling. Kiesling's 2004 paper "Dude" was widely reported in the mainstream media, to the point where people started calling him "the 'Dude' guy." In the paper, Kiesling uses recorded student observations, survey data, and discourse analysis to show how young people (especially men talking to men) use the word *dude* to do a bunch of things (greet, agree, confront, sympathize). He argues that these uses let men assert masculine solidarity while avoiding closeness that could be interpreted as homosexual in nature.

How to read: Sociolinguistically aware students usually enjoy this paper – it makes sense to them. There's not much linguistic jargon ("fronted /u/" is the sound that online writers sometimes represent by spelling *dude* as *dewd*). Terms that might be new to you are usually defined elsewhere in the paper. The footnotes will fill many possible gaps in your background knowledge (for example, why *Discourse* is spelled with a capital D).

If you liked this, you might also enjoy: Kiesling's other work, on masculinity in fraternity discourse. See also Cameron's (1997) paper "Performing gender identity," discussed in the text above, on that topic. Brave readers who want to know more about indexicality might try Silverstein's "shifters" (1976) or "indexical order" (1996, 2003) papers. The Bud Light commercials that illustrate Kiesling's point are easy to find online (e.g., on YouTube).

exercises

1. Here's a list of English terms that highlight the female-ness of the things that they refer to.
   (a) *chick flick*
   (b) *chick lit*
   (c) *women's magazine*
   (d) *drag queen*
   (e) *diva*
   (f) *girl band*
   (g) *party girl*
   (h) *girlfriend*
   (i) *girly girl*
   (j) *girl*

Be sure you know what each term means. Then try to think of its male equivalent. Is there one? Does it refer to the exact same thing except male, or do the two words have different connotations? Does one of the two terms have a narrower reference than the other? What do your observations suggest to you about how people use gendered labels?

2. Romaine (2000: 117) looks in the British National Corpus (a large linguistic corpus) to compare the number of uses of *male nurse*, *female nurse*, *male doctor*, *female doctor*, *career woman*, *career man*, *family woman*, and *family man*. Try doing the same thing using Google or a similar search engine (don't forget the quotation marks around each searched term). How do the numbers compare? What does this tell you about which combinations of gender and role are seen as worthy of comment by English speakers?

3. Google the words *woman*, *man*, *boy*, and *girl*, and the phrases (in quotation marks) *he or she* and *she or he*. How many hits for each word or phrase? How do the top 10 hits for each word or phrase differ? Discuss.

4. Google the phrases *he told*, *she told*, *told him*, and *told her* (each in quotation marks). How many hits for each? Who tells? Who gets told? Try the same thing with some other verbs (maybe *kiss*, *hold*, *hit*, and *kill*).

5. Have a chat with somebody from a different generation about how language associated with men or women may have changed.

6. Think about a couple of highly gendered communities of practice that you know. Rewrite the Pat and Sam conversation (in this chapter) as you think it would play out in each community.

7. If you speak another language, think about how gender is represented in that language, and how it differs from English. If you don't speak another language, find somebody who does, and ask them.

8. If you read Kiesling's "Dude" article, go online and find and watch the Bud Light "Dude" commercials. Describe how they illustrate Kiesling's points (or not).

9. Watch Oreskaband videos (especially *Wasuremono*) online (you can dance if you want to; it's been a long chapter). Do other aspects of how the group is presented in videos also confound gender expectations? How so, or why not?

discussion

1. A common (non-academic) response to early language and gender work (like Lakoff's) is to say that the claims may have been true once, but aren't any more. Were there any points while reading this chapter where you felt that what was being said wasn't true for you or your friends? If so, which points? Why do you think this is? Have things really changed that much? Or are you kidding yourself? Why do you think the "things have changed" response seems to surface more often for gender work than for other research?

2. The word *bitch* differs in social meaning across generations, depending on who uses it and who they're referring to (the referent). For you, which combination of user and referent (female, male, gay, straight) makes *bitch* the most confrontational? Are there any combinations where *bitch* has

positive social meaning? (If you discuss this in a very diverse group, you may be surprised by how different you all feel about the social meanings of the word.)

3. I talk a lot in this chapter about identity performance as it relates to gender, but there's no reason to stop there. Can you think of ways that other social characteristics – region, class, ethnicity – are also performed and performative?

4. Why do you think I chose to recommend a "spotlight" reading about straight guys in a chapter on language and gender?

other resources

To go back to the source, you can read Robin Lakoff's original article"Language and woman's place" (1973). Another very useful approach to *LWP* is to get the 2004 re-issue of the 1975 book version – it includes a whole lot of additional commentary and historical context.

When I teach language and gender, I use Penelope Eckert and Sally McConnell-Ginet's *Language and Gender* (2003) as a textbook. The language is pretty high-level, but there's a cool approach to making sure you have the background you need – chapter 1 is a crash course on gender, and chapter 2 is a crash course on language! For language and gender as related to community of practice, try Eckert and McConnell-Ginet's (1992) "Think practically and look locally." This is the article everyone in sociolinguistics cites about communities of practice.

A collection of influential writings on language and gender is found in *Language and Gender: A Reader*, edited by Jennifer Coates (2011/1998).

For language and sexuality, try the highly readable *Language and Sexuality* (2003) by Deborah Cameron and Don Kulick. They're also the editors of *The Language and Sexuality Reader* (2006).

There's a journal called *Gender and Language*, http://www.equinoxjournals.com/GL/index (accessed August 18, 2011), and the International Gender and Language Association (IGALA) meets every two years, http://www.lancs.ac.uk/fass/organisations/igala/Index.html (accessed August 18, 2011).

You can also go hang out in the "P120 S48" section of your university's library.

Style 8

> ## In this chapter:
>
> - Defining and measuring style
> - Why style shift?
> - Other variation within the speaker: genre, register, jargon

Over the last few chapters, we've moved closer and closer to thinking of people as active participants in the sociolinguistic process. In any social interaction, the language used is determined by more than just the social characteristics of the participants. Our communicative competence (our awareness of how language interaction works in our community) lets us express the same idea in many ways. In terms of content, "Would you please pass the remote?" means roughly the same thing as "Gimme the remote!" But the two utterances are interpreted very differently by socially capable people. People evaluate an interaction and decide which way of speaking is best suited to it, and change their language (and expectations) accordingly. Sociolinguists use the term **style** to describe this kind of **intra-speaker** ("within the speaker") variation.

Now, this means that sociolinguists have a narrower definition of style than normal people do. Normal people might say that you and I talk differently because we have "different styles." As a sociolinguist, though, I reserve the term for differences between the walk you talk in one interaction and the way you talk in another. During a relaxed conversation with friends, you may not consciously say to yourself, "Oh, this might be a good time for me to use contracted forms and fewer educated words," but your

style
Intra-speaker ("within the speaker") variation as opposed to variation across groups.

intra-speaker
Within the speaker. Intra-speaker variation is the difference in the way a single speaker talks in two or more different situations.

What Is Sociolinguistics?, First Edition. Gerard Van Herk.

language shows that you've made that decision anyway. This means that you must be carrying around information about how other people evaluate contractions and educated words, as well as how they assign social meaning to any particular type of interaction.

Style overlaps with many of the ideas covered in the past chapters, as our style choices include deciding which social characteristics to reveal or perform. In particular, we saw style shifting in how people "do" gender, and some of the ideas from that chapter, including performance, will resurface here. Style also overlaps with ideas from chapters yet to come, especially with the rules or expectations for interaction (chapter 9).

attention to speech
Labov (1972b) suggests that different levels of formality result from the amount of attention a speaker pays to the act of speaking. In some activities, such as reading aloud, speakers pay more attention to their speech, while in others, such as talking with friends, they are less attentive.

defining and measuring style

The simplest sociolinguistic conceptualization of style is degree of formality. We use formal style when we are looking for (overt) prestige, and when we pay attention to our speech; we use informal style in more relaxed situations, and/or when overt prestige is not our goal. In fact, the early sociolinguistic discussions of style (Labov 1966, 1972b) focus almost entirely on the formal/informal distinction as it relates to attention to speech. Researchers were most interested in obtaining and analyzing natural speech, so they paid attention to the style component in order to find the most natural part of their recordings, the places where speakers used casual, rather than careful, speech. Especially in the earliest work, researchers measured what they called paralinguistic channel cues (tempo, pitch, volume, breathing rate, and laughter) to identify casual speech, and used different tasks to tap into different levels of awareness of speech. The basic pattern that they identified is that the more formal your style, the more your speech resembles the prestige groups above you.

paralinguistic channel cues
Cues (e.g., tempo, pitch, volume, breathing rate, laughter) that seem to correlate with casual speech.

There are some problems, especially methodological, with an attention-to-speech model. It's hard to separate casual from careful speech. Not all speech styles fit easily on the careful–casual continuum. People can consciously shift into informal speech, as well as into formal styles. And some sociolinguistic interviewees have been known to slip into stylized vernacular "performances" (Schilling-Estes 2002: 382). Note, though, that the attention-to-speech model was never intended to explain *all* style shifting, just what was needed to evaluate data from sociolinguistic data collection methods.

Partly as a result of the limitations of the attention-to-speech model, Bell (1984) developed the idea of audience design: people shift styles to accommodate to audience members (this idea builds on research on interaction, especially accommodation theory, associated with Giles (1973) and Giles and Powesland (1975)). Basically, people try to sound more like their interlocutors, to converge toward the people they're talking to (and occasionally, if their interlocutors are jerks, or if they want to establish social distance from them, to diverge, or sound less like them). Bell takes this farther, talking about degree of closeness: interlocutors, auditors (part of the conversational group, but not addressed), overhearers (non-participants within hearing), eavesdroppers (not participants or known), and referees (people who aren't there, but act as a model for

audience design
The idea that speakers style shift on the basis of who they are speaking with or who might overhear them, that is, their audience members.

convergence
Accommodation toward your interlocutors, that is, trying to sound more like the people you're talking to.

divergence
Accommodation away from your interlocutors, that is, trying to sound less like the people you're talking to.

Different tasks, different attention to speech

Early sociolinguistic research developed a range of tasks that lead speakers to pay more or less attention to their speech, thus eliciting speech from less formal to more formal:

- The *sociolinguistic interview* is not as informal as completely casual speech among intimates, but it tries to focus speakers' attention away from language through a structure that approximates normal conversations and through questions that engage the speaker.
- *Reading passages* require people to read a paragraph or two aloud. The paragraphs are constructed to include all the sounds that might interest the researchers.
- A *word list*, to be read aloud, involves even more focus on language, as the words don't link to create meaning. Again, the lists are constructed to include all the sounds that might interest the researchers.
- *Minimal pairs* are pairs of words that differ by only one sound. This leads to even more attention to speech,

especially if the pronunciation difference between words is affected by speakers' local accent. For example, many New Yorkers are "r-less," so a minimal pair of *God* and *guard* would set off their dialect warning bells.

Of course, this only works if your informants can read, ideally fairly fluently. If not, you need to develop other tasks (such as repeating what the researcher says, or retelling a story).

The data that researchers get from this lets them determine whether speakers are actively conscious of the social meaning of a particular variable. If a speaker does more g-droppin' in an interview than in a word list, it's a sociolinguistic **marker**; if a speaker has the same pronunciation of the LOT vowel in both situations, but a different speaker has a different pronunciation, it's a sociolinguistic **indicator** (see also chapter 4).

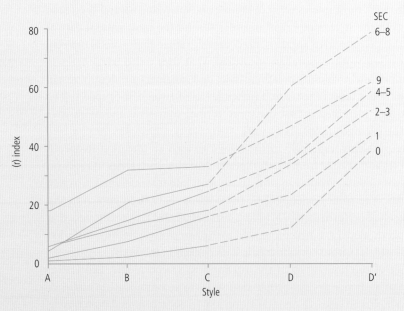

Figure 8.1.   Rates of R use, by class and formality (Labov 1972b: 114). A, casual speech; B, careful speech; C, reading style; D, word lists; D', minimal pairs.

the speaker, or an invisible judge) (figure 8.2). The "closer" the person is, the more the speaker accommodates to them. Research seems to bear this out: Trudgill (1981) analyzed his own speech in interviews, showing that he shifted toward the language of the interviewee. In a series of studies (1980, 1981, 1984), Nik Coupland looked at the language of a travel agency employee who shifted toward the (class) variety of customers. Bell also derives topic and setting effects from interlocutors (speakers associate particular addressees with particular topics and settings). Bell's hypothesis requires the amount of style shifting to decline as the "gravity" (closeness, power) of the interlocutor decreases. Thus, the model predicts that topic shifts will be smaller than addressee shifts, and this is usually the case.

marker
A variable that speakers are less aware of than a stereotype, but whose use they can control in style shifting.

indicator
A variable that can show differences by age or social group but is not subject to style shifting.

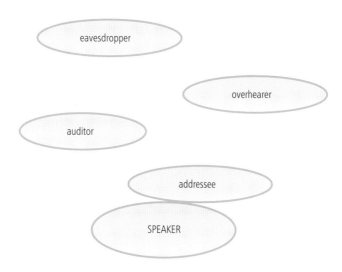

Figure 8.2. Levels of audience closeness (Bell 1984).

Bell's style axiom (1984: 151) points out that style shift seems to come from speaker prestige differences, as it's always smaller in range: "Variation on the style dimension within the speech of a single hearer derives from and echoes the variation which exists between speakers on the 'social' dimension." You may remember Labov talking about casual salesmen sounding like careful pipe-fitters. Bell's point is that the differences between casual and careful pipe-fitters will be smaller than the difference between casual salesmen and casual pipe-fitters (implicitly, because we use the differences between salesmen and pipe-fitters to teach us how to style shift).

The style axiom seems to be true most of the time, so we need to find an explanation for the exceptions to this pattern, such as studies in Ottawa (Woods 1979) or Tehran (Modaressi-Tehrani 1978) where the amount of style shift is much larger than the social shifts. Maybe these are situations or communities where deference is foregrounded? Maybe reading doesn't fit so nicely into a style continuum for some cultures or people? And maybe linguistic stereotypes show unusual behavior: Schilling-Estes and Wolfram

hyperstyle variable
A variable where there's more variation within an individual, across styles, than there is between individuals of different social backgrounds.

(1999) describe this in Ocracoke and Smith Island, isolated communities with highly distinct dialects. In fact, there may be more of these **hyperstyle variables** around than we think. After all, sociolinguistic data collection methods don't capture the full range of stylistic variation that speakers use (in particular, they usually don't capture the most casual or intimate speech styles). And some of the most style-sensitive linguistic behaviors (swearing, for example) are the kind of things that most people avoid in sociolinguistic interviews, so they're not the features we usually study.

In addition to situations like this where the model doesn't behave exactly as expected, there are potentially other problems with the audience design model. One is that we don't really know (or know how to measure) how speakers "size up" their audience in order to fine-tune their speech. The model is also entirely reactive – instead of being sociolinguistic robots whose language choices are pre-set by our social characteristics, now we're sociolinguistic robots whose language choices are set by the people we talk to! In other words, there's still not much room for speaker agency.

speaker design
Speakers using different styles to present themselves differently.

More recent work, sometimes described as a **speaker design** model, leaves more room for the conscious creation and presentation of speaker identity. Linguistic features are seen as resources, and social practice matters more than structures. In this model, all speech styles play a role in shaping all situations (Rampton 1995; Coupland 2001). For example, Coupland (2001) shows that Cardiff radio DJs use different kinds of local dialect in different joking keys (e.g., to make fun of their inarticulateness, or to connect to local themes). Schilling-Estes (1998) talks about an interviewee who uses hyper-dialect to point out the artificiality of the sociolinguistic interview. I've noticed a similar thing when sociolinguists try to interview performers (e.g., musicians), who are used to being interviewed and thus switch into "on" style in the presence of a microphone. We also see people using language to do various social work, as when Maori speakers actually use *more* Maori English male speech features when speaking to female non-Maori interviewers (Bell & Johnson 1997), because the solidarity-building value of the features trumps the identity-differentiating values.

Style shifting, authenticity, politics

Although linguists tend to consider style shifting a skill, and something we all do, it can also have negative connotations. There's a strong ideology of authenticity that relates to speech (the "keeping it real" viewpoint), in which too much shifting is seen as pandering, or at least inauthentic. During the lead-up to the 2008 US presidential election, political commentary made much of Hillary Clinton and Barack Obama sometimes adopting more Southern or African American speech features, implying that this was false or insincere. But politicians are famous for adapting to their audiences, not just linguistically. Fiorello LaGuardia, mayor of New York City from 1934 to 1945, was trilingual (English, Italian, Yiddish), and it's said that you could tell what language he was speaking from films of his speeches even with the sound off, by the way his gestures changed.

I doubt that any of these politicians consciously said, "I'm going to use a lax HAPPY vowel here" or "I think I'll use bigger gestures here." It's more likely that they pre-consciously shift their whole way of being on the basis of the audience. Sociolinguist/philosopher Pierre Bourdieu (1984) uses the term *hexis* to describe this way of carrying ourselves that can include language.

Funnily enough, the same questions of regional authenticity were rarely raised with respect to former US president George W. Bush, perhaps because he shifted less. He may have been born in Connecticut and gone to Yale, but all his hexis is from Texas.

As you might imagine, the kind of studies that teach us the most about style shifting (especially in the more speaker-oriented model) involve long-term ethnographic work returning to the same speakers (so that we get to see multiple styles) in different genres (not just sociolinguistic interviews; Kiesling 1996; Mendoza-Denton 1997; Eckert 2000). Those studies tend to look at broader features, discourse markers, even individual words, and more features at the same time. They're also often much less big-number quantitative and more discoursey. Variants are often associated with *attributes* rather than dialects/varieties (think of second-order indexing here – speakers of a particular variety may be associated with toughness or coolness, so using more of their speech features

Ahead of his time: Mikhail Bakhtin, style guru

Many sociolinguistic ideas about style (especially those of Bell) were earlier developed by the Russian thinker Mikhail Bakhtin (1895–1975), but we didn't know it. Bakhtin was the archetypal obscure academic, well respected in his own circle but not known outside it, largely for social and political reasons: he wrote in Russian, in the Soviet Union, and he wasn't popular with the government (he was exiled to Kazakhstan for six years). Some of his work may have been published under another name (Voloshinov), much of his work remained semi-finished for years, and he destroyed one of his manuscripts by using the pages as rolling papers for cigarettes, not realizing that the publisher's copy had been lost.

Bakhtin was rediscovered by Russian academics in the 1960s, and by westerners in the 1970s and 1980s. His writing has become influential in the many disciplines that now work on text analysis, but some of his ideas are especially interesting for sociolinguists (and remember, some of these go back to the late 1920s!). Among such ideas are these:

- Any language is constantly being subjected to *centrifugal* forces, which whirl it apart into dialect diversity, and *centripetal* forces, which push toward the middle and lead to standardization.
- Language involves *addressivity* and *response*. All utterances (from a greeting to a textbook) are addressed to somebody, and language results from a "reciprocal relationship between speaker and listener, addresser and addressee" (Voloshinov 1973/1929). People respond to others and expect a response in return: "I try to act in accordance with the response I anticipate" (Bakhtin 1986: 95).
- Languages involve *heteroglossia*, sometimes translated as "double voicing." Any language at any point is massively internally diverse, full of jargons and dialects, which act to flavor all components of the language: "there are no 'neutral' words and forms – words and forms that can belong to 'no one'; language has been completely taken over, shot through with intentions and accents . . . All words have the 'taste' of a profession, a genre, a tendency, a party, a particular work, a particular person, a generation, an age group, the day and hour. Each word tastes of the context and contexts in which is has lived its socially charged life; all words and forms are populated by intentions" (Bakhtin 1981: 293).

This last paragraph in particular seems to nail the issue of style and speaker identity performance. Every bit of language has social meaning derived from how it has been used and interpreted in the past, so whenever speakers make linguistic choices, they're drawing on all those social meanings to create their own mashup, which they expect to trigger a social interpretation in their listeners.

lets speakers build a tough or cool stance in a conversation). Thus, a particular feature can show group affiliation but also do conversational work, like clinching an argument (by adopting formal features) or show closeness (by adopting local or addressee features).

Which raises another question: which features can be used to do this work? Which features are most implicated in style variation? Schilling-Estes (2002: 377) suggests that researchers nowadays are more likely to look at "locally salient ways of categorizing language, people, and the world." Thus, the features involved will probably be common (Rickford & McNair-Knox 1994), salient, and strongly associated with (local) social meanings. Ironically, this brings us all the way back around to attention to speech, in that the features we can attend to are going to be the ones that we use when we're (consciously) creating our speaker identities through style shifting. In fact, sociolinguists often use style shifting as a diagnostic, to determine whether a particular variant is a sociolinguistic marker (in which case, its frequency varies depending on style) or an indicator (in which case it doesn't).

genre, register, jargon

register
A variety of language used in a particular social or economic setting, for example, legal or academic register.

genre
A category of language use recognized and usually named by the speech community, for example, *crime novel*, *sermon*. Sometimes confused with register.

jargon
A register associated with a particular occupation or activity often develops its own special vocabulary items, known as jargon.

argot
A specialized type of slang, often originally associated with thieves' talk.

Style is a shifty thing – we're always fine-tuning our output to our interlocutors and our purposes. But we also vary our language in ways that are not so split-second. The term **register**, like style, describes a type of speech, but it is more closely associated with a specific speech situation, often related to an occupation or particular pastime, so we can speak of a *legal register* or *ritual language register* or *sports announcer register*. People often speak of *recipe register*, although we can also think of *recipe* as a **genre** – it's a widely recognized category of event with its own name. Other genres might include the novel, the political speech, the lecture, or the knock-knock joke.

A register associated with a particular occupation or activity often develops its own special vocabulary items, known as **jargon**. Jargon can involve special terms, as when linguists refer to *fricatives* or *mediopassives*, or specialized meanings for existing words, as when we give particular linguistic meanings to the words *register* or *style*. Jargon makes communication more effective for in-group members – we don't need to keep saying things like "those sounds where our phonation is all hissy." But jargon also excludes non-members, or creates barriers to participation. (Sometimes this is the point, as with criminal "secret languages," often called **argot**.)

Registers and genres differ across cultures (and perhaps across speech communities). If a culture sharply distinguishes some occupations or activities, for example, then there are likely to be different registers associated with those occupations or activities. And styles and registers and genres are all associated with particular linguistic properties. The same sentiment is expressed by the formal *I shall never surrender* and the informal *I ain't quittin'!* Recipe register is full of imperatives (*Place chicken legs in bag containing*

Lots of jargon: Frequent flyers

I participate in a community of practice that just loves jargon: a discussion board for frequent flyers. Much of the jargon is borrowed from the airline industry itself, especially abbreviations and acronyms. These include airport codes (everybody writes PDX, not *Portland*), fare classes (it's J and Y, not *business class* and *economy*), airline codes (LX, not *Swiss International*), and many other terms (*GA* for *gate attendant*). Every SE (Super Elite) FF (frequent flyer) knows that an OP-UP (operational upgrade, a free upgrade to J because the airline sold too many Y tickets) is better than a LMUG (last minute upgrade, where you pay to turn your Y ticket into J). There are also terms specific to the community, such as *kettle* (a clueless hick trave-

ler, from the old *Ma and Pa Kettle* films) or *gate lice* (anybody who doesn't have access to frequent flyer lounges).

What makes this community sociolinguistically interesting is the degree to which people will use jargon whenever they can. Partly because it's efficient, I guess, but also to display knowledge or the right to claim group membership. A thread title like *CO/UA: PIT-SAN/CLD/SNA/SMF $210 a/i RT (2.6 CPM)* is meaningless to non-members. Then, on top of that, people sometimes use terms that are deliberately obscure, to tell members about loopholes or tricks without alerting airline employees using search engines. (Don't worry, FF people, I'm not going to list any of them!)

marinade) and verbs with no objects (as in *Shake vigorously*, where the shaking refers to the chicken, not you). Sports announcing is full of simple present verbs (*Subban passes to Gionta*) and subject-final sentences (*Back come the Canadiens!*). There are differences based on culture and sport, though. For example, British soccer announcers seem to prefer national origin synonyms for athletes (*It's a cracking cross from the plucky Venezuelan!*), and Spanish-speaking announcers are famous for the way they announce goals (*Goooooooooooooooooooooool!*).

passing
Adopting behaviors from another group in order to be taken as authentic members of that group.

using other people's stuff

If you have a variety of styles and flavors to draw from when presenting yourself to others, some of those styles are going to be closer to what you and your community usually use, while others are going to "belong" to other groups. In chapter 7 on gender we talked about passing, where the goal is to be taken as a legitimate member of some other group, and dragging, where the speaker and the audience are both aware that speaker is using something that belongs to someone else. Contrast both passing and dragging with crossing (Rampton 1995), a term mostly used to describe the use of language features belonging to another ethnic group (chapter 6). This falls somewhere in between. In crossing, the speaker isn't trying to pass as a member of another group, but may be claiming the right to be associated with that group. Here, it's the authenticity itself that's in question – does someone have the right to use the features associated with another group? Attempts at crossing are more likely to be remarked

As an aside: How well do we shift?

Understanding of genre differences seems to be more widespread among media-aware youth than among previous generations (trust me, my generation didn't make jokes about TV tropes). So much of the media that people consume nowadays is fine-tuned or named in some way, people interact more with their media than they used to, and people have wider choices of interlocutors. As a result, readers in their teens and twenties are probably better than people of my generation at knowing what linguistic features are appropriate in what genres or registers. Which means you know that you're not supposed to write academic papers in the same style that you would use for text messages (Baron 2008). Or in the same style that I'm using for this book, unless your prof says it's OK.

dragging
When people use features that both they and their audience know are associated with another group.

on (by members of either the target group, or the crosser's own group). A fourth option is to energetically avoid using other people's stuff at all, by **fleeing**. In fleeing, speakers make sure that audience members from their own community do not interpret their behavior as an attempt to claim membership in, or familiarity with, another group that is not highly regarded by their community.

summing up

crossing
When speakers use language features or linguistic styles associated with another ethnic group.

fleeing
Avoiding linguistic features associated with another social group.

All sociolinguistically competent members of a community have different ways of speaking in different situations. They may change their speaking style when paying more attention to their speech; they may change depending on their audience (either converging with them or diverging from them); or they may change depending on how they want to present themselves. By changing styles, people associate themselves with particular groups rather than others, and through constant style shifting (and observing the shifting of others), they define or redefine what it means to be a member of those groups. Variation between speakers can be described as style, genre, or register.

corpus linguistics
A linguistic research method based on the quantitative analysis of collections of naturally occurring language data, usually very large.

corpus (plural corpora)
A collection, usually large, of language in use, that can be adapted to allow linguistic analysis.

Where to next?

In several of these "Where to next?" boxes, I've talked about the differences between big-number quantitative research approaches and small-scale work looking at speakers as active agents. The field of **corpus linguistics** is well set up to use a large-scale approach to questions of speaker agency. Corpus linguists assemble huge collections (called **corpora**) of language from multiple sources (including conversations, newspaper and magazine articles, fiction, electronic media, and lectures). Then they do quantitative analyses of language differences across genres. Obviously these studies can't speak to what a particular language user was thinking, or trying to do, at any particular time, but they can tell us more about how members of a speech community understand the linguistic requirements of a particular genre. As sociolinguists become more aware of the masses of fairly natural speech available online, I think we'll be tempted to borrow techniques and approaches from the corpus folks.

Spotlight: The Audience

Bell, Allan. "Language style as audience design."
Language in Society 13 (1984): 145–204.

This paper is hugely influential. It's also just plain huge, 56 pages of dense text (and some references). Readers are sometimes intimidated by its length, but it's actually fairly manageable. The main point of the paper is that we change the way we talk (i.e., we style shift) in response to our audience, and that the "closer" the audience is to us, the more influence they're likely to have. So we'll change our speech more to accommodate to people that we're directly addressing (our *addressees*) than we will in order to address people who are part of the conversation (*auditors*) or who just happen to be there (*over-hearer*), or in order to sound "right" for an imagined non-present person who might be judging us (*referee*). The paper's long because it goes through each of these types of people in detail, after first explaining the limitations of earlier approaches to style (which you don't desperately need to read in detail) and laying out the basic model of audience design.

Bell's more recent work allows for a much bigger role for speaker design, for agentive identity performance. Some of these ideas are already foreshadowed in the last third of this article, and Bell proposes some ways that audience design might affect or shape speaker design (here conceptualized as *initiative shift* – the speaker takes the initiative to change styles, not simply responding to the audience).

Linguistic technical stuff: (dh) is the first sound in *then*, (th) is the first sound in *thin*, /ae/ raising is when the TRAP vowel starts to sound like *trep*, h-dropping is when *hill* is pronounced like *ill*, intervocalic /t/ voicing is pronouncing *better* as *bedder*, consonant cluster reduction is pronouncing *fast* as *fas'*. But none of this matters – the point of the article is the social distribution of those features, not the linguistic details.

Links to other readings: If you look at chapter 4 (pp. 58–86 in the second edition) of Labov's *The Social Stratification of English in New York City*, you'll better understand the perspective that Bell is arguing against.

---

exercises

1. Have a look at some of your saved emails addressed to different people (crucially, people who differ in some potentially socially important characteristic). Depending on your situation, these could include a boss, professor, friend, lover, or relative, of different ages and genders. Can you see changes in your language use from one email to the next? Do you use more text-speak, capital letters, or exclamation marks with some people? Are there some linguistic features that you would *never* use when addressing some people?

2. In the book *Exercises in Style* (1947), Raymond Queneau retells the same story (about a chance encounter on a bus) 99 times, in different styles and genres, just for fun. Try the same thing yourself (maybe not 99 times, though). Take a paragraph of writing (maybe from this book) and redo it as (say) an adventure story, talking to a baby, an online rant, or an explanation for a particularly dense friend. If you can think of a particularly odd genre or style to try, go for it.

3. Style differences are very noticeable in the news media. In fact, many of the ideas in Bell (1984) and Coupland (2001) are developed from considering the language of radio newsreaders or DJs.

Pick a big current news story. Look at the language used by different newspapers or websites to describe the events. Would you have been able to guess the source by the language choices made?

4. Watch a televised sport you've never watched before, or a discussion of a topic that you don't really follow or understand. What linguistic features – jargon or other – do you notice?

5. Ask a few friends to imitate the way people talk to different interlocutors, such as young children, foreigners, police officers, and the very elderly. Are the imitations consistent? Does everybody do "foreigner talk" the same? Are there similarities between, say, foreigner talk and talk to children? Can you describe, in linguistic terms, the differences between talk to different interlocutors?

discussion

1. Have you ever been in a situation where you (or somebody else) got the style requirements of a conversation completely wrong? What happened?

2. Are there people with whom you've interacted in very different contexts – for example, a relative who's also your teacher? How did you linguistically deal with the situation?

3. Think of a community that you're familiar with that has its own jargon. What are some of the words involved? Have you ever talked with people in the community about how odd some of the words are? Some jargony communities you might consider are workplaces, musicians or athletes or their fans (cricket people, I'm talking about you!), and gamers or other hobbyists.

4. Can you think of some hyperstyle variables, things that are extremely sensitive to style difference, across speakers from a variety of backgrounds?

5. Usually, people switch to a more formal style when they're paying attention to their speech. Can you think of situations when attention to speech would lead to people using a *less* formal style?

6. Back in the discussion section of chapter 1, I invited you to consider whether the writing and reading of this textbook could be considered an "interaction." After reading the box about Bakhtin, do you have anything new to add to that discussion?

7. Related to point 6: now that you're about halfway through the textbook, have you gotten used to the conversational style of my writing? Can you remember particular points in your reading where the style was especially noticeable?

8. Bell's observation that we style shift more when we change interlocutors than we do when we change conversational topics with a single interlocutor implies that we know that there's a limit to how much we think we can get away with, in terms of shifting in front of a particular person. Can you think of exceptions to this, situations where you might shift a whole lot in the course of a single conversation?

Eckert and Rickford's *Style and Sociolinguistic Variation* (2001) features articles and commentary from some big names in style work, including Bell and Coupland.

Bell's "Style in dialogue: Bakhtin and sociolinguistic theory" (2007) is a readable introduction to Bakhtin's sociolinguistic ideas.

For more on genre and register differences, look at Biber and Finegan (1988, 1994).

Improvisational comedy shows depend for much of their humor on the audience's understanding of genre and register. See *Whose Line Is It Anyway?* or *Improvaganza*.

Queneau's *Exercises in Style* has been translated into English (1947) and is good nerdy fun.

Interaction 9

In this chapter:

- Speech situations and events
- Analyzing conversations
- Politeness and "face"
- Solidarity versus status
- Terms of address

interactions
A relationship between two or more individuals. In sociolinguistics, it's usually pretty much a synonym for "conversation."

discourse
An extended language interaction, that is, longer than a sentence. Also, the study of such interaction.

discourse analysis
An examination of the structure of a conversation, looking for linguistic regularities.

The American sociolinguist Ralph Fasold (1990: 60) compares the way many linguists (including many sociolinguists) ignore the social purposes of language in interactions to the behavior of an automotive engineer, who might design a car without thinking (or caring) about whether it will be used for bringing home the groceries or for escaping from a bank robbery. So in this chapter, we continue our move away from explaining language choices by looking at the social characteristics of speakers or linguistic influences on the utterance, and toward seeing how language is used to do things – in this case, how language is used to make sure that interactions between speakers work as they're supposed to.

This is not to say that social characteristics like gender or class don't matter. But they don't "do" anything to language until we deal with other people. We reveal (or perform!) our social roles in extended language interaction, or discourse. And societies have rules, or at least conventions, about how discourse should proceed. Discourse analysis lets linguists look at the structure of a conversation and what it reveals about the roles of

What Is Sociolinguistics?, First Edition. Gerard Van Herk.
© 2012 Gerard Van Herk. Published 2012 by Blackwell Publishing Ltd.

the participants. In fact, you can often recognize discourse analysts when you meet them because they tend to say things to you like "What's *that* supposed to mean?"

ethnography of communication

Ethnography of communication is a way to analyze discourse by using the same sort of methods that anthropologists might use to study other aspects of a culture, such as religious practices. Within **speech situations** (circumstances involving the use of speech), cultures have developed conventions governing interactions, or **speech events**. Ethnography of communication analysis pulls apart speech events into their component parts. Eight basic components have been identified; the acronym SPEAKING may help you remember them (Hymes 1974b). Consider, for example, the following speech event:

> A mushroom walks into a bar. The bartender says "We don't serve your kind here." The mushroom says, "Why not? I'm a fungi."

Table 9.1 demonstrates how the components of this appallingly bad joke can be identified. In a real conversation, we would also expect each of these components to affect the language that is used, and the structure of discourse. You may be familiar with a game popular in improvisational comedy or theater, where actors begin a scene, somebody shouts *freeze!* and one of these components is changed – for example, a conversation between two theologians (*participants*) is suddenly performed in the style of an episode of *Glee* (*genre*). We can laugh at the adaptations made by the actors, because we share with them an understanding of the often unspoken rules that govern discourse. In other words, we (and they) have **communicative competence**

ethnography of communication
The study of discourse in relation to extralinguistic variables that identify the social basis of communication.

speech situations
The circumstances and context surrounding the use of speech.

speech events
A group of speech acts or interactions.

communicative competence
Native speakers' ability to produce and understand grammatically acceptable and situationally appropriate sentences.

Table 9.1. Components of a speech event.

	component	explanation	analysis of sample
S	setting, scene	place, time, social occasion	a bar
P	participants	who was there, including audience	bartender, mushroom
E	ends	purpose of event and goals of participants	mushroom: to get a drink bartender: to refuse
A	act sequences	content of interaction and related forms	request, refusal, explanation
K	key	emotional tone, mood	hopeful, later annoyed
I	instrumentalities	mode (spoken, written), type (dialect, style)	spoken, casual speech
N	norms	conventions of interaction	request addressed, refusal acknowledged
G	genres	category/name of event	conversation (and "X walks into a bar" joke)

speech acts
A communicative activity or utterance that does something.

scripts
In Saville-Troike and Klefgen (1989), the social expectations that people bring to an interaction.

codes
In Saville-Troike and Klefgen (1989), the content and form of an interaction.

(Gumperz 1972) – we know "how to do things with words" (Austin 1962) beyond stringing them into grammatically acceptable sentences. We know the linguistic forms and strategies that are appropriate in our community to request, question, criticize, command, inform, warn, joke, greet, ignore, praise, comfort, defer, suck up, turn down, freak out, chat up, clue in, and relate to other people in a hundred other ways, or speech acts.

Researchers can use the SPEAKING framework to identify the socially significant components of any particular speech event. For example, a change in instrumentality (from speech to writing) might have a smaller effect in some genres (such as academic papers) than in others. It's possible that some SPEAKING components usually "trump" others. For example, Saville-Troike and Kleifgen (1989) look at interactions between English and non-English speakers in schools and find a large role for the social expectations that people bring to an interaction, which they call scripts, and a smaller role for the content and form of the interaction, which they call codes. So if your script (understanding of norms and genres) predicts a particular outcome, but the code (actual language used) does something else, you try to fit that code into your script. In that particular study, kids with limited English still did what was expected of interactions in the classroom, even without understanding the language involved, because they had classroom scripts that worked without any linguistic knowledge.

As an aside: Communicative competence across languages

Gumperz's (1972) work on communicative competence has been influential in the field of second language teaching, as it became clear that it's not enough to just give people the raw linguistic components of another language. They also have to know how to appropriately use that language in different speech situations.

Notice how few of these things have much to do with a science-nerd definition of the function of language, "to get information from the speaker to the hearer" (a referential function). We use language to do a bunch of other things – to express our feelings (an expressive function), to try to get someone to do something (a directive function), or to express empathy or solidarity (a phatic function; Malinowski 1923; Hymes 1974a).

One way to investigate the conventions of conversation is through conversation analysis. Among other things, this method lets us search large collections of recorded natural speech to discover patterns in the distribution of utterances. One very common structure is the adjacency pair, a sort of minimal act sequence in which a specific type of utterance by one speaker is followed by a specific type by someone else. An obvious example is *question–answer*, but other recurring examples include *compliment–acceptance* and *offer–refusal*. Sometimes the first part permits more than one response: in a store, an offer (*Can I help you?*) can trigger either acceptance (*Yes, I'm looking for a Black Lips t-shirt*) or refusal (*No, just browsing*). Sometimes one utterance type can be interpreted as another. For example, in cultures where direct requests are discouraged, an overt compliment (*What a nice hat!*) will be interpreted as a request (*May I have it?*). In other cultures, the same compliment may be interpreted as an attribution of wealth (*You must be rich to afford such a hat*) leading up to a request for money, thus requiring a denial (*This old thing? I've had it forever*).

conversation analysis
Among other things, this method looks at the sequential organization of conversation and how participants manage the conversation using strategies like turn-taking.

adjacency pair
A single stimulus-plus-response sequence by participants, that is, one in which a specific type of utterance by one speaker is followed by a specific type by someone else.

Conversation analysis also deals with who speaks when. It includes identification of conversational openings (*How are you?*) and closings (*Well, gotta get back to work*). As well, it studies turn-taking. At the end of a conversational "turn," the speaker may try to determine who should speak next (for example, by asking a question), or "open the floor" to any participant who has something to contribute. If nobody takes over, the original speaker may continue. Sometimes, the cues for boundaries between turns are subtler, including intonation or the use of discourse markers. For example, I and other English Montrealers (and many other people) can use *so . . .* or *but . . .* at the end of a discourse turn to mean something like "Well, I bet you can figure out the implications of what I just said." For example:

Other person: Did you go into school to work on your sociolinguistics textbook?
Gerard: I was going to, but it was raining, *so . . .*
Other person: You are so slack.

Here, even though *so . . .* would usually imply that I had something else to say, I intend it as the marker of a turn boundary, and the other person knows it's time to say something. Cross-culturally, differences in turn-taking cues may cause confusion. Linguists have identified communities with a high involvement style, such as eastern European Jews in New York or radio talk show callers in Jamaica (Tannen 1984; Shields-Brodber 1992). Here, turns will often overlap (one speaker will start before another finishes). In other communities, including among the Kuna of Panama (Sherzer 1983), a longer pause is required to signal the end of a turn. A speaker who hadn't developed communicative competence in these communities might be seen by Jamaicans as unwilling to participate, and by the Kuna as monopolizing the conversation. An ethnography of speaking might also consider whether any talking at all is appropriate. For example, among the Western Apache (Basso 1972), silence is an appropriate strategy for dealing with uncertainty in human relationships, in situations such as responding to criticism, or meeting strangers. Contrast this with the advice frequently given in mainstream American culture that people should "talk out" their differences.

openings
In conversation analysis, openings begin the interaction.

closings
In conversation analysis, closings end the interaction.

turn-taking
Part of conversation analysis that looks at how speakers share the conversational floor, or right to speak.

discourse marker
A word or phrase that isn't really part of sentence structure, but that helps an interaction along. Examples include *well, y'know, I mean, like, know what I'm sayin'?*

high involvement style
In conversation analysis, a type of interaction involving frequent turn changes, interruption, and overlapping speech.

Method: Ethnography as a research practice

Once a researcher assumes that speakers are going to use language differently in different kinds of interactions, she will need to adopt research methods that let her consider how interactions work in the community under study. Ethnographic methods usually require participant observation – the researcher becomes a part of the community, to whatever degree that's possible or permitted, in order to observe it. This usually involves intense engagement with the community over an extended period of time, in some role that makes sense in the context. Longer periods of engagement not only let the researcher observe more and different behavior, but also are likely to encourage the community to trust the researcher, or at least get used to her, so that they don't act like there's a stranger nearby (the Observer's Paradox, remember that?).

Participant observation as a research practice is most closely associated with anthropology, and anthropologists are famous for considering and reconsidering their methods, so it's no surprise that practitioners have spent a lot of time figuring out exactly how broad they want to make their claims, on the basis of their intense engagement with a very specific community. Ethnography of speaking tends to produce detailed and perceptive descriptions of what's going on with language use in a particular place (e.g., Ochs 1974), but its practitioners are more hesitant to generate big guiding principles about what people do with language, a tendency that can be seen as either a strength or a weakness. There's also the issue of how to interpret what you observe. As an outsider to a community, you're likely to notice many phenomena of interest (basically, all the stuff that's different from how you do things back home), but it may be hard to tell what those phenomena mean to the community without either interviewing or consulting community members, or spending long enough in the community that meanings begin to reveal themselves.

Linguistic anthropologists who have produced work based on extended participant observation include Hill and Hill (1986) and Lindenfeld (1990). Sociolinguists who have adapted ethnographic methods include Hazen (2002), Bucholtz (2011), and, most famously, Penelope Eckert (2000), whose long-term participation in the daily life of a Michigan high school led to her work on communities of practice (see chapter 2).

face

politeness theory
Based on the notion of face, politeness theory argues that people use strategies of positive politeness and negative politeness to negotiate personal interactions (cf. Brown & Levinson 1987).

face wants
The desire to protect one's positive face and negative face. Also called *face needs*.

face threatening acts
Actions that threaten people's face wants.

Understanding what counts as polite is, like other aspects of sociolinguistic behavior, something that young members of a society learn over time. "Politeness" as we use the term here means more than just following the rules of formal etiquette – it's more like "behaving appropriately in a given situation" and/or "treating your interlocutor appropriately." Brown and Levinson's **politeness theory** (1987) analyzes how we deal with each other's **face wants**. You've probably heard people use the expressions *to save face* or *to lose face*, meaning to preserve your status or respect or to have them damaged. These uses of the word *face* (which English has borrowed from Chinese) are what Brown and Levinson have in mind. They divide people's face wants into two types, negative and positive. **Negative face** is "the want of every competent adult member of a community that their actions be unimpeded by others" – (Brown & Levinson 1987: 62) – in other words, the right to be left alone, to not be imposed on. **Negative politeness** strategies are ways of dealing with this by, for example, minimizing interactions, or apologizing for bothering someone. Negative **face threatening acts** might include giving advice, or trying to act too friendly with somebody who isn't really your friend. **Positive face** is "the want of every member that their wants be desirable to at least some others" (Brown & Levinson 1987: 62) – in other words, the right to have yourself and your opinion valued. **Positive politeness** strategies are ways of dealing with this by, for example, complimenting someone, or using in-group language or nicknames. Positive face threatening acts might include interrupting, disagreeing, or being inappropriately formal with somebody who is your friend.

The focus on "appropriate" behavior and social learning is a hint that what counts as polite can vary greatly from one situation to another, and from one culture to another.

It's often argued that cross-cultural misunderstandings result from different ideas of what counts as polite and appropriate, including a tendency for different cultures to prefer negative or positive strategies. For example, Bailey (1996) looks at differences between Korean American shopkeepers, who focus on negative face wants and thus keep conversations to a minimum in service interactions, and their African American customers, who focus on positive face wants and thus treat service interactions as a chance to be friendly. The mismatch leads to customers interpreting shopkeepers' behavior as deliberately antagonistic. We probably don't want to assume that *all* differences in interaction between cultures can be explained in this way, but it's a reasonable explanation of how the two cultures involved had different face expectations for this particular type of interaction.

> ### *As an aside*: You're so negative!
>
> Students often have trouble with the idea of positive and negative face, interpreting positive as "being nice" and negative as "not being nice." That's not what this is about. Negative face and negative politeness strategies are about being nice by backing off or butting out; positive face and positive politeness strategies are about being nice by being casual or friendly.

solidarity and power

Even when participants in a conversation share norms, the conversation may be somewhat unbalanced, depending on the relative social standing of each participant (the **power** relationship). Participants may express closeness and intimacy, or shared status (**solidarity**); or, they may maintain a difference and highlight their social distance (**status**). One clear example of this is found in **forms of address** – what the participants call each other.

   Many languages can express power relationships through the choice of pronoun meaning *you*. Generally, the **T form** (from the French *tu*) is used reciprocally among family and close friends, while the **V form** (from the French *vous*) is used reciprocally among people of roughly equal status, but who are not close (Brown & Gilman 1960). When participants are of unequal status, the powerful use the T forms to address the less powerful, while the less powerful use V forms to address the powerful. This distinction carries so much significance that languages sometimes have a verb meaning "using the T form." In German, it's *dützen*; in French, it's *tutoyer*. People will sometimes formally admit somebody into their friendship circle by saying, "You may *tutoyer* me." Analysis of T/V usage can often reveal how speakers feel about the relationship between participants in a conversation. For example, Placencia (2001) looked at the language of White or Spanish-identified mestizo (mixed ethnicity) employees of Bolivian public institutions (such as hospitals) during service encounters, and found that clients who were indigenous people were usually addressed with the familiar (T) forms. Those clients were also spoken to with more direct instructions and fewer politeness formulas. All of these linguistic behaviors suggest that the employees perceived indigenous people as lower-status. Placencia concludes that use of T forms to indigenous people "seems to be so ingrained in the linguistic behavior of white-mestizos that they are not even aware of it" (Placencia 2001: 123).

   Different societies have different ideas about where to draw the line between people who need T-ing or V-ing; for example, Québec French speakers will use *tu* more readily

power
An unequal or non-reciprocal relationship between two or more speakers, predicting who (or whose norms) will dominate an interaction.

solidarity
Closeness or intimacy, or shared status.

status
Social positions that society assigns to its members, or the differences between social groups, in terms of the prestige associated with them by others.

forms of address
The way in which conversation participants call (or address) each other.

Solidarity and childbirth

The choice of T and V forms can be used to create solidarity. Here's an example from a Canadian French speaker from the Ottawa-Hull region:

J'emploi le vous formel avec mes supérieurs ou avec des personnes en position d'autorité. Je l'utilise aussi avec mes clients (je suis infirmière). Le seul moment ou je me permets de déroger à cette règle est quand ma cliente est en train d'accoucher et qu'elle est en période de transition (à partir de 7 ou 8 cm). Une fois l'accouchement terminé et le placenta expulsé, je retourne au vouvoiement.

"I use formal *vous* with my superiors or with people in positions of authority. I also use it with my clients (I'm a nurse). The only time I let myself break this rule is when my client is in labor and she's dilated (from 7 or 8 cm onward). Once childbirth is over and the placenta is expelled, I return to using *vous.*" (Ottawa-Hull Corpus, Ottawa University Sociolinguistics Laboratory; my translation)

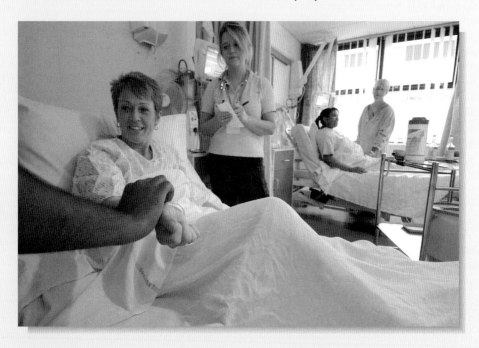

than European French speakers. In addition, the boundaries between T and V can change within a society over time. In French, T seems to be expanding its domain, while in English, V won out to such a degree that hardly anybody says *thou* or *thee* (the old T forms) any more. And within a community, T/V use can be a strong way of positioning yourself with respect not just to your interlocutor, but to the society as a whole. In 1960, Brown and Gilman could say "A Frenchman could, with some confidence, infer that a male university student who regularly said T to female fellow students would favor the nationalization of industry, free love, trial marriage, the abolition of capital punishment, and the weakening of nationalistic and religious loyalties" (Brown & Gilman 1960: 175). That's a lot of meaning for one pronoun to carry!

English no longer has an active T/V distinction, but as in many other languages, English-speaking participants in a conversation can express solidarity and status through other forms of address: the names that we call people. For example, we can express solidarity through reciprocal naming, as when friends call each other by their first names. Where there is a perceived power difference, as with age differences or work relationships, we often use non-reciprocal naming. A teacher or boss may call students or employees by their first names, while students or employees may use title and last name: *Professor Bubenik, Mr. Kadonoff*. If you've worked in factories, you've probably observed a gradient form of address: a fellow worker named Rupen Pandya is *Rupen* or *Roop*, a foreman of the same name is *Mr. Rupen*, while the "big boss" would be *Mr. Pandya*. In this system, last-naming behaves a little like V, first-naming like T.

There are other naming choices available to us. In some varieties of English, such as here in Newfoundland, many speakers use affectionate terms like *my duck* or *my darling*, even with strangers (and some uptight non-Newfoundlanders find this overly familiar). In many cultures, people refer to older friends and neighbors as *auntie* and *uncle*, even though there is no genetic relationship. Sometimes, we call people by their job title. *Doctor* or *Professor* (without an actual name) is respectful, but distant. On the other hand, in V. S. Naipaul's *A House for Mr Biswas* (1961), Indo-Caribbean characters insult people by calling them by the names of their low-status current or former jobs (*crab-catcher, grass-cutter*). In many varieties of English, we can take an antagonistic stance through the sarcastic use of former solidarity address forms like *pal* or *buddy*.

Sometimes we're not sure what to call somebody. Do professors really want to be called by their first names? Do we know them well enough to be first-naming them? Do we want to? What do we call our partner's parents? And does it change over time, or if we marry? What do we call our *ex*-partner's parents? Sometimes speakers choose to cop out entirely, and find ways to address somebody or to get their attention without using any address form at all. This is usually known as no-naming (Ervin-Tripp 1972). Wardhaugh (2006: 270) cites a nice literary example of no-naming from the novel *Jasmine* (Mukherjee 1989: 77): the wife can't bring herself to call her husband by his name (instead of the traditional pronoun form), and so she gets his attention by coughing, or saying "Are you listening?"

We can also express solidarity and power relationships through style shifting (see chapter 8). Informal or casual speech usually indicates a degree of solidarity or affiliation. Formal style is usually associated with social distance, and perhaps unequal status. In particular, the higher-status participant in a conversation might expect formal speech from the lower-status speaker, as evidence of both accommodation (to upper-class-associated formal variants) and negative politeness strategies (not getting too friendly or uppity). Or, at the very least, the higher-status speaker might get to determine what level of style will be used. I see this when secretarial staff at my university send me emails that begin *Dear Dr. Van Herk* and sign off with their first names, and only switch over to *Hi, Gerard!* after I've signed off with *my* first name at least once.

reciprocal naming
An expression of solidarity, as when friends call each other by their first names.

no-naming
Addressing somebody or getting someone's attention without using any address form at all.

Table 9.2. Level differences in Javanese.

level	Are	you	going	to eat	rice	and	cassava	now?
3a	menapa	pandjenengan	bade	dahar	sekul	kalijan	kaspé	samenika
3	menapa	sampéjan	bade	neda	sekul	lan	kaspé	samenika
2	napa	sampéjan	adjeng	neda	sekul	lan	kaspé	saniki
1b	apa	pandjenengan	arep	dahar	sega	lan	kaspé	saiki
1a	apa	sampéjan	arep	neda	sega	lan	kaspé	saiki
1	apa	kowé	arep	mangan	sega	lan	kaspé	saiki

In some languages, the boundaries between styles are so sharply marked that speakers have to make all kinds of complicated decisions about both the relative status of participants and all the other stuff associated with Hymes' SPEAKING model. Speakers of Javanese, for example, have to decide between high, middle, or low style, as well as between the use or non-use of honorifics, words associated with people and the things they do. Geertz (1960: 250) lays out six possible ways to say exactly the same sentence in Javanese (table 9.2). And you're not allowed to shift styles in the middle of an utterance – forms associated with one style have to all be used together (thanks to what are sometimes called co-occurrence restrictions).

co-occurrence restrictions
Constraints on which forms or styles can be used together.

So how do you know which form to choose? Geertz (1960: 257–8) lists a few relevant factors: the age, sex, kinship relation, occupation, wealth, education, religious commitment, and family background of the speaker, as well as the social setting, content of the conversation, whether you've quarreled with the interlocutor . . . and then, depending on who you are and how much clout you have, you might decide that the whole thing is silly and use low style with almost everyone.

summing up

Discourse analysis and ethnographies of communication let us identify the relevant patterns that recur when speakers interact with others. Communicative competence in a language requires knowing not just the words and the grammatical rules, but also the interactional rules of that language. Linguistic choices in interactions can reveal a great deal about the relationship of the participants, including their closeness and their relative status. Many languages have elaborate systems of status marking, including style shifts, address forms, pronouns, and names.

Where to next?

Understanding the rules of interaction for a linguistic community involves also understanding how those rules govern many different interactional situations, so it's hard to research just by collecting language data from one context, such as a sociolinguistic interview. As a result, researchers often directly ask people what they would say in a particular situation. As we get access to bigger and bigger collections of actual interactional data (online, for example, or in the collections of corpus linguists), we're seeing more work looking at multiple authentic interactions. This might lead to new, quantitatively based ideas about language interaction.

exercises

1. Ask your profs if there are particular things that they dislike being called by students (aside from the obvious ones, like "Bozo"). Is there any correlation between their preferences and their social characteristics (age, sex, region) or field of study?

2. Describe a function – referential, phatic, directive, or expressive – for each of the following utterances. If there's more than one, describe a situation in which it could be used in each way. For example, *The window is open* could be referential (a statement of the openness of the window), or directive (if the speaker wants the window closed, but doesn't want to appear too bossy).
   (a) How are you feeling?
   (b) It's a beautiful day!
   (c) The University of West Virginia is located in Morgantown.
   (d) You've told this story before.
   (e) I'm glad you're here.
   (f) Most octogenarians don't try break-dancing.
   (g) I can't see the blackboard.
   (h) Will you be around at 3:30?
   (i) Did you see that Sidney Crosby goal?
   (j) Shut up!

3. Each of the following situations might threaten somebody's face. Which of them might threaten positive face wants, and which might threaten negative face wants? How do you know?
   (a) You ask somebody you haven't met for a while what they're doing now.
   (b) You call a friend's dad "Sir."
   (c) You call the queen of Great Britain "Liz."
   (d) Your prof has a picture of people (presumably family) on her desk, and you comment to her on the people in the picture.
   (e) You wear headphones on the plane so that the passenger next to you won't talk to you.

4. Words meaning "to use the T form" are also found in Dutch, Finnish, German, Polish, Romanian, Russian, Spanish, and Swedish. If you don't speak those languages yourself, find people who do and ask them what the word is. Pay attention to whether you have to explain what you're asking about in great detail, or whether they understand right away what you want. What might this say about how important the distinction is in that language, or for that person?

discussion

1. What naming practice do you use with your professors? First name? Professor + Last Name? Doctor + Last Name? Does it vary from professor to professor? If so, why?

2. Have you ever been in a situation where you weren't sure which name to use for someone? What did you do?

3. Can you see ways in which positive/negative face wants relate to convergence and divergence? To status and solidarity? To T and V?

4. Have you ever been involved in a service interaction where you and the other person clearly had different ideas of what counted as appropriate? Could the difference be explained by considering negative and positive face wants?

5. I do a lot of simplification in this chapter, especially about differences across cultures. Even within a single culture, people often have very different discourse and politeness strategies. Have you ever been in a situation (within your own culture) where, looking back on it, you wish you'd been a little more Western Apache and kept your mouth shut? Or been a little more Jamaican and spoken up?

6. Has your communicative competence ever let you down when you were talking to people from another culture or linguistic community? What happened?

7. Do you have any friends that you can call by their last name alone, like *Hey, Jackson!* What does doing this say about your relationship to that person? Do you think this has changed over time? Do you think it's different depending on social characteristics like gender, class, or region?

8. How do the ideas about address terms relate to using nicknames with people?

9. Many people (especially those along the autism spectrum) have trouble with the meanings of utterances beyond the referential. Thus, they misunderstand sarcasm, and often don't pick up on hints that a conversation is over. Has this happened to you? How did you interpret what was going on?

10. If you're comfortable discussing stereotypes of national and ethnic groups: are there groups that some people in your culture see as too friendly, too impersonal, too pushy? How much of this might be due to different politeness strategies?

11. For education students in particular: how could you use scripts and codes to help you understand (or improve) classroom interactions with ESL (English as a second language) students?

other resources

Bucholtz and Hall's "Identity and interaction: A sociocultural linguistic approach" (2005) is an influential (but difficult) article that brings together many of the ideas about interaction, performance, and identity introduced over the last few chapters.

Hymes' "Ways of speaking" (1974b, frequently reprinted) explains the SPEAKING model in greater detail, while also laying out many of the ideas that sociolinguists work with, but from more of an anthropological perspective.

Journals:

Research on Language and Social Interaction, http://rolsi.lboro.ac.uk (accessed August 30, 2011).

Journal of Linguistic Anthropology, http://www.wiley.com/bw/journal.asp?ref=1055-1360 (accessed August 30, 2011).

All the hits: Duranti, *Linguistic Anthropology: A Reader* (2009).

10 Multilingualism

This chapter is about the different ways that multilingualism can play out socially, at both the societal and the individual level. So far, we've been looking mostly at individual speech communities, in which all members speak fairly mutually comprehensible varieties of a single language. Around the world, however, this monolingual situation is not the norm. Most of the planet's people live in multilingual societies. Naturally enough, if people are used to multilingualism as the norm of their society, they will have different ways of thinking about it than people from monolingual societies, for whom competence in multiple languages sometimes seems like an amazing (or freakish) skill. Some interesting sociolinguistic situations can develop as a result. Multilinguals who grow up thinking of multilingualism as the norm are more likely to see the boundaries between languages (and their speakers) as fluid. They may acquire bare functional competence in many additional languages, or not really worry about what level of ability is required to be considered competent in a language (see Sridhar 1996). They

As an aside: Multilingual enough

A nice example of multilinguals' casual attitude toward acquiring additional languages is described for Kenya by Sedlak (1983): at one point most low-cost cinemas showed mostly Hindi-language films, so in each town a handful of people learned enough Hindi to describe the film plots to their friends, who in exchange for this service would pay for the translator's ticket.

What Is Sociolinguistics?, First Edition. Gerard Van Herk.
© 2012 Gerard Van Herk. Published 2012 by Blackwell Publishing Ltd.

may also be so used to the idea of switching between languages for different tasks, or to talk to different people, that they barely notice that they're doing it. And they may end up using two or more of their languages in a single utterance, a phenomenon usually called *code-switch*ing (see below).

multilingual societies

There are different ways that a society can be multilingual. In some multilingual societies, including much of South Asia and sub-Saharan Africa, most members of the community are themselves multilingual, using different languages for different purposes. In other societies, the political entity is bilingual or multilingual but individual speakers tend to be monolingual – multiple communities with different languages co-exist in a single society, sometimes clustering in different regions (that's the way things work in Belgium and Canada). In many multilingual societies, we find something in between. Maybe the more mobile or accommodating members of the society learn languages other than their mother tongue. Or maybe there's asymmetrical bilingualism, where the less powerful linguistic groups are expected to adopt the language of the powerful group in order to gain access to education or government services or jobs. (The idea that there are social and power imbalances among languages should come as no surprise after all this time talking about the same imbalances among dialects of the same language!) And, of course, there are different ways that a society (or political entity) can become multilingual in the first place:

asymmetrical bilingualism
A bilingual situation in which the less powerful linguistic groups are expected to adopt the language of the powerful group in order to access education or government services or jobs.

- *Population movements*, such as immigration or displacement due to war or famine, can lead to speakers of new languages moving into an area.
- *Boundary drawing* between countries can lead to linguistically distinct regions being cut apart, or stuck in with other linguistic regions. This was a widespread occurrence in the European colonial powers' division of sub-Saharan Africa.
- *Exogamy*, a societal requirement that requires people to "marry out" of their cultural or linguistic group, can lead to situations like that among the Tukano of the Amazon, where all the men have wives who speak various other languages, so all the children grow up surrounded by multiple languages.

diglossia

diglossia
A situation in which two distinctly different language varieties co-exist in a speech community, acting as social registers, in which the high variety is used in formal situations and the low variety among friends.

In some multilingual societies, distinctly different varieties serve social roles, similar to the way that different styles or levels of formality work in monolingual societies. This is known as diglossia (Ferguson 1959). In diglossic situations, the high (H) variety is used in formal situations, the low (L) variety among friends. What really makes diglossia diglossia is that you can't mix a bit of one language and a bit of another (reminiscent of the co-occurrence restrictions in Javanese mentioned in chapter 9). The choice of which language to use is highly constrained by the social context of use, or domain, and these constraints are fairly similar across diglossic situations. Sometimes the use of a language in a particular domain is required by law (see a broader discussion about how societies officially regulate which language should be used where in chapter 13). Usually, though, diglossic situations arise through generations (or centuries) of societal multilingualism, multiple languages co-existing in a single community. H language is usually found in formal domains, including classroom lectures, formal religious rituals, literature, government, law, newspaper editorials, and TV news. L language is usually found in informal domains – the home, the schoolyard, the market, the street, newspaper cartoons, and jokes. H language is for strangers, bosses, and teachers; L language is for family, close friends, and subordinates. The original conceptualization of diglossia required the H and L languages to be related, either fairly closely (as with Standard German and *Schwyzerdütsch* in Switzerland, or Standard and local Arabic (*darija*) in Morocco) or more distantly (as with French and French-based creole in Haiti), and for the H language to be largely school-learned, rather than natively acquired. Most researchers since have been willing to use the term to describe situations where the languages are not related (as with Spanish and Guaraní, an indigenous language, in Paraguay), as long as they fulfill the expected social roles.

How do people in diglossic contexts decide which language to use in a particular context? The answer seems to relate to Hymes' SPEAKING metric (see chapter 9); in particular, speakers consider *where* they are, *who* they're talking to, and *what kind* of speech activities are involved. Bilinguals in Paraguay use Guaraní in rural areas, and in non-serious discourse among intimates, but they use Spanish in urban areas for formal conversations and for informal conversations with non-intimates (Rubin 1985: 119). For serious but informal conversations with intimates in urban areas, Paraguayans choose on the basis of a speaker's preference and first language learned, as well as assumptions the speaker makes about the listener's language proficiency. Another possibility is that a change in language can signal a change in the roles of the speakers, as when a Norwegian uses Ranamál (the local L dialect) to inquire after her neighbor's relatives, then switches to Bokmál (the local H dialect) to ask for her professional advice about tax forms.

Because the constraints on language choice in diglossic situations are so clear (as are the differences between the languages involved), a strong effect can be produced by breaking the rules. Paraguayans can "lighten up" a serious political discussion (in Spanish) by inserting a witty comment (in Guaraní; Rubin, 1985). Hungarian-speaking grandparents can get their Hungarian-speaking grandchildren to behave by giving an order in German (H), even if nobody involves actually understands German (Gal 1979). Caribbean newspaper columnists can write in the local creole language (L) to indicate that their opinions are common sense, or shared by the masses, while Caribbean rum-shop philosophers can switch to Standard English to lend authority to their arguments. In each case, speakers accomplish two things by switching: they get their listeners' attention, and they borrow the social traits associated with the language variety (casualness, reliability, authority, etc.). Speakers can also make a social or political point by deliberately using the "wrong" variety. As the H variety is usually associated with political power, using L in H contexts (especially in writing) can be interpreted as a challenge to the established political order, especially during times of social or political change.

domain
The social or institutional context of language use.

societal multilingualism
When multiple languages co-exist in a single community.

As an aside: Demonizing the demotic

In Greece during the switchover to the use of Demotiki (demotic Greek, the L variety) in more and more contexts, many people assumed that anyone using Demotiki in expository writing or in a university lecture was a provocateur or political radical (and centuries ago, people probably thought the same about Chaucer and Dante when they wrote in English and Italian, rather than French or Latin). In 1941, the Greek minister of education suspended a university professor for two months for publishing two academic articles in Demotiki (Frangoudaki 2002: 106). Earlier, in 1901, conservative elements rioted in the streets when a Demotiki version of the Bible was produced.

(By the way, Standard Demotic Greek became the official language of Greece in 1976.)

Researchers generally use the term "diglossia" when the domains of use of two languages are clearly defined. In practice, of course, things don't always play out that cleanly. For example, Moroccan Arabic is one of the classic examples used in Ferguson's original article (1959) on diglossia, but in Morocco and elsewhere in the Arabic-speaking world, nowadays there's usually a variety intermediate between Classical Arabic and the marked local dialect. This middle variety is generally spoken by urban people and the middle classes, and the relationship between the dialect and the middle variety is very similar to the sociolinguistic situation in dialect continuum situations all around the world (Al-Wer 1997). Another possibility is that two languages can split the work of the H variety, as in Luxembourg, where German is used in government, French in law, and the local dialect (Lëtzebuergesch) in L contexts (Hoffmann 1981). More often, especially in postcolonial situations, a multilingual society will involve one H language (often the former colonial language) and a number of local languages, each of which serves as L for its speakers. In this situation, the H language can fill an additional social need, as a way of distancing the speaker from strong regional or tribal loyalties when interacting with people from another linguistic group (if you want a loan and you and the bank manager are from different groups, maybe you don't want to underline that fact by using your home language at the bank). And sometimes, even in fairly classic diglossic situations, the domains don't line up exactly as expected. For example, usually H languages are associated with religion, but in some places the L language may be closely associated with the traditional local religion. Or schoolteachers may use H for the content of a lecture, but L to help students understand, or to get them to behave.

And, of course, there are many non-diglossic multilingual societies (although if you stretch the definition of diglossia far enough, most multilingual societies involve one or two languages that are more closely associated with power, money, and education than the others). And there are many situations of **unstable multilingualism**, where you wouldn't expect "real" diglossia to develop, because the relationship between the languages doesn't get a chance to coalesce, and competence in both languages involved doesn't spread through the whole community.

unstable multilingualism
Temporary or fleeting instances of social multilingualism.

code-switching
When people alternate between at least two languages or language varieties in a single conversation (across sentences or clause boundaries). Sometimes called *code-mixing*.

code-switching

A far more common outcome of widespread multilingualism than diglossia is **code-switching**, when people switch between two (or more) languages ("code" here is an all-purpose term to refer to languages and distinct dialects). The kind of language switching I described in the previous section – where the components of SPEAKING play a big role – is usually known as **situational code-switching**. Situational switching generally involves one language being seen as appropriate for a particular conversation or interaction – in other words, the whole exchange happens in one of the speakers' languages. Factors influencing language choice in this kind of situation include domain (as we saw above with diglossia), but also interlocutor, the roles or relationships between speakers, the venue (setting), the channel of communication (writing vs, speech, telephone vs. face-to-face), or type of interaction (Clyne 1997).

But code-switching is often motivated by more volatile components, such as topic, or the speaker's attitude toward the topic, or identity creation, or solidarity (see phatic functions, chapter 9). Consider the following often-quoted example (Holmes 1992: 49–50), in which Alf, a Samoan–English bilingual, discusses his diet problems (the parts that he says in Samoan are in italics):

> My doctor told me to go on a diet. She said I was overweight. So I tried. *But it was so hard, I'd keep thinking about food all the time.* Even when I was at work. And in bed at night *I'd get desperate. I couldn't get to sleep. So I'd get up and raid the fridge. Then I'd feel guilty and sick.*

What leads Alf to switch languages in the middle of the story? It seems like he's using English for the hard expository of the story, and using Samoan to express his ambivalent feelings about the diet, or to deal with his guilt, or to elicit the listener's sympathy. In other words, the multiple languages are a sociolinguistic resource for him – he uses them to do "social work." This kind of switching is sometimes called **metaphorical code-switching**. To do this kind of switching, Alf has to know both languages well enough to draw on them, and he also has to know what social meaning each language carries in the multilingual speech community that he inhabits.

In other words, this kind of code-switching is a skill, not a shortcoming. People who criticize this kind of mixed language (which is often given a name – Spanglish, Franglais, Chiac) might think it results from lack of ability in one of the languages. But Alf clearly knows both languages well. In communities with many multilinguals, you can get truly virtuoso switching. Studies of Puerto Rican Spanish speakers in New York ("Nuyoricans") and Tamil–English bilinguals in India and Canada (Poplack 1980, 1987) often find dozens of switches in a couple of hundred words. In these communities, it's the code-switching itself that represents (and builds) community identity. In other words, code-switching is not the kind

situational code-switching
When code-switching is constrained by the social context. Also known as *domain-based code-switching*.

metaphorical code-switching
When code-switching is used as a sociolinguistic resource, rather than just to respond to context.

matrix language
The dominant language in code-switching.

As an aside: The linguistics of code-switching

Once sociolinguists fully realized that heavy-duty code-switching operated in much the same way as monolingual speech did, they began to work toward understanding the distinct rules that govern the location and purpose of the switches. The **matrix language** hypothesis (Myers-Scotton 1993b) suggests that at any one point in a conversation, one of the languages acts as the frame into which material from the other language is inserted. The **free morpheme constraint** and the **equivalence constraint** (Poplack 1980) suggest that there are predictable places within sentence structure where switching is likely to happen.

Researchers debate whether single-word switches, like "Please pass the *poi*," are really code-switching, or just **nonce borrowing**, a kind of temporary grabbing of a word from elsewhere. Luckily for me, a fuller discussion of these issues is beyond the scope of this book. But whether we're talking borrowings or switches, there are definite linguistic tendencies at play when single words from one language are inserted into the other. Nouns are the most commonly inserted words, followed by verbs (often paired with a word meaning "do"), then adjectives, adverbs, and grammatical function words.

free morpheme constraint
A proposed constraint on code switching. Simplified version: switching can't happen between bound morphemes, word parts that can't stand on their own.

equivalence constraint
A proposed constraint on code switching. Simplified version: switching tends to happen where the sentence structure just before and just after the switch are possible in both languages involved.

nonce borrowings
Individual words from another language that are inserted, often being changed to obey the rules of the matrix language.

of "make it up as you go along" mess that monolingual observers (or people terrified by linguistic or cultural mixing) sometimes take it for. (More on the actual linguistic results of languages in contact in chapter 11.)

Much of the language-switching decision-making process described here may remind you of things that we've already discussed with respect to style shifting or T/V choice. In fact, many researchers have commented on the similarities between a monolingual choosing a style and a bilingual choosing a language. The same kind of factors come into play in both situations. A major difference, though, is that dialect or style differences *within* a language are often subtle or gradient. Your listener may not be consciously aware that you've shifted, unless you use a very marked form. Actually *changing* languages is obviously more noticeable. Another difference is the issue of mutual intelligibility. In many contexts, it's quite possible that your interlocutor doesn't understand one of your languages, or understands it less well. In that case, usually whoever can switch the easiest (or is assumed to be able to switch) is expected to do so: even one or two monolinguals in a group can lead a large group of bilinguals to change languages. Human nature probably plays a role here, too. Gal (1979) describes a situation where a table full of monolingual Germans in the bilingual Austrian town of Oberwart asked Hungarian-speaking strangers at the next table to switch to German, "because we're all Austrians here." This could be to encourage solidarity, or impose norms; it could also be because some people worry that anybody they can't understand must be talking about them!

summing up

Most of the world's societies or political entities are multilingual, at either the state or the individual level. The choice between languages is influenced by complex combination of social forces. In multilingual societies, different languages often fill the sociolinguistic roles that different styles or dialects do in monolingual contexts. Diglossic situations, with a high (H) language for formal and official contexts and a low (L) language for familiar contexts, tend to arise as a result of longstanding societal multilingualism. Individual multilinguals move between languages (code-switch) depending on the situation or the speaker's social and conversational goals.

Where to next?

I'm oversimplifying here, but there has been a tendency for research in and on multilingual societies to focus on sociological issues like language status and planning (see chapter 13), while research on the social forces influencing linguistic content tends to happen in monolingual (but multi-dialectal) societies. A notable exception is in the area of code-switching, which seems to bridge the gap in terms of research interests. If the nature of multilingualism changes over the next couple of generations (with "tiny languages" disappearing and a few big languages like English expanding), the nature of multilingualism may change, and so too might the research. Multilingual speakers may be able to draw from a different linguistic repertoire, with different assumptions about the social meanings of what they're doing.

Spotlight: Phat comme un sumo

Sarkar, M., and L. Winer. "Multilingual codeswitching in Québec rap: Poetry, pragmatics and performativity." *International Journal of Multilingualism* 3, no. 3 (2006): 173–200.

This article is a clear illustration of one of the big ideas of this chapter – that many multilinguals use multilingualism itself (in the form of code-switching) as a language variety that helps them build or perform their identity. The paper includes a useful summary of existing research that considers multilingualism and code-switching to be the norm, rather than freaky exceptions.

One of the cool things about Québec (especially Montréal) in recent decades is that because there's no obvious dominant language (English and French are used by different people for different things), third languages have a chance to survive longer than you'd expect. Combine that with all the kinds of French and English used in the province and in hip-hop, and you get a lot of linguistic resources that performers can draw from: English and French standard varieties, non-standard varieties (Quebec French and African American English), and creoles (Haitian and Jamaican), as well as other immigrant languages such as Spanish.

Reading: Easy, with occasional gusts of postmodernism later on. People with no background knowledge of global hip-hop should be OK (I was). The authors occasionally use phonetic symbols for the sounds involved in rhymes. The sound involved is usually obvious from the examples or context, but just to reassure you: /o/ is the vowel in *snow*, /e/ in *play*, /i/ in *teen*, /a/ in *spa* (sort of).

Also read: The authors have continued this line of research in more recent papers, some of which aren't in print yet but might be by the time you read this. See also the work on global hip-hop mentioned in chapter 3.

exercises

1. You may be familiar with *decision trees*, where the answers to one question branch off to other questions and further branches, ending eventually with proposed decisions (they're sort of the academic equivalent of "choose your own adventure"). Go back to the discussion of Spanish and Guaraní in the diglossia section, and turn the language options that I describe into a decision tree. (You can also find some decision trees for code-switching in Meyerhoff 2006: 118–19.)
2. Try to think of as many languages as possible in which you know at least one word. Write down the language and the word. Compare your list with someone else's. What (if anything) do you notice about the words/languages that are on both lists?
3. Ask a bilingual friend or relative to teach you the words in their other language for *house, grandmother, bread, coffee,* and *hat.* Write the words down. Then ask the friend/relative to relax and form a mental image for each word that you read. Read back the words, in English and the other language, in random order. Afterward, talk to your friend/relative about whether the images were the same or not, and why. (Note that this is a bit of a hit-or-miss activity; for some people, it'll spark a really engaged conversation, and for some, it's a complete non-starter.)
4. If you're multilingual (lucky you!), spend a few days paying attention to the sociolinguistic context of code-switches that you hear. Who do you hear switching, where, and why? What kinds of things get said in each language? Do your observations match what I claim in the above sections?

discussion

1. Aside from the question of intelligibility, to what extent can we talk about switching between languages in the same way that we talk about style shift? What are the different social implications of code-switching and style shifting? How are they the same?
2. Have you ever been in a situation where you (or or someone else) had an emotional response to other people speaking a different language to each other in your presence? Did that response include the worry that other people were talking about you/them?
3. If someone who's mostly monolingual uses a word or two from another language, does that count as code-switching?
4. In a bilingual society, what's the "speech community"? Is it all speakers of one language? Should bilinguals be thought of as a separate speech community? What about in diglossic situations?
5. How might changes in the relative social or economic status of speakers of a particular language affect how that language fits into the social structure of that community? Would your answer change if the community was diglossic?

6. Do people expect you to speak particular languages, because of your name, or your appearance? How do you deal with that?

7. In recent years, people have criticized scholars of diglossia for describing it as a sort of natural language phenomenon, rather than pointing out that it results from long-term social inequality (somebody has to be in charge for their language to become the H language). What do you think?

8. A common **Discourse** in older literature about multilingual or multicultural people (especially immigrants) is "caught between two cultures" or "not really this, not really that." Do you think this is an unavoidable consequence of the nature of immigration? Do you think it reflects a monolingual assumption of how culture and language work?

9. Sarkar and Winer (2006), and some of the people they cite, claim that contemporary multilingual music (including hip-hop) acts as a counter-Discourse to the one I describe in the previous discussion question. Does this argument work for you? Do you think that your response depends on how familiar you are with such music?

Discourse

A society's way of talking about something that reflects underlying assumptions of the dominant group; these tend to become seen as "common sense" and thus are barely noticeable, despite the influence they have..

---

other resources

A good general introduction is John Edwards' *Multilingualism* (1994).

Li Wei's *The Blackwell Guide to Research Methods in Bilingualism and Multilingualism* (2008) is one of a number of recent books on how to do the work of particular fields.

For more on the linguistics and sociolinguistics of code switching, try Poplack's "Sometimes I'll start a sentence in Spanish" (1980) and Myers-Scotton's "Common and uncommon ground: Social and structural factors in codeswitching" (1993b).

There are many case studies of multilingualism in particular countries out there, and books on multilingualism from an applied linguistics perspective tend to include a sociolinguistic discussion.

Journals:

International Journal of Bilingualism, http://ijb.sagepub.com (accessed August 20, 2011).
Journal of Multilingual & Multicultural Development, http://www.tandf.co.uk/journals/rmmm (accessed August 20, 2011).
Multilingua, http://www.degruyter.de/journals/multilin (accessed August 20, 2011).

Language Contact 11

contact
When speakers of a language or language variety interact with speakers of a different language or language variety.

dialect leveling
The process by which the regional features of the speech of a group of people converge toward a common norm over time.

We've already considered the role that isolation (physical, social, or linguistic) could play in the formation and maintenance of distinct language varieties (in chapter 3). The other side of isolation, of course, is linguistic contact – with speakers of other varieties or of other languages. Sometimes we see dialect leveling, where similar dialects that come into contact with each other tend to keep their shared features and get rid of the things that are different (usually by adopting the variant found in the socially or numerically dominant language). But there are also linguistic phenomena that can happen when speakers of different *languages* meet and move toward bilingualism (see also chapter 10).

code-switching and borrowing

You'll remember from chapter 10 that code-switching is a common phenomenon when people who share more than one language get together and use two (or more!) languages

What Is Sociolinguistics?, First Edition. Gerard Van Herk.
© 2012 Gerard Van Herk. Published 2012 by Blackwell Publishing Ltd.

(or "codes") to communicate. Not surprisingly, bilinguals sometimes decide that only one of their languages is appropriate for a particular situation. An example of this **situational code-switching** would be the use of English in a workplace, or to talk about work-related topics, and the use of one's native language among friends and family. Some communities are famous for switching back and forth constantly during a single conversation, and the mix that results sometimes gets its own name, usually intended to be derogatory. Spanish-English switching in the US is often called Spanglish, while Canadian French–English switching is Franglais.

Monolinguals often assume that this kind of switching happens because speakers are not competent in one of their languages – a sort of deficit hypothesis – or because a concept just can't be expressed in one of the languages – a sort of **lexical gap** explanation. Analysis of recorded multilingual speech doesn't support these ideas, however. Speakers who code-switch the most often are usually those who are the most fluent in both of their languages, and there are linguistic rules about where in a sentence a switch can happen. The switching becomes a linguistic resource in many communities, used by speakers to signal a bi-cultural identity or to evoke attributes associated with one of the languages, such as sophistication or identification with local values. Some neighborhoods in northern Toronto boast particularly skilled code-switchers – young people born in Russia, brought up in Israel, and now living in Canada. They're *triple* switchers, moving effortlessly between Russian, Hebrew, and English (Levitski 2005).

Sometimes switches involve long stretches of each language, as in *Sometimes I'll start a sentence in Spanish y termino en español* (Poplack 1980). Some researchers reserve the term code-switching for only this type of switch. More often, a single language will dominate (sometimes called the **matrix language**; Myers-Scotton 1993b), and individual words from another language will be inserted, often being changed to obey the rules of the matrix language. Some researchers call these **nonce borrowings** – "one-offs" that don't really involve a change of language. If particularly useful nonce borrowings happen often enough, eventually they get picked up by monolingual speakers of the matrix language. Then they're just called **borrowings**.

Presumably, borrowings result from other contact situations as well – speakers of one language adopt terms from another language to describe new things and activities associated with that new language (for example, animals, geographical features, or foodstuffs). Some types of words are far more likely to be borrowed than others – nouns are especially common, followed by verbs and the occasional adjective or adverb. Grammatical function words (like *that* or *and*) tend not to be borrowed – they occur too often in our first language to be displaced, and we rarely run into a concept that requires a new pronoun, or preposition.

English is known as a language that borrows a lot. At various times over the past 1,500 years, it has been a

---

code-switching
When people alternate between at least two languages or language varieties in a single conversation (across sentences or clause boundaries).

situational code-switching
When code-switching is constrained by social context.

lexical gap
When a particular language doesn't have a word for a particular concept (and thus usually adopts a word from another language), for example, *schadenfreude*.

matrix language
The dominant language in code-switching.

nonce borrowings
Individual words from another language that are inserted, often being changed to obey the rules of the matrix language.

borrowings
A linguistic form taken from one language or dialect and incorporated into another, such that monolingual speakers of the latter use it, sometimes with new associations.

As an aside: **When is something fully borrowed?**

There's a point in the borrowing process where the new word hasn't fully penetrated the recipient language. For example, I consider *dim sum* (Chinese dumplings) to be an English word, but some of my older relatives might not. And my sons consider *desi* ('from our country, from the Indian subcontinent') an English word, while I was surprised to hear them use it as if it was.

nativization
When a word borrowed from another language is changed so that it behaves like a word from our language.

folk etymology
A change in a word's form based on a mistaken understanding of its meaning or composition.

sprachbund
A group of (usually unrelated) languages that have become more similar because of geographical proximity.

language of peasants (looking up and out to French and Latin as models for formal speech), as well as a language of colonialists and explorers (imposed on other language groups and adapted to new situations). As a result, it's not hard to find traces of other languages in it, aside from the obvious code-switching situations. Back in the peasant days, English speakers adopted thousands of words from the French nobility (especially legal words and anything fancy-sounding, but also everyday words like *beef* or *station*). Later, during the Enlightenment, English created its science words out of Greek and Latin (sometimes via French), or borrowed existing Arabic terms. And exploration and colonization led to borrowing from many languages, especially for things that didn't exist "back home." Even very English-sounding words like *sofa*, *boondocks*, or *tomato* have their roots in languages from far away (look them up in an etymology dictionary!).

But almost everything "non-English" in English is at the lexical word level. Today's little grammatical function words have almost all been part of English for ages, as have English sentence and word structure rules. Some scholars argue that the language underwent some mild creole-like simplification about a thousand years ago, from the contact between older English and the linguistically related Norse in the north of England (where speakers dealt with the differences in word endings between languages by just getting rid of the endings). But that simplification process was already underway, and might have happened anyway.

Sometimes, grammatical structures can be borrowed along with individual words. For example, the Acadian French of the Maritime provinces nonce-borrows many verbs from English and adapts them to French morphology, as in *J'ai parké* for 'I parked' (King 2000). Verb + preposition combinations, however, also keep some of their English structure, as in *J'ai hangé around*, 'I hung around.' In communities where both verbs and prepositions are borrowed, even all-French sentences can end up with English-like word order not found elsewhere in French, as in *le gars que j'ai donné la job à*, 'The guy that I gave the job to' (King 2000). This kind of contact effect, however, seems to be more common if there are similar forms in the recipient language to act as a model. It also seems to require a *lot* of contact, often for long periods of time. Historical linguists call a situation where unrelated languages become more alike from sharing a geographical region a **sprachbund** (from the German for 'language union'). For example, Albanian, Romanian and Bulgarian share many linguistic features, even though they come from different language families, because they're Balkan near-neighbors.

As an aside: Changing borrowings

Once we take a word into our own language, we treat it like one of our own, a process often called **nativization**. We make it follow our pronunciation rules, replacing sounds that our language doesn't have, or adding or removing sounds if they don't "belong" together in our language (for example, the Japanese borrowing of *strike* is pronounced something like *sutoraiku*, to avoid clustering consonant sounds together). We slot the new word into our grammatical system (English people say *two souvlakis*, not *two souvlakia*), adding whatever our system requires (for example, when new words are borrowed into French, they usually get assigned masculine gender).

Sometimes we misinterpret a borrowing as a combination of words from our own language, or adapt it so that it becomes one (for example, the French *chaise longue* ('long chair') is often called a *chaise lounge* in English, because, well, you lounge in it). This last process is called **folk etymology** (it can also happen with non-borrowed words, as when *buck naked* becomes *butt naked* because, well, your butt is involved). Sometimes borrowed words become harder to spot over time, as they participate in sound or meaning shifts in their new language.

contact languages: mixed languages, lingua franca, pidgins, creoles

Occasionally, in heavy code-switching communities such as New York City Puerto Ricans or Canadian Tamils, you can get sentences where virtually all the content words (nouns, verbs) are borrowed and adapted, while all the function words are from the matrix language. As an extreme example, when I worked as a shipping clerk in Montreal, I once heard a co-worker say, *Tu peux pas* <u>parker</u> *ton* <u>truck</u> *dans le* <u>spot</u> *du* <u>station wagon</u> *du* <u>boss</u> ('You can't park your truck in the spot reserved for the boss's station wagon'). If that sort of process became the norm in a language contact situation, you might eventually end up with a **mixed language**. One strong candidate for mixed language status is **Michif**, still spoken in western Canada and nearby states among the Métis, people of mixed Cree and French ancestry. In Michif, most nouns and the words associated with them are derived from French (they're in upper case in the example), while most verbs and the words associated with them are derived from Cree (they're in lower case).

PAR LA QUEUE	apoci-pit-ew	kihtwam	LE LOUP	ase-kiwe-pahta-w
by the tail	*inside-out-pull-he/him*	*again*	*the wolf*	*back-go-home-run-he*

'He pulled him inside out by the tail, and the wolf ran home again.' (Bakker & Mous 1994: 30)

Mixed languages are not common, and researchers who work on language contact argue (often fiercely) over whether they really exist, and what they tell us about language.

mixed language
A language that shares components of two or more languages, generally in equal proportions.

Michif
An example of a mixed language still spoken in and near Manitoba among the Métis, people of mixed Cree and French ancestry.

As an aside: How much does contact actually change languages?

Researchers at the University of Ottawa (Poplack et al. 2004) investigate many changes to the grammar of English and French in Canada, changes that are often attributed to contact between the two languages. Quantitative analyses suggest that the changes involved have been going on independently of the contact (i.e., the same changes are happening in non-contact varieties, and increased contact doesn't mean increased change). Even superficial changes, such as borrowings, happen far less often (on a per-thousand-word basis) than people think. For example, English Québeckers (like me) use only a handful of French words regularly: *depanneur* ('corner store'), *autoroute* ('highway'), and *CEGEP* ('junior college').

This is a situation where linguists and real people may have different ideas about what counts as "frequent," though. If people have very strict monolingual norms about the purity of their language, they're likely to notice (and maybe worry about) words intruding from other languages. *Linguists* who interpret any change as evidence of contact effects, on the other hand, are sometimes dismissively termed "contact romantics."

lingua franca
The language used when people who speak different languages need to interact on a regular basis, but have languages that are not mutually intelligible.

pidgin
A language variety that is stripped down to its essentials, that is, not very linguistically complex. Pidgins arise in language contact situations, for example, trade, and are used as a lingua franca.

lexifier language
The language that supplies most of the vocabulary (i.e., lexicon) for a pidgin or creole.

creole
A language variety that develops out of a pidgin in a language contact situation. Unlike a pidgin, a creole is spoken as a first language of some group of speakers, and can be used in the entire range of social settings.

Bajan
A casual term for Barbadian English.

Non-linguists sometimes assume that creole languages are mixed languages. Linguists, however, use the creole label for the outcome of a very different situation of language contact, which goes something like this: when people who speak different languages need to interact on a regular basis, they will often come to choose one particular language to communicate between groups. A language used this way is called a **lingua franca**, named after the language used centuries ago in the Mediterranean by traders from different language backgrounds. A lingua franca can be the native language of one of the interacting groups, or a "neutral" language that is not the home language of the groups involved. A neutral language may have social advantages in that it doesn't favor any one group. For example, in postcolonial situations, the former colonial language may act as a lingua franca, despite its historical connotations, just because the different language groups in the country want a linguistically level playing field (see chapter 13).

Some linguistic contact situations lead to the formation of a **pidgin**, a language stripped down to its essentials. Such a heavily simplified language is capable of conveying the basic information needed for many cross-linguistic purposes. Linguistically, pidgin languages consist of a small set of content words and very little grammatical complexity.

Socially, pidgins tend to develop in two different contact situations, each of which involves one or more groups having limited access to the **lexifier language**, the language that supplies the basic word stock for the pidgin. Trade is one such situation: people from very different backgrounds come together to accomplish specific business tasks that can be done with a limited vocabulary (if you've traveled much, you can probably think of situations where you've bought something through using very basic language). Australian Pidgin English or Chinese Pidgin Portuguese are trade pidgins that developed from European lexifier languages. In the Pacific northwest, North American indigenous groups developed the trade language Chinook Jargon.

The other common pidgin formation situation is where people from many language backgrounds are brought together to work on large plantations, as slaves or indentured workers. Tok Pisin, a language of the south Pacific that is now a full **creole**, originally developed this way. Presumably, so did the ancestor languages of Caribbean creoles. Richard Ligon, who travelled to Barbados in the 1640s, later described how slaves from different language groups were mixed together in a way that typically leads to a pidgin: "They are fetch'd from several parts of Africa, who speak several languages and by that means, one of them understands not another: For, some of them are fetch'd from Guinny and Binny, some from Cutchew, some from Angola, and some from the River of Gambia" (Ligon 1970: 48).

If a pidgin is only required for limited kinds of work, as in trade situations, it may persist in its simplified form for a long time. In plantation situations, though, the children of the original pidgin speakers may learn the pidgin as a first language, and bring their full first language acquisition skills to bear on it. As a result, it may become the native language of the new community. When this happens, the pidgin becomes a full-fledged language known as a creole. Creoles greatly expand the number of lexical items and grammatical rules found in the original pidgin, and make them more regular.

Barbadian English, or **Bajan**, is sometimes described as a mesolectal or near-acrolectal variety (see the box below on 'Acrolect, mesolect, basilect'), and is often assumed to

Table 11.1. Some features of Barbadian (Creole) English.

linguistic feature	example
done to show or foreground that an action is completed	It <u>done</u> set there since last year
present tense *-s* absence	He <u>send</u> somebody
similar forms for past and present tense	Two day before she <u>pass</u> away, I <u>tell</u> her to start crying now
copula (*be* verb) absence	<u>She lucky</u> that I ain't throw it on her
ain't in many contexts	It <u>ain't</u> concern you
possessive forms without *-'s*	You know some <u>people</u> cake, you cut it here, you find a lump
object forms as subjects	<u>Them</u> ain't want to hear you
subject forms as objects	I ain't mind <u>she</u>

Source: Van Herk (2003).

show little variation. In Barbados, however, as elsewhere, we find a range of creole features. Table 11.1 shows a few, drawn from my own fieldwork there.

Worldwide, creoles share many grammatical characteristics, despite developing in different situations from different lexifier languages. Several theories have developed to account for the similarities between creoles. One argument is that creoles all over the world have developed from a single template language, which acted as a sort of structural frame into which the actual words of different lexifier languages were slotted. This frame might have been a **proto-pidgin**, perhaps spread by sailors and slavers, or a stripped down version of one or another West African language. This scenario is called the **relexification hypothesis**. Another widely held viewpoint is that the similarities in creoles happen when they become the first languages of children, in that all children have access to an innate biological program that leads them to restructure the very basic input of each pidgin in the same way. This is known as the **language bioprogram hypothesis**. It's also possible that some similarities result from universal or near-universal tendencies involved in learning another language, or in simplifying your own language to be understood by others ("foreigner talk"). And, of course, we have to allow for influences from the first languages of the people learning the pidgin or creole (often called the **substrate**), as well as from the different varieties of the lexifier language itself (often called the **superstrate**).

As pidgins and creoles have tended to develop without documentation, it is unlikely that any one hypothesis will garner conclusive proof. Observations of the development of Tok Pisin into a full-fledged creole (and the official language of Papua New Guinea) in recent years confirm that major changes occur when a language gets native speakers, consistent perhaps with a weak version of the bioprogram.

proto-pidgin
Part of the relexification hypothesis, this is the template language into which the actual words of different lexifier languages are slotted.

relexification hypothesis
The argument that similarities among creoles arise because creoles all over the world have developed from a single template language, which acted as a sort of structural frame into which the actual words of different lexifier languages were slotted.

language bioprogram hypothesis
The argument that similarities among creoles arise because all children have access to an innate biological program that leads them to restructure the very basic input of each pidgin in the same way.

substrate
A variety that has influenced the structure or use of another, more dominant variety.

superstrate
A variety that has influenced the structure or use of another, less dominant variety.

Often, especially with the passage of time, creoles end up co-existing with a local version of their original lexifier languages. For example, many people in Jamaica speak the local Creole at home, but need Caribbean Standard English in schooling or other formal situations. This can have two effects. Speakers may reduce the number of creole features in their speech (**decreolization**). As well, or in addition, multiple levels of the creole can develop, between the most creole-like, called the **basilect**, and the least creole-like, the **acrolect**. Intermediate stages are called **mesolects** (see the box on 'Acrolect, mesolect, basilect'). This range is known as the **creole continuum**.

In table 11.2 we see how seven speakers are situated along the continuum according to how they use six different variables. This arrangement is called an **implicational scale** – a speaker who uses one acrolectal variant will also generally use the acrolectal variant of each variable to the left of it; a speaker who uses a basilectal variant will generally also use the basilectal variant of each variable to the right.

We often assume that the basilect represents something close to the original creole variety, with mesolects reflecting a wearing away of those deep creole features under the influence of the acrolect – a sort of "bottom-up" explanation. This scenario is supported by evidence that basilectal features "drop out" as we move up the continuum, sometimes replaced by a form that looks like the standard, but continues to behave like the original basilectal feature. In other cases, however, there seems to be a break in the middle, as when bare forms like *she see him* represent a single event at the basilectal end, but a recurring or habitual one in the high mesolect. In those situations, a combination of "top-down" and "bottom-up" explanations may be needed.

decreolization
A reduction in the number of creole features in the speech of an individual or community.

basilect
A term used in creole studies to refer to the most creole-like variety, that is, the most distant from the acrolect . See also creole continuum.

acrolect
A term used in creole studies to refer to the least creole-like, or most standard or prestigious variety. See also mesolect, basilect, creole continuum.

mesolect
A term used in creole studies to refer to the intermediate variety between basilect and acrolect. See also creole continuum.

creole continuum
Subvarieties of creoles fall along a continuum, ranging from basilect, the least standard, to acrolect, the most standard. Mesolect varieties fall in the middle.

implicational scale
A scale or ordering that implies that a feature associated with a particular point will also be associated with all points to one side of it.

Table 11.2.   The creole continuum in practice: Jamaica.

speaker	variables					
1	eat	granny	didn't	child	thin or *tin*	then or *den*
2	eat	granny	didn't	child	thin or *tin*	*den*
3	eat	granny	didn't	child	*tin*	*den*
4	eat	granny	didn't	*pikni*	*tin*	*den*
5	eat	granny	*no ben*	*pikni*	*tin*	*den*
6	eat	*nana*	*no ben*	*pikni*	*tin*	*den*
7	*nyam*	*nana*	*no ben*	*pikni*	*tin*	*den*

Italics = basilectal variant.
Sources: DeCamp (1971: 355); Rickford (2002: 146).

Acrolect, mesolect, basilect

These are specialized terms used by researchers studying creoles, although they're sometimes generalized to other sociolinguistic situations because the idea of a continuum is useful to us.

The *acrolect* ("high," like *Acropolis*) is the variety most like the local standard, and sometimes we use the term to refer to that local standard. Acrolects tend to differ from their lexifier languages in terms of accent, plus some local words or expressions. Sometimes a few grammatical structures or function words may be "camouflaged" versions of more creole-like speech. For example, Barbadians often say *She did go* or *She had gone* where Standard English speakers elsewhere might say *She went*. This may be a camouflaged version of the very creole *She bin go* (Blake 1997).

The *mesolect* ("middle," like *mezzanine*) is the in-between variety, sometimes associated with more urbanized areas, but definitely less Standard-like than the acrolect. Sometimes, researchers describe some quite non-standard varieties as "mesolects," perhaps because they're hesitant to claim that they've managed to access the deepest, most divergent speech of an area.

The *basilect* ("bottom," like *base*) is the variety that diverges the most from the Standard variety of the lexifier language. If we assume (as many researchers do) that creoles start out very different from their lexifiers (due to the processes described elsewhere in the chapter) and then slowly decreolize, then basilects should be taken to represent the earliest, "purest" variety of any particular creole. If, however, we assume that all languages are always changing, then all three lect levels may include innovations not found during the original years of creole formation.

summing up

Languages that are in extended contact eventually grow to resemble each other in some ways, just as people start to look like their dogs. But most of this linguistic resemblance is at the level of words, not grammar. Bilinguals who code-switch are likely to introduce borrowings, words from one language, into their other language. If these borrowings catch on, they can be completely integrated into their new language. Some language contact can lead to the creation of new languages. These can be mixed languages, but in situations where speakers have limited access to a language, it's more likely that a pidgin will develop. When a pidgin gets native speakers, it becomes elaborated into a creole, which may decreolize over time, and a creole continuum may develop.

Where to next?

The major recent theoretical debate in creole studies has been over whether creoles are linguistically distinct, with features that mark them as behaving the same as each other but differently from other languages, or whether the collection of language varieties that we call creoles are sociologically or historically similar, but linguistically diverse. This debate has been extremely vociferous at times, and I don't think I'm out of line when I say that it has scared researchers away from the field. At the same time, ironically, people who research non-creoles have become more comfortable using creole terminology, as the creole continuum represents clearly visible (or audible) community language variation. We may see people using creolist ideas without talking about creoles!

Spotlight: English makes you do things you were going to do anyway

Silva-Corvalán, Carmen. "The gradual loss of mood distinctions in Los Angeles Spanish." *Language Variation and Change* 6 (1994): 255–72.

There are no easy sociolinguistic scholarly articles about language contact effects, because the evidence that people use to argue, in either direction, is found in the fine details of the linguistic conditioning on variation. This article is a good example of that – Silva-Corvalán looks at whether contact with English leads speakers to prefer a Spanish linguistic variant that looks the most like what people do in English. The situation is complicated by the fact that Spanish seems to be heading toward that variant anyway. Silva-Corvalán argues that it happens faster in contact situations, on the basis of an analysis of groups of Los Angeles Spanish speakers with different amounts of contact with English.

Reading: There will be bits you don't get, even if I try to explain it here. The subjunctive is a form used in many languages for situations that are not fact (e.g., wishes, impossibilities), as in the English *if I were you*. The indicative is the non-subjunctive variant. You might as well just think of them as "two variants of something" while reading the paper. The protasis is a name for a clause that starts with the word *if*. You may want to rush through some of the methodology section and focus on the results, from p. 264 onward. It turns out the subjunctive is still healthy in places where Spanish requires it, but not so much elsewhere, and speakers with more English contact have less subjunctive. But it takes more than just contact for change to happen; Silva-Corvalán describes some of the other requirements.

Link to other readings: Similar studies of French in Canada (Poplack 1991) show a variety that's farther advanced in the "clumping-up" of the subjunctive – it's restricted to a handful of contexts, but it's almost obligatory in those particular contexts. That paper argues that this is just something that French is doing, and that English contact is not responsible.

exercises

1. Ask a bunch of (non-linguist) people to define "creole languages." See how many of them talked about mixed languages.

2. Write down how you would simplify the following sentences in order to be understood by somebody who speaks very little English. When you finish, compare your simplification with those of other people. Do you find shared strategies?

   The sentences:
   (a) *I don't want to eat in your restaurant.*
   (b) *Tomorrow I will visit the site of the battle of Hastings.*
   (c) *What is the fare for a trip to the airport?*
   (d) *Emmanuel's partner has grown corpulent through the over-consumption of high-fat items.*
   (e) *I like you, but not in a physical sense.*

3. Here are some words from other languages (along with their original meanings) that have been borrowed into English (sometimes via a third language) and have undergone some nativization or folk etymology. Try to figure out the English word that resulted in each case.
   (a) *Bangla* ('in the Bengali style')
   (b) *blinyets* ('little pancake')
   (c) *crevisse* ('small crustacean')
   (d) *girasole* ('sunflower')
   (e) *kraal* ('enclosure')
   (f) *la reata* ('the rope')
   (g) *Shah mat* ('the king is dead')

4. Hubert Devonish, at the University of the West Indies, has demonstrated the suitability of creole languages for academic discourse by sometimes publishing scholarly work in English-based creole. Try translating the following paragraph from a 1998 article into Standard English. Hints: "ee" represents (roughly) the FACE vowel, "ii" the FLEECE vowel; try reading it aloud.

   In dis worl hee, yu gat konchrii wa don set op aredii, bot we di piipl-dem no fiil dem iz wan neeshan kaaz dem taakin aal kain a difrent wee. An den yu gat piipl wa fiil se dem iz wan neeshan bot no gat konchrii. Dem hoslin fo chrai set op konchrii fo aal huu biilangs to dem neeshan.

   You can check your results, and read the rest of the article, in *Kyk-Over-Al* 48 (1998): 136-52, or on Devonish's home page at http://www.mona.uwi.edu/dllp/jlu/staff/devonish.htm (accessed August 20, 2011).

discussion

1. Have you ever been part of a conversation where somebody used an unfamiliar word from another language that they just assumed everybody knew? What happened?
2. Do you know of other words like *Spanglish* or *Franglais* that describe heavily code-switched speech?
3. Do you know people who salt their speech with words from other languages? What are some examples? How is this received by their listeners? Do you associate this with particular speech situations?
4. Have you ever *accidentally* used words from one language when speaking another one? What happened?
5. Because languages that develop out of pidgins often use heavily streamlined grammars (*Me see him* for *I saw him*, for example) and creative combinations of restricted vocabularies (such as *grass-belong-face* for *beard*), they superficially resemble child language. Do you think that this contributes to a tendency to view speakers of such languages as child-like, or do you think that's just colonialism and racism at work?
6. Where, if at all, do you hear creole languages used, either in media or in your daily life?
7. If you tried the creole-to-standard translation exercise in question (4) above, you probably noted that not only does Devonish represent creole pronunciation and grammar, but he also uses vocabulary that is different from the standard version. How is it different? What effect does this have?
8. If you read the Silva-Corvalán article and aren't really familiar with subjunctives, did that make it much more difficult to grasp the point of the article? Do you think it's possible to let go of anxieties about Understanding Every Word when doing academic reading, in order to grasp the main point? Or does that go against everything you've ever learned?

other resources

Books on studying language contact include Holm and Michaelis' *Contact Languages: Critical Concepts in Language Studies* (2008), which collects a bunch of writings on contact languages, with a focus on creoles, and Winford's *An Introduction to Contact Linguistics* (2003). Hickey's *Handbook of Language Contact* (2010) and Singler and Kouwenberg's *Handbook of Pidgin and Creole Studies* (2008) both cover a lot of ground. Siegel's *The Emergence of Pidgin and Creole Languages* (2008) looks at the possible origins of creoles. A broader look at the languages of the Caribbean is found in the essays collected in Simmons-McDonald and Robertson's *Exploring the Boundaries of Caribbean Creole Languages* (2006). Note that many of the sources listed here describe creole or contact language stuff mostly from a linguistic, rather than sociolinguistic, background.

There are many published studies of individual varieties (such as Jamaican Creole) or groups of varieties (such as Asian contact languages). Some of these are more sociolinguistic in focus, such as Patrick's *Urban Jamaican Creole: Variation in the Mesolect* (1999).

Journals:

Journal of Pidgin and Creole Languages, http://www.benjamins.com/cgi-bin/t_seriesview.cgi?
series=jpcl (accessed August 20, 2011).

Journal of Language Contact, http://cgi.server.uni-frankfurt.de/fb09/ifas/JLCCMS/index_en.html
(accessed August 20, 2011).

Attitudes and Ideologies 12

Attitudes toward language have been implicitly involved in most of what we've covered so far. At varying levels of awareness, every time speakers use one linguistic form rather than another, they're drawing on their attitudes toward those forms, and toward the people that they think use them. In this chapter, I'll look more closely at language attitudes, and how they play out in the representation of languages and language varieties. Depending on how (and how much) you've thought about these issues, parts of this chapter may either depress or annoy you. This is partly due to the unquestioned nature of many of our language attitudes. Although we don't always acknowledge it, people tend to think that there are two kinds of language, "normal" (what we have, or wish we had) and "wrong/odd" (what other people have) – although nowadays, we often replace these terms with their mild-mannered equivalents, "appropriate" and "inappropriate." This seems to be particularly true when it comes to attitudes toward regional or ethnic dialects and their place in society. Or maybe it's just dialect attitudes that sociolinguists have written the most about.

What Is Sociolinguistics?, First Edition. Gerard Van Herk.
© 2012 Gerard Van Herk. Published 2012 by Blackwell Publishing Ltd.

One way to find out what people think about a language variety, of course, is to ask them. Attitude surveys have been used for decades to track changing perceptions of non-standard varieties. For example, Trudgill and Tzavaras (1977) used a questionnaire to trace the declining status of Arvanitika, the Albanian dialect of Greek, among Arvanites (members of that sociocultural group). They found a steady decline across the generations in the number of respondents who liked to speak the dialect, who thought speaking it was a good thing and an advantage. One unusual finding was that younger speakers were *more* likely to agree that it was necessary to speak Arvanitika to be an Arvanitis, even though they were far less likely to actually speak it (or enjoy speaking it). Trudgill and Tzavaras explain this by saying that old speakers see the language declining but think that people can be Arvanites in other ways (kind of like Louisiana Cajuns who no longer speak French). Younger speakers, on the other hand, expect both the language and the group distinction to disappear – that is, they think that you need to speak Arvanitika to be an Arvanitis, but that it's not a big deal that people are less Arvanitis-like than they used to be.

Probably the best-known work on attitudes toward regional varieties is by Dennis Preston, who uses techniques borrowed from cultural geography to show that Americans have a strong shared sense about which areas of the country are linguistically distinct. Given blank maps to label, a full 94 percent of university students from Michigan outlined the south, and a further 61 percent outlined the Great Lakes area, their own region (which many labeled "normal"; Preston & Howe 1987) (figure 12.1). When the results were combined to produce a consensus list of regions, and students were asked to rate the speech of those regions, researchers found virtual mirror images in ratings for the two areas: southern speech was described as casual, friendly, and polite; northern speech was normal, fast, and smart, but also noted for its absence of marked traits – it had "no drawl" and "no twang."

A more direct state-by-state assessment (Preston 2002: 58-61) asked respondents to score states for language correctness and pleasantness. Michiganders rated their own state highly as the most correct, and fairly highly as the most pleasant. They rated Alabama (and surrounding states) the lowest on both scales. This naturally led the researchers to wonder: what do people in Alabama think? It turns out that Alabamians don't see their own state's language as particularly correct (after all, they're often reminded of its "faults" in media and popular representations), but they rank it no worse than that of many other states – including Michigan! Alabamians do give high scores to their own state for language pleasantness, though, and see Michigan speech as among the least pleasant. Preston argues that this shows that Alabamians and Michiganders are invested in different aspects of language, a sort of language ideology that foregrounds the self-perceived strong points of each group's own language variety.

But all this is very "macro." While it's useful to know how people feel about a language (variety) as a whole, which is the approach often adopted in other fields (such as social psychology – e.g., Tajfel 1978), Preston (2002: 43) and others point out that it would be

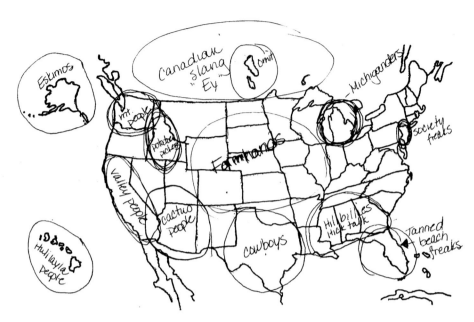

Figure 12.1. A map of perceived dialect areas, from a participant in Dennis Preston's language attitudes research.

more useful for sociolinguists to know about attitudes toward individual features of a particular variety. This could provide clues as to how features are deployed by speakers when they build their sociolinguistic identity. That, of course, assumes that speakers can actually identify different varieties by the features used, and it seems they can. Purnell et al. (1999) show that Californians are able to correctly identify the ethnic variety (African American English (AAE), Chicano English, Standard American English (SAE)) used by recorded speakers about 70 percent of the time just from hearing a single word – "hello."

Another study that demonstrates how strongly listeners can respond to a single speech feature, if it's the right one, is Labov (1966), looking at the highly stigmatized New York English feature of post-vocalic r-deletion (*cah* for *car*, mentioned way back in chapter 2). He had New Yorkers pretend to be personnel managers, and to rate voice samples for "occupational suitability" (Labov 1966: 411). Even a single missed /r/ dropped people's ratings from three to four levels on a seven-point scale – and working-class/lower-class raters were harsher judges than people from the higher classes! In a well-known study that combines surveys of attitudes and language use, Trudgill (1972) compared whether people claimed to use a local pronunciation of the NEAR vowel with their actual rates of use of the variant. Women over-reported their use of the British Standard English pronunciation; men, on the other hand, over-reported their rates of use of the local pronunciation. From this, Trudgill developed the influential concept of covert prestige – the men were attracted to the working-class, local, non-school connotations of the non-standard variant (see also chapter 4). Preston (2002: 47) points

covert prestige
A norm or target that speakers unconsciously orient to, with a sort of hidden positive evaluation that speakers give to other (presumably non-standard) forms. The linguistic equivalent of *street credibility*.

out the methodological utility of this study: people *can* evaluate their language use on a per-feature basis (accurately or not).

But how much of people's language attitudes actually reflect their responses to linguistic input, and how much results from completely non-linguistic beliefs or expectations? You may remember studies discussed in chapter 6, in which respondents "hallucinated" hearing a foreign accent on a recording if presented with a picture of a non-white speaker at the same time. The same tendency toward hallucination seems to surface with non-ethnic distinctions. In a clever study of how expectations can affect how people perceive language, Niedzielski (1999) played Detroiters samples of another Detroiter's pronunciation of the MOUTH vowel and asked them to match it to one of three synthesized speech samples. The speaker on the tape had a "raised" (*mehwth*) pronunciation, the one used by many Detroiters and most Canadians. When respondents were given an answer sheet with the word "Canadian" written on it, they usually correctly heard the vowel as raised; when the sheet said "Michigan," most respondents heard no raising, and a full 38 percent matched the vowel to a *lowered* sample, the opposite of what they had actually been played. We can draw two conclusions from this: one, non-linguistic information can have a huge influence on what people hear, or think they hear; and two, as mentioned earlier, weirdness is usually associated with other people (in this case, Canadians).

Of course, with any attitude questionnaire, there's always the concern that people aren't revealing their true feelings (although many people are a lot more willing to describe a language variety as lazy, sloppy, or limited than they are to describe its speakers using those terms). The matched guise test, first developed in Canada (Lambert et al. 1960; Lambert 1967) tries to get past people's professed viewpoints to gauge deeply held language attitudes. In this kind of test, subjects are played multiple recordings of people speaking, and asked to rate the speakers on a scale according to traits like social class, intelligence, and friendliness. What the subjects don't know is that they're actually listening to the same speaker or speakers several times, using different accents or speaking different languages. As the only thing that differs between recordings is the accent or language, any differences in ratings are taken to reflect differences in attitudes toward the language varieties involved. Early Canadian experiments (e.g., Lambert 1967) showed that both English and French speakers rated French-guise recordings lower in intelligence. In the years since, matched guise studies have fairly consistently shown a split between status and solidarity. Standard speakers score higher on status measures – they're seen as more competent, smarter, even taller! Non-standard speakers score higher on solidarity measures – they're seen as warmer and friendlier. Matched guise studies in the USA have shown that human resources personnel are likely to recommend lower-status jobs for speakers with AAE features, as well as for speakers with Hispanic or Asian accents (Henderson 2001).

One of the problems with matched guise tests is that ideally you need the content of the speech samples that you're comparing to be roughly the same, to be sure that your subjects aren't responding to the message, rather than the language variety (obviously, you need to have multiple scripts, so that the raters don't have to listen to the same content 20 times). But if Arabic raters hear a conversation about, say, friendship in both

matched guise test
A test designed to gauge unexpressed language attitudes by asking subjects to rate recorded speakers on a scale according to traits like social class, intelligence, and friendliness; however, subjects are actually listening to the same speaker or speakers several times, using different accents or speaking different languages.

status
Social positions that society assigns to its members, or the differences between social groups, in terms of the prestige associated with them by others.

solidarity
Closeness or intimacy, or shared status.

Method: Matched guise studies

Matched guise studies need quite a lot of advance planning, but let researchers get at language attitudes that might not otherwise be expressed. A fairly typical study might go like this:

1. Decide which language varieties will be of interest to the community that you're going to study. A study in New Zealand, for example, might contrast Maori-accented English with Pakeha (non-Maori) English.
2. Find people who can sound fairly authentic in those different varieties. This is important – you can't really have different people speaking each variety, because listeners may pick up on other aspects of their speech, such as gruffness of tone or swoopy pitch. Sometimes actors are used for this.
3. Record your speakers using each accent to read passages designed to include the variation of interest. The logic behind reading passages is that you want to be sure listeners aren't responding to the content of the recording, rather than the accent. Ideally, you record a bunch of different passages, so that individual listeners don't hear the same passage over and over, which would also focus their attention on the form. (Remember, you don't want listeners to guess what you're really after!)

4. Design a questionnaire to get listeners (often called "judges") to rate the people in the recordings according to various personal traits. These might include friendliness, intelligence, competence, honesty, and industriousness. The rating method used is often a Likert scale – there's a range of possible answers where "1" might mean "very very friendly" and "7" might mean "not friendly at all."
5. Find a bunch of people who are willing to be judges. Ask them for whatever demographic information you think you'll need (age, sex, education, region, employment, whatever). Play them the recordings and get them to rate the speakers. You might also ask open-ended questions, to get at attitudes that are hard to put into a scale. Remember, they're rating recordings of the same people, but with different accents ("guises").
6. Debrief the judges afterward! It's unethical to fool people without explaining afterward why it was necessary.
7. Analyze the data you collect. Did particular guises score higher for particular traits? Did different types of judges have different (or stronger) attitudes?

Likert scale

A scale often used in questionnaires, usually to let respondents indicate how much they agree with or accept a particular statement

Standard Arabic and a local variety, their judgments might be responding to the incongruity of using Standard Arabic for such a topic, rather than revealing their general attitudes toward that variety. Some studies that consider this possibility do seem to show a topic-appropriateness effect. For example, Carranza and Ryan (1975) recorded people reading two paragraphs in both Spanish and English – one about a mother preparing breakfast, one about a teacher giving a history lesson. They played the recordings to both Hispanic and Anglo students at a high school in a Mexican American neighborhood in Chicago, and asked the students to rate the speakers on a status scale (education, intelligence, success, and wealth) and on a solidarity scale (friendliness, goodness, kindness, trustworthiness). There was no difference in scores from the two groups of student judges, which the authors attribute to the Anglo students taking the point of view of the Hispanic students. But there were significant differences in the scores based on which paragraph was read (higher scores for English with the school paragraph and for Spanish with the home paragraph), and for scale type (higher scores for English on the status scale, roughly equal scores on the solidarity scale). These findings remind us that respondents react to the appropriateness of a language for a particular topic, as well as to the characteristics that they associate with a particular language and its speakers.

The matched guise test can have real-world applications: in California, Purnell et al. (1999) called prospective landlords and used African American, Hispanic, and SAE accents to say, "Hello, I'm calling about the apartment you have advertised in the paper." The SAE speaker guise got an appointment to see housing about 70 percent of the time; the other two guises, only about 30 percent. Other well-known work in this area is by the linguist John Baugh (2003), whose team uses a similar approach to collect evidence to be used in actual landlord discrimination cases.

language beliefs (myths, ideologies)

People's search for objective evidence to support their linguistic attitudes and prejudices sometimes leads to odd language myths. These include the once-popular idea that the features of AAE resulted from its speakers having large lips, or the belief of some Korean parents that having their children undergo tongue surgery (called a *frenulotomy*) will give them more flexible tongues and lead to accent-less English. Many of the language myths that people cling to are less bizarre, but potentially equally harmful (Bauer & Trudgill 1998; Wardhaugh 1999; Niedzielski & Preston 2000). Wardhaugh (2006: 53) summarizes: "[People] believe such things as certain languages lack grammar, that you can speak English without an accent, that French is more logical than English, that parents teach their children to speak, that primitive languages exist, that English is degenerating and language standards are slipping, that pronunciation should be based on spelling, and so on and so on." Some of these myths are widespread, especially the idea that some language varieties have tiny vocabularies, or are not capable of expressing complex or abstract ideas. The opposite notion is also popular – that certain languages have massive vocabularies for particular items. This is sometimes known as the Great Eskimo Vocabulary Hoax (also the title of a book on the subject; Pullum 1991), after its most commonly expressed example. This seems to be one of those situations where people believe what they want to believe. The linguist/anthropologist Franz Boas started the ball rolling in 1911 when he listed *four* Inuktitut words for snow; from there, the number just started growing in the retelling, like some out-of-control academic fish story. Recent (completely unsupported) references mention up to a hundred words!

Presumably this particular myth has not caused irreparable harm, leading to a generation of Inuit youth who feel insecure about the size of their snow-related vocabulary. But many of the language myths that Wardhaugh mentions have widespread consequences. They serve to reinforce the higher status of the standard, at the expense of other varieties, and presumably reassure people who want to dismiss those particular language varieties, or limit their domains of use (see chapter 13). The very idea of a standard language (especially if "standard" means "default against which other stuff is

language myth
Widely held beliefs about language (that are usually not supported by empirical evidence).

measured") legitimizes this marginalization. Citing Oakley (1974) – "The primary function of myth is to validate an existing social order" – Lippi-Green (1997: 53-62) suggests that the idea of the standard is itself a myth, especially as it relates to pronunciation: there is no such thing as an accent-less, more objective variety of the language. Rather, a small group of dictionary-makers, pundits, style guide writers, and others with access to channels of influence decide what the "standard" contains, and it just happens to match the way that this group of people speaks. Although the resulting variety is *sold* as if it had been chosen on objective linguistic grounds, this is clearly not the case – as Bonfiglio (2002: 23) puts it, "There is nothing in the particular language itself that determines its worth: it is the connection of the language in question to the phenomena of power that determines the value of that language and that contributes to the standardization process."

So, how is the standard "sold"? Lippi-Green (1997: 68) sets out the components of what she calls the language subordination process:

language subordination process
The process by which some language varieties are built up and others are put down.

- *Language is mystified:* your mother tongue is so complex that you need expert guidance to understand it.
- *Authority is claimed:* we are the experts – we've studied language and write well.
- *Misinformation is generated:* our language variants are historically, esthetically, or logically better than yours.
- *Non-mainstream language is trivialized:* your language is cute or funny.
- *Conformers are praised:* see how much you could accomplish if you conformed, too!
- *Non-conformers are vilified:* see how willfully stupid, deviant, or unrepresentative people who talk like you are!
- *Promises are made:* do things our way, and employers will take you seriously.
- *Threats are made:* do things your way, and they won't.

A couple of things really jump out at me about this model of the process. The first is the claiming of authority, which for some reason works for pundits and newspaper columnists, but never seems to extend to linguists, people who, uh, actually study language. I remember being at a talk once where a well-known sociolinguist complained that people will believe almost anything scientists say about cold fusion, or deep space, but not what other scientists say about language variation. The difference, of course, is that very few people are deeply invested in a particular view of deep space that is challenged by science. But people *are* invested in their views of "bad" language.

The second point is that non-conformity is associated in this model with being *willfully* stupid, or deviant, or whatever. This is a recurring theme in standard language ideology (or, more accurately, in anti-non-standard ideology): the idea that people could speak differently if they just tried a little harder. Much research that we've looked at in previous chapters suggests that this is just not true, at least when it comes to accent changes in adults. Imagine what would happen if you moved to another dialect area right now, and were suddenly expected to sound like everyone around you, or else be considered uneducated. Your odds of success would be low. Imagine, for example, living in Philadelphia, like the people studied by Payne (1980), who couldn't figure out the local "short A" vowel system *even if they were born there*, unless their parents were born there too! Yet, on the other hand, we've also looked at research that suggests that people do a lot of active identity work with language, that they use language choices to build their sense of gender, or local-ness, or ethnicity. That kind of behavior clearly requires some kind of conscious choice. Studies of minority and immigrant groups show big differences in the degree to which different groups show convergence to the local main-stream variety. Bourhis and Giles (1977) played recordings of third-generation West Indian immigrants in Cardiff (Wales) to local (White) residents, and 78 percent of the West Indians were judged to be White. The authors contrast the level of convergence to the local variety in Wales with the maintenance of AAE speech features in the USA. Obviously the motivations and opportunities for convergence are different in the two situations, but the finding does remind us that we're not talking about absolutes of ability here. Rather, what the standard language ideology does is to impose a massively steeper burden on speakers of some varieties than on others. When people say that speakers of a non-standard variety "could change if they wanted to," they are in effect saying, "even though it would require a massive effort, erasure of their identity, and rejection of their home language and community norms, and *even then* it would still not be completely successful."

It may have struck you while reading the steps of the language subordination process above that you very rarely hear people saying those things in that particular way. But the "public conversation" (or Discourse) about language and attitudes goes on all the time. When I first began teaching in Newfoundland, I was surprised at the vigor with which my liberal university-oriented students would put down people that they called *skeets*. This word is not related to the sex-related American slang term – it's a local (and fairly recent) term for urban working-class youth (especially men) who have a sort of swagger, are big on (commercial) rap music and conspicuously brand-named clothes, are generally unemployed, and tend to have high (even exaggerated) rates of use of some local speech features (depending on where you're from, your community may have names like *bogan*, *chav*, or *ned* to cover the same basic idea; see also chapter 4). My students insisted that they were putting down people on the basis of their behavior, their choices, rather than their class or social origin. Then I'd ask them if there were particularly "skeety" first names, and they would tell me a few (sometimes including *Gerard*, as it turned out). When I pointed out that this meant that their definition of skeet clearly didn't just include people's behavior (as we don't name ourselves), they would see my point, and were usually kind of concerned that they had bought into this unexamined form of linguistic class prejudice. That's what makes some of these processes so effective – they become automated, part of what Bourdieu (1998) would call habitus, so that power is maintained not through the overt threat of

convergence
Accommodation toward your interlocutors, that is, trying to sound more like the people you're talking to.

Discourse
A society's way of talking about something that reflects underlying assumptions of the dominant group; these tend to become seen as "common sense" and thus are barely noticeable, despite the influence they have..

habitus
Socially learned ways of being that are so ingrained that we don't notice them (cf. Bourdieu 1977).

As an aside: The power of noticing

It can be liberating for people on the receiving end of linguistic prejudices just to hear someone point out that those prejudices are arbitrary, rather than based on linguistic fact. I remember once guest-lecturing in a class and saying that linguists consider code-mixing to be a skill, evidence of linguistic ability, rather than a shortcoming, and I noticed several multilingual students smiling and high-fiving each other.

punishments (although there's that, too), but "by the internalization of the norms and values implied by the prevailing discourses within the social order" (Mesthrie et al. 2009: 316).

reading and responding

If language ideologies that promote inequality get their power from being below the radar, it's possible for motivated sociolinguists to level the playing field, just a little, simply by noticing things. Since chapter 1, you've been encouraged to engage with your *sociolinguistic angel*, the little voice that helps you notice interesting sociolinguistic behavior in your daily lives. If your angels go to university and learn some Marxist theory, they might end up engaging in critical discourse analysis (CDA) or critical language awareness (Fairclough 1989). The underlying assumption of CDA is that texts promote or reproduce ideologies, and that people can be trained to critically read these texts, to be aware of what these texts are doing to them. Much of this work is done by looking at mass media and advertising. Granted, different texts can be read in different ways, and it's hard not to have your own ideology get in the way (see Widdowson (1995) or Blommaert (2005) for critiques of CDA). But once you start, it's amazing how much in the way of underlying assumptions or ideology you can find when you pull apart a yogurt commercial (see Sarah Haskins' *Target Women* videos) or a news story (for example, you rarely see investment fraud described as "White-on-White crime"). The producers of texts can get really cranky when you do this – media groups in Ontario (Canada) strongly objected when that province introduced a course in media awareness into the high school curriculum.

> critical discourse analysis (CDA)
>
> The assumption that texts promote or reproduce ideologies, and that people can be trained to critically read these texts, to be aware of what these texts are doing to them. Also known as critical language awareness.

Attitudes toward language varieties are also found in (and reinforced by) the representation of dialect in literature and other writing. Many authors represent non-standard speech through the use of non-standard spellings or punctuation. Authors often struggle with the balance between accurate representation of what someone says and readability. Sometimes, for those unfamiliar with the dialect, the result makes for difficult reading. Consider the following passage, in which Glasgow writer Tom Leonard (1984: 73) writes about how to represent local speech in print:

> *Yi write doon a wurd, nyi sayti yirsell, that's no thi way a say it. Nif yi tryti write it doon thi way yi say it, yi end up wi thi page covered in letters stuck thigithir, nwee dots above hof thi letters, in fact yi end up wi wanna they thingz yi needti huv took a course in phonetics ti be able ti read. But that's no thi way a think, as if ad took a course in phonetics. A doant mean that emdy that's done phonetics canny think right – it's no a questiona right or wrong.* (cited in Macaulay 1991: 281)

Here, both the content and the form of the paragraph speak to Leonard's efforts to faithfully represent speech. He represents the local pronunciation of such words as *down* (*doon*), *yourself* (*yirsell*), and *cannot* (*canny*). He also represents what Preston

As an aside: Princesses vs. hyenas

Language attitudes can also be revealed by deconstructing entertainment media images. What accents do you hear from characters who are supposed to be stupid? Criminal? Wise? Pretentious? Lippi-Green (1997) looked at accents in Disney animated films, and found that (as you might expect) major characters and attractive characters tend to have mainstream English accents. Foreign-accented characters are more likely to have negative motivations than British and other English-accented characters, who in turn are more likely to have negative motivations than US English-accented characters. Speakers of AAE are more likely to be fun-loving, unemployed, and/or animals (listen to the crows in *Dumbo*). French-accented characters are "those persons associated with food preparation or presentation, or those with a special talent for lighthearted sexual bantering" (p. 100).

(1985) calls "allegro speech forms," things most of us do in normal rapid speech: *and you* (*nyi*), *and if* (*Nif*), *want to* (*wanna*), and *anybody* (*emdi*). Leonard avoids pronunciation-based spellings of unusual words that would completely throw the reader off (*course in phonetics*). But he also uses non-standard spellings to represent pronunciations of individual words that match those of almost all English speakers: *things* (*thingz*), *word* (*wurd*).

This last process is usually known as eye dialect – some writers use nothing but eye dialect to represent non-standard speech. When that happens, the intent of the writer seems to be solely to send the message, "this person sounds different," without actually

eye dialect
The use of non-standard spellings to represent pronunciations of individual words that match those of almost all English speakers, for example, *duz* (*does*), *wurd* (*word*).

As an aside: Ideologies of the non-standard

Of course, not all language ideologies are about promoting and defending the standard. There are competing language attitudes and ideologies out there, things that speakers take into account when calibrating their language use. Violate local community norms by sounding *too* standard and you might be accused of disloyalty to the community, through the use of terms like *oreo, apple, banana,* or *coconut* (various colors on the outside, white on the inside). These ideas operate within community discourses about loyalty, survival, and authenticity that can be just as strongly held as standard language ideologies, and just as contentious (note the audience response to Barack Obama's line in his address to the 2004 Democratic convention about "the slander that says a Black youth with a book is acting White"). Again, however, the ideological burdens or barriers create more work for members of some communities than others. There's no food term equivalent to *oreo* for, say, Dutch immigrants who act too Anglo (and it's hard to imagine what that food would be – a cheese filled with instant macaroni, maybe?).

indicating any difference. This can be problematic. The default assumption for a reader is standard spelling and pronunciation; anything else can distance the reader from the viewpoint of the eye-dialected or non-standard-spelled characters (Preston (1985) shows that for many people, this is true for *any* non-standard written representation of speech). This would tend to marginalize non-standard characters (and, by extension, the communities they represent). Authors struggle with this issue regularly. One interesting strategy is adopted by Toni Morrison in the novel *Beloved*: non-standard representations are reserved for the speech of some White characters; the book's main (African American) character speaks/thinks in very standard English.

Another issue authors struggle with, of course, is accuracy of representation. Just how good are authors at capturing the details of non-standard language use? The answer, sometimes, is "very good." For example, a study of the works of Québec playwright Michel Tremblay, famous for his use of local French, shows that he not only accurately represents the variation between future tense forms in the language, but also captures the linguistic constraints on the choice of forms (Fonollosa 1995).

And not everybody buys into standard language ideologies. Researchers point out the presence of covert resistance to standard language ideologies, including **anti-languages**, ways of speaking that reverse or twist the standard meaning of words for social or political ends (Halliday 1978). One example is turning *oppress* into *down-press* in Rasta talk (or "I-talk") in Rastafarian communities. And Scott (1985) reminds us that people not in power may use the language of power around powerful people, but drop it as soon as they can – for example, Malaysian peasants who never call landowners *kaya* ("rich") to their faces, but use that term among themselves. *Overt* resistance, in the form of "professional noticing" or CDA, has been widespread, and is often successful enough to provoke a backlash. Mesthrie et al. (2009: 329-32) discuss the jokes about anti-sexist language initiatives that often surface (usually involving overextending suggestions, so that *manhole* becomes *personhole* and the like). The term **political correctness**, originally used in a self-deprecating way within feminist groups, has since become more popular among defenders of the social status quo as a way to trivialize or dismiss advocates of change.

anti-languages
The language used by oppositional subcultures within a society, usually used to reverse or twist the standard meaning of words for social or political ends.

political correctness
A term used by defenders of the social status quo to describe (and disparage) social changes and the people who advocate them.

Language attitudes underlie the linguistic choices we make, and the way we evaluate other people and their speech. At their most extreme, attitudes toward language harden into language myths. A variety of research techniques (especially matched guise tests) have enabled researchers to get at people's beliefs about language. People tend to see their own speech as unmarked (unless they speak a variety that's been heavily stigmatized over the years) – that is, people think that other people talk funny. The standard variety in particular gains its power from its apparent unmarkedness. However, the status of the standard requires constant reinforcement, and CDA can peek into some of the ways that this happens.

Where to next?

The basic toolbox of language attitude research (including mapping exercises and matched guise tests) continues to be applied in new settings, letting us learn more about attitudes in different cultural and social situations. It seems likely that the increased accessibility of survey tools (especially online) and people's increasing comfort and familiarity with answering surveys will lead to growth in this area. It would be fun to see what language attitude researchers could do with a full battery of electronic tools, such as the clickers used to track audience response to political debates and advertising.

1. Encourage your sociolinguistic angel to watch television (especially comedy or cartoons) with you, and note the accents associated with particular characters. What social or personal characteristics do you think the makers of these shows intended each accent to represent?
2. The color-outside-white-inside food words that I describe above presumably derive from the African American use of *oreo*. Do you know of any other words like this? Have a look online for discussions that involve these words (you'll probably want to search for a combination of the relevant food word and the ethnic group that it is intended to represent). How are the discussions that you find organized? What kinds of situations or people are described using these terms?
3. Read one of the Preston dialect attitude map studies described in the chapter, and see what kinds of terms the students use to describe the different dialect areas. What kind of emotional or value judgments are involved?
4. Ask people around you which accents they consider the most beautiful, correct, ugly, or incorrect. Ask them what in particular about the language makes them feel that way. Note their answers.

discussion

1. Consider again the things that Wardhaugh (2006) describes as language myths:
    (a) Certain languages lack grammar.
    (b) You can speak English without an accent.
    (c) French is more logical than English.
    (d) Parents teach their children to speak.
    (e) Primitive languages exist.
    (f) English is degenerating and language standards are slipping.
    (g) Pronunciation should be based on spelling.
    Do some of these seem more myth-like to you than others? If so, why?
2. Can you actually understand the Leonard passage above? Is it easier if you read it aloud?
3. Are there particular linguistic "errors" that drive you (or people around you) nuts? Which of them are actual errors (of spelling, punctuation, etc.), and which are part of non-standard language varieties?
4. If you live in a community where people do a lot of code-mixing (using two or more languages together), what are the attitudes toward that mixing?
5. If you were going to do a matched guise study in your community, what would it be about?
6. Consider how Alabamians and Michiganders feel about each other's speech, as described by Preston. How would your interpretation of this material change if you knew that many African American migrants to Detroit had their roots in Alabama?

other resources

Lippi-Green's *English with an Accent: Language, Ideology and Discrimination in the United States* (1997) will tell you more about standard language ideology and the representation of accented English. Bonfiglio's *Race and the Rise of Standard American* (2002) explains why that standard doesn't come from New York City.

Pullum's *The Great Eskimo Vocabulary Hoax and Other Irreverent Essays on the Study of Language* (1991) is what it says it is. For other language myths, check out Bauer and Trudgill's *Language Myths* (1998). There's a good academic look at language ideology by Woolard and Schieffelin (1994) called "Language ideology." (Do you see a titling theme developing here?)

As far as I can tell, there is no journal called *Language Attitudes*, but articles on the topic crop up regularly in sociolinguistics journals. Readers interested in language and ideology might try the *Journal of Language and Politics*, http://www.benjamins.com/cgi-bin/t_seriesview.cgi?series=JLP (accessed August 20, 2011).

13 Language as a Social Entity

In this chapter:

- Language maintenance
- Language policy and planning

Over the last twelve chapters, our discussion has moved from the linguistics end of sociolinguistics toward the socio end. On the whole, we've taken *language* as our object of study, and looked at how social forces can shape it. But society can also treat language the same way it treats immigration, the arts, or business – as a thing to be debated and regulated. In this chapter (and a bit of the next), we consider how societies approach language as a *social* object. Doing this brings us close to our sister discipline, the **sociology of language**.

In particular, we'll be concerned with the choice among languages. How do societies (and their members) decide which language is theirs? Which languages will survive, and prosper, and which will be abandoned, or even repressed? These are questions that have very little to do with the details of the language itself – a language variety can change its social or political status over a generation, or even overnight, independent of any alteration of its linguistic content. What changes is how people and their governments see and evaluate the language.

We'll start by looking at how languages survive (**language maintenance**), and then move on to how government and other institutions affect the role and status of

sociology of language
The branch of sociology concerned with language. Unlike sociolinguistics, this approach studies the social contexts of language without recourse to analysis of linguistic structure.

language maintenance
The study of how languages survive, or the continuing use of a (minority) language in the face of a more regionally, socially, or politically dominant language.

What Is Sociolinguistics?, First Edition. Gerard Van Herk.
© 2012 Gerard Van Herk. Published 2012 by Blackwell Publishing Ltd.

language policy
Sometimes used synonymously with language planning, language policy refers to the goals underlying the language planning process.

languages (**language policy** and **language planning**). Language maintenance happens at the individual level, but in response to social (and economic and political) forces. Language policy and planning happen at the societal/political level. And they assume an even more overt choice – (long-term) evaluation of the available alternatives, and the conscious choice of one of them.

language maintenance, shift, revitalization

language planning
Conscious efforts by government, society, organizations, etc. to affect the role and status of languages.

My father Willem came to Canada from the Netherlands with his parents and siblings in 1953. He soon moved to Montréal, where he met and married my mother Cynthia (from England). When he arrived in Canada, Dutch was very much his first language (although he also spoke German, French, and English). But I grew up speaking only English, later learning French. My friend Lidia's family story is very similar to mine, but she speaks both her parents' languages (Spanish and Polish), as well as English and French. So then why is it that don't I speak Dutch? Aside from my own shortcomings, are there social reasons why Dutch doesn't last long in Canada?

ethnolinguistic vitality
Rooted in the social psychology of language, this term refers to how widely a language or variety associated with a particular culture or ethnicity is spoken.

In fact, many researchers study the **ethnolinguistic vitality (EV)** (Giles et al. 1977) of languages – how likely they are to survive. These researchers have identified a number of factors that can influence language retention (Tabouret-Keller 1968; Dressler & Wodak-Leodolter 1977; Gal 1979; Dorian 1980, 1981; Timm 1980):

- *Institutional support:* Is the group's language used in local education? Government? Churches? Media? Where I grew up, education was available in either English or French. There were no Dutch "Saturday schools," where Canadian children of immigrants get a day (or half day) a week of instruction in their parents' language. And there was no Dutch Reformed church in town.
- *Power and prestige of languages:* How prestigious is the group – in their own eyes, and in the eyes of the larger society? One of my parents' languages, English, was also a language of school and work, so I was exposed to a lot of it. It was also the language of all the cool stuff around me – movies, music, books, TV. And it was the language of upward mobility. So it made sense to my parents that English would be the language that my brothers and I would grow up using. In a sense, it overpowered Dutch. (In Lidia's case, neither Spanish nor Polish played a big role in work or school, so neither language had an unfair advantage. She grew up in a classic "one parent, one language" bilingual family situation, then picked up French and English at school and in the community.)
- *Demography:* How big is the group and other language groups around it? How dispersed are the speakers? Are people marrying out of the group, or having a lot of children? Are new migrants continuing to arrive? In my case, there weren't that many Dutch-speaking people in small-town Québec. My dad had already married out. Most of my Dutch relatives lived far away, and there was no "Dutch-town" neighborhood to hang out in (although that would have been cool). Pendakur and Kralt

(1991), working from census data, show that living in a large linguistic or ethnic enclave (such as a Chinatown) encourages retention of immigrant languages.

- *Community choices:* Often, an accumulation of individual choices about assimilation and change lead to a speech community shifting to a new language. Even among Canadians who learned Dutch as their first language, only 12 percent still speak it at home (Statistics Canada 1989). Sometimes it seems that Dutch people as a whole have decided that English is the language of their future – in the Netherlands, citizens strongly support English as the second language taught in schools, and if you go there you'll hear a lot of very competent English. English is now becoming the preferred language of Dutch academics, none of whom seems to feel that this will lead to the extinction of Dutch from other domains of language use.

Put together, these forces have led my family to **language shift**, the gradual replacement of one language by another (Weinreich 1953: 68). Most immigrant families shift to the language(s) of their new country over two to four generations. The speed of the shift depends on the factors described above, and sometimes others. For example, German speakers in North America switched to English fairly quickly during and after World War I, when German was the language of the other side. Recent immigrants to Montréal tend to have trilingual children, as neither English nor French exerts enough influence there to win out as the language of choice. Sometimes, large groups of refugees maintain their home language because they believe or hope that they'll be returning to their country of origin (Ogbu 1978). Sometimes, enough speakers of one particular language move to a new place that they can maintain their original language for hundreds of years, especially in cases of social isolation (see chapter 3). And sometimes, for example in colonial situations, newcomers to a place have no intention of learning the majority language, and have enough political, economic, and military power to force the locals to learn their languages.

How tragic is it that I don't speak Dutch? I can't say I lose a lot of sleep over it, although I do occasionally miss the ability to plug into another language group (usually during World Cup). My equanimity comes at least partly from my sense, shared by many Dutch Canadians, that my identity doesn't require me to speak another language (a similar attitude has been described for Yiddish-speaking immigrants to North America in the early 1900s – their sense of *Yiddishkeit* ('Jewishness') didn't require actually speaking Yiddish, and the language declined rapidly across generations). I'm also reassured by the knowledge that there are millions of Dutch speakers in the world (they even have their own country!).

But for many languages that are losing speakers, there is no safe homeland. These are mostly languages spoken by small numbers of people who don't wield much political or economic power. These communities face the prospect of **language death**, a complete shift in which the original language is no longer used by anyone, anywhere. Some researchers (Robins & Uhlenbeck 1991; Crystal 2000: 19) predict that about half the world's languages will die out over the course of this century. The situation is especially dire for many indigenous languages in the Americas and Australia, some of which now have fewer than 100 native speakers. Overall, 52 percent of all the world's languages are spoken by fewer than 10,000 people each (Coulmas 2005: 150).

language shift
The gradual replacement of one language by another as the primary language of communication and socialization within a speech community.

language death
A complete language shift in which the original language is no longer used by anyone, anywhere.

domain
The social or institutional context of language use.

How does language shift happen? In most cases, it's not because individuals entirely change languages during their lifetime. Instead, there are two incremental processes at work. At the societal level, the community starts using the old language in fewer and fewer institutional contexts (what Fishman (1964) and others call domains). These domains are made up of particular combinations of people, places, topics, and situations. Examples include family, friendship, neighborhood, transactions, education, government, and employment (this division of domains may remind you of the discussion of diglossia in chapter 10). Survey-based studies of Spanish–English bilingual communities in the USA (Greenfield 1972; Laosa 1975) found domain-based use that was about what you'd expect: lots of Spanish at home, less in recreational contexts in school, and less still in the classroom. Greenfield's results can be summarized as "Spanish for intimacy, English for status." Laosa found that the gap in Spanish use between home and school was much larger than the gap between the different in-school contexts, which supports other findings that sometimes one language *dominates* a domain – respondents strongly agree that it "belongs" there. This is especially true of the link between the family domain and the mother tongue. Parasher's (1980) work in India comes to a similar conclusion. Although Parasher's survey respondents spoke multiple languages (English, mother tongue, regional language, Hindi, and sometimes other languages), they divided their domains sharply between two languages, for the most part: their mother tongue at home, English everywhere else – although in that case, it was partly because most of them had friends with a different mother tongue, and English was the shared language that eased communication.

At the individual or family level, shift happens because languages are not transmitted from one generation to the next (Lieberson 1972, 1980). This is easy to see in the case of immigrant languages. Generally, the first generation speaks the old country's language; generation 2 is bilingual; and generation 3 speaks only the language of the new country. Different immigrant groups shift at different rates, though: Clyne's (1991) study of immigrant groups in Australia found that after three generations, competence was down to under 2 percent for some immigrant languages (mostly northern European ones), while it ranged from 60 percent to 80 percent for others (mostly Balkan and southeast Asian languages). The different rates presumably result from some of the factors described above. Language mainte-

As an aside: Death

A language dies when its last speaker dies. In the yard of the parish church of Paul, in Cornwall, is the following inscription:

Here Lieth Interred Dorothy Pentreath who Died in 1777
Said to have been the last person who conversed in the ancient Cornish.
The regular language of this county from the earliest records till it expired in the eighteenth century in this Parish of Saint Paul.
This stone is erected by the Prince Louis Bonaparte in Union with the Revd John Garret Vicar of St Paul. June 1860
Honour thy Father and thy Mother that thy days may be long upon the land which the lord thy god giveth thee Exod XX12
Gwra perthi de taz na mam de dythiow bethenz hyr war an tyr neb arleth de dew ryes dees Exod XX12

In fact, Cornish (a language in the Celtic family, related to Welsh) may have been spoken by others in the neighborhood, but Dorothy was mentioned as the last speaker in a letter to London's Society of Antiquaries in the 1760s. Cornish today is nobody's native language, but there are revival efforts underway, including lessons and Cornish-language radio programs and newspaper articles.

nance or shift as a measure of acculturation to a new society isn't absolute – it depends on what the host and immigrant society think, and how much pressure is put on immigrants to conform.

It's important to remember that although language shift and decline is a macro-level (society-wide) process, it results from a series of micro-level (individual) choices. Individual speakers decide what language(s) they (and sometimes their children) will use in a given situation. We've looked at a few major forces, but how these forces play out on the ground can vary, depending on the individual circumstances (this is why it's hard to *predict* exactly how "safe" individual languages are). Real people respond to local situations, not big international forces. A new factory in the neighborhood, a discount store, the starting (or ending) of funding for local schools in a particular language: these and many more events can affect how speakers deploy their linguistic repertoire. We probably also need to remember that when people make choices about what language to speak (or to teach to their children), they base these choices on their *perceptions* of the EV of the languages involved. People who speak a language with low perceived EV will generally be more likely to use the dominant language, eventually leading to language shift.

age grading
When differences between age groups repeat as each generation ages, that is, when all speakers in a particular community favor a particular variant at one age and then a different variant at another. People sometimes change their (reported) behavior over the years as their life situation changes.

Being careful with language shift data

There's a couple of reasons to be cautious when discussing and analyzing data about language use and shift. Most work is based on census or survey data, and it often uses the apparent time construct to examine change. This can lead to sensationalistic claims, as languages appear to be in sharp decline. You'll recall that a problem with apparent time data is age grading – people sometimes change their (reported) behavior over the years as their life situation changes. Lieberson's (1972) analysis of multiple censuses in Montréal showed that an apparent increase in English ability among younger French adults – implying a community-wide move over time away from French – was actually an age effect that recurred with every census, and reflected the fact that young people were just coming onto the job market, where bilingualism was an asset. His interpretation was that people use English when they have to, in the workforce.

Remember, too, that we're dealing with how people self-report their language use and ability on a census. Governments make very particular choices about what questions to ask on a census, and respondents make very definite choices about how to answer. As an Anglophone (the preferred local term for an English speaker) growing up in Québec in the 1970s, I wouldn't have dreamed of describing myself as bilingual. My French wasn't good enough to live up to the exacting standards of that linguistically and socially turbulent time. But here and now in Newfoundland, most people would say that I speak French – even the native speakers in the French department, upstairs from me. And in Québec, most Anglophones now claim to be bilingual. Many of them probably actually are more bilingual than their parents; but they're also more willing to *see* themselves as bilingual. This is because many Anglophones who have stayed in Québec see themselves as adapting to the language and culture of the Francophone majority – they also tend to be "more French than the French" when it comes to eating (pork!) and drinking (red wine!). So if Québec Anglos are doing all this identity work on the Canadian census (which is considered "best practice" (Mesthrie et al. 2009: 383) as language census forms go – it asks a lot of questions and permits multiple responses), how certain can we be about making claims on the basis of other census data? And how much should such data influence language planning decisions?

We also need to remember that some languages are simply more dominant than others. Communities are rarely equal in terms of financial or political power, and at a global level, a handful of languages have spread far beyond their original borders through colonization and conquest. Coulmas (2005: 148–50) points out that only 1/2 of all French speakers, 1/10 of all Spanish speakers, 1/13 of all Arabic speakers, and 1/20 of all Portuguese speakers live in their language's country of origin. Contrast that with (the many varieties of) Chinese, which, despite being the world's most-spoken language, is concentrated almost entirely in and near China – its use elsewhere is as an immigrant or enclave language.

Overall, the world's top 10 spoken languages account for almost half of the world's population. The concentration of linguistic power in a few languages is especially noticeable in what may turn out to be the most sociolinguistically influential domains. According to 2010 estimates (www.internetworldstats.com/stats7.htm, accessed August 21, 2011), 82.2 percent of all online language populations were speakers of only 10 languages – English, Chinese, Spanish, Japanese, Portuguese, German, Arabic, French, Russian, and Korean. As of 2003, a staggering 96 percent of all the world's population was being educated in one of only 20 languages, all of them European or Asian.

Particularly noticeable is the worldwide shift to English, which is seen more and more as the ticket to participation in global culture and the global economy. Some scholars (notably Phillipson 1992) situate the growth of English firmly within the (neo)colonialist policies of English-speaking countries (especially the USA and the UK); others (such as Crystal 1997) see it more as a bottom-up process. Either way, the perceived value of English is massive, and success breeds success. English is powerful enough that it can afford to borrow words from other languages, which increases its expressive range (and the uses to which it can be put); it's the language of a number of powerful, wealthy countries, and of their cultural exports; and it's often the (supposedly) neutral choice when speakers of two other languages get together, in person or online.

So, what can linguists and others do about the perilous state of so many of the world's smaller languages? Obviously, that depends to some extent on how far along the path to extinction they are (the languages, not the linguists). Most languages seem to be at what Fishman (1991: 87–92) calls stage 6 on his 8-stage Graded Intergenerational Dislocation Scale (GIDS), a domain-based description of where and how languages are used (see table 13.1). At stage 6, intergenerational continuity in the home or community is the basis for language transmission, and the language is surviving across the generations. Contrast this with languages that are widely used in education, mass media, work, and government, on the one hand, and languages that have very few (or no) surviving

Sapir–Whorf hypothesis

A theory about language and thought that argues that the way a particular language describes the world actually affects its speakers' view of reality.

As an aside: Diversity of languages and worldviews

One of the arguments for language revitalization is that each language (or, presumably, language variety) encompasses a worldview shaped by the collective experiences of its speakers. For some theorists, the way a particular language describes the world actually affects its speakers' view of reality (this is usually known as the **Sapir–Whorf hypothesis**, after its developers). Although strong versions of this idea haven't met with much empirical support, it's clear that popular language ideologies see the world this way – I remember posters in Montréal's subway system, reminding us that *Il y a des choses qui ne se disent qu'en Français* ("There are some things that can only be said in French").

Table 13.1. The Graded Intergenerational Dislocation Scale (GIDS).

level	the language is:
1	used in education, work, mass media, and government, nationwide
2	used for local and regional mass media and government services
3	used for local and regional work, by both insiders and outsiders
4	transmitted through education, literacy
5	used orally by all generations and written effectively throughout the community
6	used orally by all generations and learned by children as their first language
7	used by the child-bearing generation with their elders, but not transmitted to their children
8	known only by members of the grandparent generation

Source: Adapted from Fishman (1991).

speakers and are used in very few domains, on the other (although by the time a language hits that last stage, we're probably talking less about language maintenance and more about language documentation, with possible re-introduction of the language into a limited number of domains). In Fishman's intermediate stages, such as stage 6, work can be done to enhance the status of the language, and perhaps increase its domains to outside the home, so that young speakers don't see it as unsuitable for public use. Building up languages in this way is just one of the goals of language planning and policy workers, as described in the next section.

language policy and planning

Language policy is the overall viewpoint that a government or some other organization has concerning the use of languages. It often reflects the language ideologies of the organization (or at least of those with power in the organization!). Language planning is the way that language policy gets put into effect.

What is language planning?

An influential definition of language planning is that of Weinstein (1980: 56), who describes it as "a government authorized, longterm, sustained, and conscious effort to alter a language's function in a society for the purpose of solving communication problems." We'll adopt a slightly broader definition here, in terms of who can do language planning, and why it's done – perhaps something closer to that of Wardhaugh (2006: 357), who defines it as "human intervention into natural processes of language change, diffusion, and erosion." Or maybe even broader still – perhaps language planning includes the choice to *not* intervene, to let market forces have their way, to allow (often linguistically uninformed) choices to be made.

Who can do it?

So, who can "plan" a language, or affect its status and shape? Depending on how broadly we define language planning, all kinds of people can be involved (Haugen 1966a; Ray 1968; Jernudd 1973: 18–19; Rubin 1973; Fasold 1984: 251):

- *Governments* are the subjects of much language planning research. National governments choose national (official) languages, and decide how those are defined and maintained (much more on this below). Local governments often affect how languages are treated in a particular region.
- *Non-government* commercial or professional groups such as the Chamber of Commerce, or large corporations, can influence the language of the workplace, or push for the introduction of language tests as part of hiring or certification practices.
- *Churches* decide on the language of religious observations and texts, and whether translations will be permitted. The decision of the Catholic church in 1964 to move away from Latin as the language of the Mass was a major instance of language planning.
- *Dictionary-makers* decide which words are acknowledged. In 1961, Merriam-Webster moved to include many vernacular terms (including *ain't*) in *Webster's Third New International Dictionary*, to a great uproar.
- *Pundits* can include newspaper columnists, bloggers, advice columnists . . . When it comes to language use, everyone's an expert, and widely read works (such as Lynne Truss' 2003 book *Eats, Shoots and Leaves*) can change the shape of language.
- *Writers* can choose to write in one language (variety) rather than another, thus changing the status of that language – Dante in Italian instead of Latin, Ngugi wa Thiong'o in Gikuyu instead of English, Michel Tremblay in vernacular Québec French instead of standard French.
- *Educators* (at all levels of the system) have a major influence on language choices, and education is often a major tool in language planning (more on this in chapter 14).
- *Printers, publishers, and editors* choose one spelling or grammatical construction over another when consigning language to print. The best-known example in English is probably William Caxton, who as the first person to introduce a printing press into England made all kinds of decisions about how English words were going to be spelled.
- *Independent political and social groups* can have an effect. For example, the "English Only" movement in the USA has encouraged state legislatures to declare English their state's (only) official language.

- *Individuals*, even those with limited political or social influence, can affect perceptions of a society's position on language. For example, during the most contentious years of Québec's linguistic debates, the English on stop signs was often painted out, and I remember anti-bilingualism graffiti in Montréal that read *Seuls les monstres ont deux langues* ('Only monsters have two tongues').

Why do it?

As Coulmas (2005) points out, there are far more languages in the world than there are countries, which means that somebody's language probably will be overpowered at some point, either politically, demographically, socially, or economically. He further notes that most of the world's countries put language policy at the heart of their political being, by including language provisions in their constitutions – 163 countries studied did so, compared to only 22 that didn't (most of which were smallish or fairly monolingual or both). Coulmas sees this as evidence that language policies are largely intended to manage diversity and dissent — you don't need to say what your country's language is if everybody already agrees on it. Cobarrubias (1983) identifies four typical language planning ideologies:

language planning ideologies
The four main motivations for language planning or language policy: linguistic assimilation, linguistic pluralism, vernacularization, and internationalization.

- *Linguistic assimilation:* Everyone should learn the dominant language. This has traditionally been the view in France and the USA, and was behind policies of Hellenization and Russification in Greece and the USSR respectively. This ideology is also behind policies of language banning, such as the banning of Basque and Catalan in Spain under Franco, or the banning of Kurdish in most contexts in Turkey.
- *Linguistic pluralism:* Societies and their governments should recognize more than one language (either nationally or in the regions where a particular language group is numerous). Linguistic pluralism is seen as a resource, rather than an obstacle to participation in the (dominant) society. This is the viewpoint behind many moves toward societal multilingualism.
- *Vernacularization:* An indigenous or less-powerful language should be "promoted" to official status. This is the ideology behind much of the governmental language planning that we'll look at in the next section. Languages that have been promoted in this way include Tagalog (Philippines), Hebrew (Israel), Tok Pisin (Papua New Guinea), Bahasa Indonesia (Indonesia), and Quechua (Peru).
- *Internationalization:* A non-indigenous language (usually English or French) should be encouraged – perhaps as an official language, perhaps not. This viewpoint is often promoted in highly multilingual societies, where an "outside" language (often a former colonial language) might be perceived as neutral, or a way to avoid giving an unfair advantage to the speakers of any one local language.

How to do it?

Many researchers working on language planning look at the efforts of governments and societies to increase the status and use of a local language. Although their terminology may differ, they generally describe two main kinds of planning (Kloss 1967; Jernudd 1973).

Status planning, also known as *language determination*, is concerned with choosing between available languages or language varieties and promoting one over another. Status planning often includes the declaration of an **official language**, a language declared the language of a particular region or country as a result of legislation. When a language is made an official language, it often affects the political and economic power of the ethnic group that speaks that language. In some cases, official language designations are a response by a majority group to a perceived threat from the increase in status or power of a minority group, as when "English-only" groups try to have English declared the official language of the USA (presumably because of a perceived threat from immigrant languages, especially Spanish).

The other major kind of planning, **corpus planning**, also known as *language development*, is concerned with the internal structure of the language, with choosing between available variants within that language in order to build up the language to the point where it can be used for all the requirements of a modern society. Obviously these two types of planning are linked – for a language to have a particular status and do a particular job, it needs certain stuff in it (including a technical vocabulary and an agreed-upon writing system).

In terms of the actual work involved, researchers describe some typical steps (Haugen 1966b, 1987; Ferguson 1968):

- *Selection:* Even once the decision is made to promote a local language, planners need to decide which language (variety) will be the norm. When choosing among dialects, it is often the central or more powerful one that wins out (as when the Île-de-France dialect of the Paris region became the template for Standard French). In Somalia, the northern dialect was chosen, partly because it had many speakers, and partly because much poetry had already been composed in that dialect (Andrzejewski 1980). In the Basque region of Spain, "Unified Basque" was created starting in the late 1960s by bringing together aspects of the four main Basque dialects (Mahlau 1991).
- *Codification:* If a language is to be used in law and politics and education, and frequently written, norms need to be established. These include graphization (choosing or developing a writing system), grammatication (establishing grammar rules and norms), and lexicalization (building or refining vocabulary, often by getting rid of loan words, as happened with the "Sanskritization" of Hindi in India; Coulmas 1989: 11).
- *Elaboration:* Also known as *modernization*, this involves making sure that a language can do all the things it needs to in a modern society. This is done largely through development of vocabulary – it's hard to imagine that many languages, if any, lack the *grammatical* resources to do all the jobs of a modern language. Elaboration often involves choosing between regional variants. This has been particularly true in the codification of modern Standard Arabic.

- *Implementation:* Once people come up with all this stuff, they then actually have to make it happen. Implementation might include the creation of books, newspapers, and other written material in the newly codified variety, plus its introduction into new domains (especially education). Recent decades have seen an increase in the number of books, especially those aimed at younger people, produced in lesser-spoken languages (whether they're official languages or not). This has the effect of (somewhat) increasing the domains in which the language can be used. Implementation also involves a fair amount of marketing, to encourage the acceptance of the newly promoted variety. For example, Québec's *Office de la langue française*, the body responsible for the promotion and standardization of local French, has produced posters with the French words for exotic items (such as tropical fruits and vegetables), to encourage shop owners to avoid using loan words for these things.

> ## *As an aside*: Let me elaborate
>
> McIntyre (1991) describes some of the ways that language elaboration has been done for Hausa, a language of Nigeria. Strategies used include borrowing from other languages, extending the meaning of an existing term, and **coining** – creating new words, often through compounding. For example, Hausa *gwamnatì* is borrowed from English *government*; the already-existing Hausa word *jàkaadàa* (important palace messenger) is extended to mean *ambassador*; and the awesome new Hausa compounded word for *helicopter*, *jirgin samà mài sàukar ungulu*, literally means something like "vehicle from above that lands like a vulture."

coining
Creating new words.

Does it work?

In other words, do language planning initiatives achieve their goals? There are some fairly clear language planning success stories, usually when there has been a powerful (often nationalist) desire on the part of a population for a policy to succeed. In the 1920s, Turkey successfully changed its writing system from an Arabic-based script to a Latin-based one, as part of a broader move toward a European orientation. Over the course of the twentieth century, Hebrew has been transformed from a ritual or religious language (similar in status to Latin) into the national language of Israel. Over the past two centuries, many European countries have built their own languages out of what were once considered dialects (the poster child for this process is Norwegian). In each case, the society (or its dominant members) saw the benefits of the change for themselves, and pushed hard for its adoption. The situation is less clear for lesser-spoken languages that don't have the luxury of a national boundary or government on their side. In Canada, the province of Québec has worked since the 1960s on language planning, culminating in the Charter of the French Language, which regulates the languages used in education, signs, and the workplace, and is described as "perhaps the best-known example of status planning for work" (Cooper 1989, 118–19).

> ## *As an aside*: English bitters
>
> Québec's Charter of the French Language is seen as a success and a model in much of the language planning community, and among Québec's Francophone (French-speaking) majority. This is less true for a subset of Québec Anglophones (English speakers), especially older monolinguals, who tend to complain bitterly about the Charter (and the *Office de la langue française*, which oversees its application). In fact, there's even a local slang term for this group: *angryphones*.

It's not entirely clear that a European-like model will work everywhere. A lot of language planning is based on the idea of choosing between two or more things that can be called different languages, and on the assumption that those languages are actually different (a viewpoint steeped in European nationalist traditions). In much of the world, though, the boundaries between languages are more gradient or fluid, as are people's linguistic affiliations. Even in North America, it's hard to argue that Louisiana Cajuns or Montréal Ashkenazim see themselves as less Cajun or Jewish than their French- or Yiddish-speaking ancestors – they've just chosen to use different ways of expressing their Cajun-ness or Yiddishkeit.

Spotlight: Language policy and neo-colonialism

Ricento, Thomas. "Historical and theoretical perspectives in language policy and planning." *Journal of Sociolinguistics* 4, no. 2 (2000): 196–213.

How much difference is there between western linguists telling developing countries that they need a standardized (probably European) language, and western botanists telling them that they need factory farms and a whole lotta chemical fertilizer? Not much, judging by Ricento's summary of 50 years of language policy and planning. Ricento describes three stages. First, sociolinguists prescribe unifying languages for nation-building; then, other sociolinguists note that these processes reinforce inequality within societies; then, yet others note that these processes help the imposition of western (especially North American) ways on other cultures, and call for active work on rights of linguistic minorities. Ricento ends by drawing parallels with early anthropology, where it took politically committed scientists to overthrow the dominant idea that inequality was caused by racial deficiencies.

Help with reading: There's no linguistic terminology in here. Language really is treated like any other aspect of culture or economy. Readers with a background in political science or postmodernism will have an easier time. Others should look up definitions of *epistemology* and *hegemonic* before starting.

Links to other readings: This is a summary of other people's work, so it's a great place to get the big ideas and to situate other readings before starting on the work of the major names in the field (say, Phillipson, Tollefson, and Skutnabb-Kangas).

summing up

Scholars of language and society often deal with the status and security of languages within a particular society. In cases of language shift, the move to a new language can lead to language death for the old language, sometimes slowed by policies of maintenance and revitalization. Language vitality can be affected by prestige, demography, and community choices. Societies often overtly address the vitality of a language through language planning, deciding which language varieties will have which status, and planning the vocabulary of the language.

Where to next?

Language endangerment is a huge issue for linguists (and, obviously, for speakers of endangered languages). Even theoretical linguists who aren't part of the sociolinguistic mainstream tend to have a social component to their work when it comes to helping languages to survive. A growing area of discussion is the involvement of speakers of languages (especially "small languages") in making decisions about what needs to be studied and preserved for a language, and who gets to do it.

exercises

1. Pick a language variety that is undergoing some form of language revitalization or other planning process (options might include Basque, Cayuga, Cornish, Dhanggati, Inuktitut, Innu-Aimun, Maori, Navaho, Ulster Scots, or Welsh). Read up on it. What strategies are being used to support the language? Who is involved in the decision-making? What are the major forces leading to decline of the language?

2. If your family is somewhere in the middle of language shift, talk to older family members who have retained more of the original language (how much language depends, of course, on how far along the shift your family is). How do they feel about the shift? Has their language use changed over the years? Try to get them to teach you some words or phrases that you don't know.

3. If your family has pretty well completed language shift, are there still a couple of words or phrases that you know in your ancestral language? What are they? Why do you think those particular words or phrases have survived?

4. What language maintenance activities are available in the place where you live or study? Are there courses, preschools, "Saturday schools"? Who runs them?

5. The last speaker of the Beothuk language (an aboriginal language of Newfoundland) was named Shanawdithit. See what you can find out about her.

6. Read up on how linguists are talking about the responsibilities they have to speakers of the languages that they study (hint: the name "Kenneth Hale" may help you find something).

7. Watch the film *The Linguists*.

discussion

1. Revitalizing languages is expensive, requiring dictionaries, grammars, teaching materials, teacher training, and facilities. How do you think language revitalization funding should be allocated? Should some languages get more than others? Why, or why not?
2. Can you think of any *economic* counter-arguments to the "revitalization is expensive" viewpoint?
3. Do you think countries (including your own) need an official language? Why, or why not?
4. Are there endangered languages in your part of the world? If so, what do you know about them?
5. Do you feel that *dialects* that are in decline deserve some or all of the same efforts at preservation and revitalization that languages get? What if the dialect was called a language, or if its speakers fought for its recognition as a separate language?
6. A comparison of internet language users between 2003 and 2010 shows Arabic, Portuguese, and Spanish moving "up the charts." Why do you think this might be?
7. Language maintenance and documentation are often undertaken by linguist missionaries, with the goal of producing religious materials in the relevant language. How do you think this could affect the work that gets done, and how it is received?

other resources

Two recent and useful introductions to language policy are Ricento's *An Introduction to Language Policy: Theory and Method* (2006) and Spolsky's *Language Policy* (2004).

Phillipson's *Linguistic Imperialism* (1992) is a full book, but you might want to start with chapter 3 (theoretical foundations, pp. 38–77).

Likewise, you can get a taste of Fishman's *Reversing Language Shift: Theoretical and Empirical Foundations of Assistance to Threatened Languages* (1991) by reading his 1990 "What is reversing language shift (RLS) and how can it succeed?"

For work on educational policy (and linguistic inequality), try Tollefson's *Language Policies in Education: Critical Issues* (2001), or Skutnabb-Kangas and Phillipson's 1995 book *Linguistic Human Rights: Overcoming Linguistic Discrimination* (at least the introduction, pp. 1–22).

Journals:

International Journal of the Sociology of Language, http://www.degruyter.de/journals/ijsl (accessed August 21, 2011).

Language Policy, http://www.springer.com/education+%26+language/linguistics/journal/10993 (accessed August 21, 2011).

Language Problems and Language Planning, http://www.benjamins.com/cgi-bin/t_seriesview.cgi?series=lplp (accessed August 21, 2011).

14 Education

> ## In this chapter:
>
> - The school as community
> - Home language(s) and schools
> - Languages in education
> - The effect of school on language

In the past chapters, we've considered many ways that society and language affect each other (and we've noted again and again that all these topics interact). In what's left of the book, I draw the connections between topics tighter, to see how an understanding of many of these ideas can illuminate how language and society relate in particular communities.

In this chapter, we take a multiple-perspective look at the educational system, which is a sort of superheated sociolinguistic environment:

- students are at the right life stage to be building their own identities;
- school gives many people their first intense exposure to (and socialization in) the language practices of the mainstream;
- people in school spend many hours interacting with each other; and
- groups outside the school see it as a place where particular language ideologies can be implemented or resisted.

What Is Sociolinguistics?, First Edition. Gerard Van Herk.
© 2012 Gerard Van Herk. Published 2012 by Blackwell Publishing Ltd.

the school as a sociolinguistic community

How many years have you spent in school? If you're reading this book at the university level, let's assume 14 to 20 years – perhaps 25,000 hours? That's an awful lot of time to spend with other people: fellow students, teachers, school staff. Since you were small, those people have shaped your language behavior, and you've used language to shape how you would like them to see you and to treat you.

Sociolinguists have always been interested in schools, but sociolinguistic practice in the schools has recently been of particular interest to people who work on language and gender identity (Eckert 2000; Bucholtz 1999; Mendoza-Denton 1994). This work focuses on language practices in middle schools and high schools, which are when the **heterosexual marketplace** (Eckert 1996) really kicks in – which makes sense, as students in these schools are developing into young adults. Combine that age-specific focus with the typical intensity of adolescent expression and the number of hours that students spend together, and it comes as little surprise that people in schools develop sharply defined ways of being (in fact, the use of non-standard language features tends to increase during this time – see the discussion of the adolescent peak in chapter 5).

These school-related ways of being, or social roles, are often similar in a broad sense from place to place, and tend to include *elites, athletes, deviants,* and *academics.* Ethnographic studies of adolescent culture clump these ways of being into "keepers of the institution" and "rebels against the institution" (Sussman et al. 2007). Keepers tend to be middle-class, but they don't have to be; they work within the institution of the school, are successful in officially sanctioned ways, and are more likely to continue in school. Rebels tend to be working-class, but don't have to be; they don't define success in terms of the overt goals of the school. Although these groups occur in many schools, details of group membership, description, and practice are locally generated: keepers of the institution may be called *jocks* or *cafeteria people* or any other local name; rebels may be called *burnouts* or *smokers* (or any other local name); people who distance themselves from both groups may be called *nerd*s or *gamers* (or, again, any other local name; Eckert 2000; Gardner 2010; Bucholtz 1999). These labels reflect the poles – the extremes of expected social behavior in the school. Other students situate themselves with respect to these poles.

It's not just the labels that are locally generated, though: the things that group members do vary from place to place, including their language. In Eckert's study of a suburban Michigan high school (Eckert 1989, 2000), the burnouts were more likely to meet up with urban Detroiters in parks or while driving around, and thus had more contact with incoming sound changes (like the Northern Cities Shift). So burnouts had more heavily shifted vowels, girl burnouts shifted even more (if you forget why, refresh your memory in chapter 7), and the burned-out burnouts (those who behaved the most like burnouts) shifted the most of all.

That's not to say that contact is the only thing that drives this kind of language change, in schools or anywhere else. Students presumably use language features to show where they fit in with respect to the communities of practice active in their schools.

heterosexual marketplace
The (media-driven) institutionalization of heterosexuality and traditional gender.

Shifting your vowels isn't just something burnouts do; it's something people do in order to be burnouts. This is illustrated nicely by some research here in Atlantic Canada, where rapid social change is really pushing language change. In Gardner's (2010) study of high school students in Cape Breton Island (an economically and demographically declining area of Nova Scotia), most of the smokers (rebels) used local features, as we would expect. But so did people who ate their lunch in the cafeteria, the local keepers of the institution. Gardner attributes this to the fact that their futures are fairly clearly determined. In other words, they could afford to sound local, because their status wasn't in question. The students who *avoided* local stigmatized forms were a subset of the smokers who intended to go to university – they were the group that most needed formal, non-local language to establish their social and educational aspirations.

---

what students bring to school

Schools are interesting to us because they're places where sociolinguistic practices develop, but they're also interesting because they're where different sociolinguistic ways of being come together. Students (and their parents) and teachers come to school with particular ways of talking and interacting, and particular attitudes toward language use, and these aren't going to be the same for everybody. Mismatches between students can lead to misunderstandings. Often, though, thanks to the way neighborhoods work, most of the students will actually share a lot of linguistic and sociolinguistic traits (in my son Willem's kindergarten class, for example, all except three students had Somali as their first language).

If there is a significant language mismatch in schools, it's more likely to be between the home language of many of the students and the language of the school and the teacher. There are severe consequences to this mismatch. Studies around the world describe worse school outcomes for students who haven't been brought up speaking the language or language variety that the school values (Romaine 2000: 206–9; Rickford 1999: 305; Green 2002: 28).

One influential attempt to explain the school failure of non-standard speakers is found in the work of Basil Bernstein (1961a, 1972), who argued that middle-class and lower-working-class communities are so different from each other that their language varieties help their speakers construct different views of the world. Working-class families tend to be part of closed, multiplex social networks (Ammon 1994) – because of their limited resources, they depend on each other in many ways (see chapter 2). Perhaps as a result of the large overlap in shared experience, this favors the use of a "language of implicit meaning," which Bernstein called a **restricted code**. The linguistic features that Bernstein associated with restricted codes included "poor" (that is, non-standard) grammatical constructions, which are short, grammatically simple, and often unfinished, with few conjunctions, little subordination, dislocated presentation of information, limited numbers of adverb and adjective types, infrequent impersonal pronoun subjects, and frequent comprehension requests (like *y'know?*).

restricted code
Restricted codes, typically associated by Bernstein (1961a, 1972) with the working class and closed, multiplex social networks, involve non-standard grammatical constructions that are short, simple, and often unfinished.

elaborated code

Elaborated codes, typically associated by Bernstein (1961a, 1972) with the middle-class and broader, less multiplex social networks. Involves standard syntax and complex sentences.

Middle-class speakers can use this code, but their broader, less multiplex social networks involve far more contexts where they can't rely on shared knowledge, so they also make use of an elaborated code. This involves "accurate" (that is, standard) syntax, complex sentences (with subordinate clauses and stuff), prepositions, lots of "I," a wide range of adjectives and adverbs, and a lot of qualifying language. This was said to be "a language use which points to the possibilities inherent in a complex conceptual hierarchy for the organizing of experience" (Bernstein 1961b: 169). As schools use a lot of elaborated code, lower-working-class students, who are unfamiliar with it, are at a disadvantage, and they have trouble changing, because that change would involve trying to change cultural patterns.

Bernstein's work obviously dovetails easily with standard language ideologies (chapter 12). It remains influential in Europe, and at first struck a responsive chord in North America, especially with respect to the school problems of African American English (AAE) speakers. Bereiter and Engelmann (1966: 39), for example, described AAE speakers as showing "a total lack of ability to use language as a device for acquiring and processing information. Language for them is unwieldy and not very useful." Educational initiatives to remediate this perceived deficit included the Head Start program, which led to (among other things) *Sesame Street*.

But other initiatives addressing the educational barriers facing African Americans included funding early sociolinguistic studies of AAE. Those sociolinguistic researchers described a language variety that was nothing like what Bernstein and others were talking about, and set out to demonstrate what Labov (1972c) called the logic of Non-Standard English. "There is no reason to believe that any nonstandard vernacular is in itself an obstacle to learning," he wrote. "The chief problem is ignorance of language on the part of all concerned" (including, presumably, teachers and pundits). These studies found that young AAE speakers who seemed monosyllabic and disengaged during stressful school and experimental situations were far more eloquent on their own sociolinguistic turf. As Labov (1970: 84) puts it in what is clearly a shot at Bernstein, "the cognitive style of a speaker has no fixed relation to the number of unusual adjectives or conjunctions that he uses."

Now, that's not the same as saying that the mismatch between the sociolinguistic situation at home and at school isn't a problem (and more of a problem for some people than others). After all, by the standards of everyday speech, classroom conversational conventions are kind of odd. Teachers sometimes ask students to answer "in complete sentences," so that the answer to "What is the father doing?" is not "walking the dog," as it might be in real life, but rather "The father is walking the dog." Teachers also ask questions that they already know the answer to, which is something sociolinguistically competent adults rarely do in daily life – *unless* they're middle-class parents (Holmes 1992: 360), who often do teacher-like talk: "What's that? A ducky! Yeeeeeeessss!"

As an aside: Talking and learning

The school–home mismatch can extend to the very act of talking versus silence, as in the often-quoted exchange between a White Canadian teacher and an Inuit parent in the north, where the community tradition is that children learn by observing quietly (Crago 1992: 496):

Teacher: Your son is talking well in class. He is speaking up a lot.
Parent: I am sorry.

Mismatches in how language works at home and in school can also lead to teachers underestimating the language-related ability of students because they don't realize *how* students are using language. Heath (1983), in a detailed ethnography of a southern mill town, shows that the purposes and ways of using literacy relate to how people function in social networks. Some students who seemed to have very little to do with "school literacy" did all kinds of writing and reading outside the school.

And, of course, standard language ideologies reinforce assumptions of student short-comings, by encouraging links between the use of salient non-standard features and lack of school ability (see, for example, Cunningham 1976–7). Charity et al. (2004: 1352) remind us that "people (including teachers and teachers in training) readily make attri-butions about a speaker's intelligence, education, and other personal characteristics solely on the basis of listening to a brief excerpt of the individual's speech or oral reading (Cross et al. 2003, Tucker & Lambert 1969)." This, in turn, can lead to self-fulfilling prophecies, as teachers have lower expectations for those "weaker" students, and give them less instruction, and so the students actually end up doing worse.

While people generally agree that speakers of non-elite languages and language varie-ties tend to do worse in school, students and parents often object to strictly language-based approaches to fixing that problem, even though some programs involving the use of students' home dialect in the classroom seem to have been very successful at helping with literacy (Rickford & Rickford 1995). Parents may fear that a focus on language will shift the blame for school failure to the students and their home environments and away from other barriers to education – things like ethnic or class prejudice, underfunded schools, or a lack of teacher training. In particular, the use of dialect readers as bridges to literacy in the standard is interpreted as suggesting that dialect speakers have a com-prehension barrier when it comes to Standard English (which, generally, they don't – if they do, we need to rethink a lot of the previous 13 chapters). What *does* cause trouble for speakers of non-standard dialects is knowing which language features are part of school language and which ones aren't. And we know that this is the kind of thing where only a couple of mistakes can sink you.

To address this problem, some sociolinguists (e.g., Charity 2007) have worked on school programs that overtly address dialect differences. These generally involve some sort of contrastive analysis – a method now out of favor in second language acquisition, but useful in this context, in which students are trained to notice the precise ways in which the standard is different from the language that they use outside of school. There is some evidence that non-standard-speaking students who can imitate Standard English are better at reading (Charity et al. 2004); so if the awareness underlying this ability can be taught, perhaps this will lead to higher literacy rates.

self-fulfilling prophecy A prophecy that causes itself to become true. The term is often used in education to suggest that high teacher expectations for a particular student lead to success for that student.

contrastive analysis A method, now little used in second language acquisition, that focuses on the similarities and differences between two varieties.

languages of education

So far, we've been talking mostly about students who speak a different (non-standard) variety of the same language as the school. What happens when students come to school speaking a completely different language? Clearly, this is a barrier to their learning. What

As an aside: Code-switching in the classroom

It may be easier to introduce multilingual education in societies where multilingualism is the norm. Serpell (1989) describes an experiment in Zambia, where a grade one teacher switched among three languages (Bemba, English, and Nyanja) when discussing home life, games, and books. The students were more fluent in English (the usual school language) during the book discussion than during the other two, which suggests that they don't usually use English for non-school conversations. More interesting is that out of 40 students, only two commented on the code-switching at all, and then only by claiming that they didn't speak Bemba. But then the same students were able to answer questions asked in Bemba!

immersion
A teaching method in which students who speak one language (usually the socially dominant one) are taught content in another language by (bilingual) teachers.

heritage language
A language that is acquired by individuals raised in homes where the region's dominant language is not (exclusively) spoken.

structured immersion programs
Where students who don't speak the dominant language are taught that language and taught in that language.

dual-language programs
When two languages are used for instruction for a fairly long period.

societies choose to do about this problem varies across time and region. Traditionally, educational systems have been monolingual, in the language of the elite (Lewis 1976). Either that, or teaching has been done in a high-status language that was nobody's first language, as was the case with Latin in Europe until a few centuries ago.

The USA has a tradition of bilingual education going back to the earliest days of European settlement, with its heyday in the 1800s, as many immigrant groups wanted to preserve aspects of their culture (Pearlmann 1990). In the early 1900s, the growth of compulsory (government-funded) education, accompanied by a world war and a rise in anti-immigrant feeling, led to more monolingual education.

Around the world, the pendulum swung back in the 1960s, with heightened interest in ethnic identity leading to mother tongue use in schools. For example, the Welsh Language Act of 1967 legalized the use of Welsh in teaching (Baker 1991). New Zealand has had Maori language preschools (*kohanga reo*, 'language nests') since 1982, and these have served as a model for groups elsewhere. Schools in India tend to operate in three languages – English, Hindi, and a regional language (Sridhar 1991) – while in Tanzania, students often learn in their mother tongue for three years, then switch to Swahili, the language of wider communication (Abdulaziz 1991). Canada features language **immersion** programs, in which students who speak one language (usually English) are taught content in the other official language (usually French) by (bilingual) teachers. Many Canadian immigrant kids are also familiar with **heritage language** classes (Cummins 1992), usually called "Saturday school." These programs, usually after school or on weekends, often meet in schools or community centers and aim to maintain or develop students' competence in the language their parents brought to Canada.

In the USA, the language-of-education pendulum seems to have swung back and forth more quickly than elsewhere. The Bilingual Education Act (1968) allowed for transitional bilingual education, where the goal was to move students toward English instruction. In 1974, the court case of *Lau v. Nichols* found in favor of Chinese-speaking parents who had taken the San Francisco school board to court on the grounds that their children were not getting an equal educational opportunity. In 1980, the Bilingual Education Act extended funding to **structured immersion programs** (where non-English-speaking students are taught the English language and also taught subject material in English) and **dual-language programs** (where both English and another language are used for instruction for a fairly long period). A generation later, however, 2001's No Child Left Behind Act overturned the Bilingual Education Act, and in 2009 a Supreme Court majority opinion stated that "research on ELL [English Language

Learner] instruction indicates there is documented, academic support for the view that SEI (Structured English Immersion) is significantly more effective than bilingual education."

The debate over bilingual education in the USA is highly polarized and politicized, in part because it's usually about Spanish–English bilingualism, and thus takes place within a larger debate about immigration and the fears that it raises for some people (although the USA actually has a far smaller percentage of non-English speakers now than at earlier times in its history, especially around 1900). A couple of themes recur, though, and are worth a sociolinguistic glance.

A first theme is that everybody involved claims that their position is supported by research, but it's sometimes hard to tell what research people are comparing their favorite approaches to. There are many different types of bilingual education – García (1997: 410) lists 14 of them, with different educational and linguistic aims and different mixes of participants. So we need to be careful not to claim that what worked in one place is "the same" as a model that we happen to like, without comparing both the educational and the sociolinguistic contexts in which programs happen. Most Canadians, for example, wouldn't recognize what we call "immersion" if we looked at programs of the same name in the USA. It's not clear that "English immersion" for a Spanish speaker in an English community is the same as (say) French immersion for Canadian English speakers in English Canada, where their English is maintained and supported everywhere else in their lives.

A second theme in much of the debate involves the goal of such educational programs. Often, the debate seems to be entirely about how quickly students can become proficient (enough) in English. This is based on two underlying though often unspoken assumptions, common in monolingual societies: that any use of one language hinders the learning of another, and that retaining your mother tongue slows your assimilation into mainstream society. In other words, bilingualism is seen as a problem, rather than a goal. This, despite the fact that research seems to show a number of advantages to bilingualism: cognitive advantages (Hudson 1968), metalinguistic awareness (Bialystok 1987), and communicative sensitivity (Genesee et al. 1975), if people are bilingual enough (Cummins 1981), as well as greater inter-group understanding (Cummins 1988) and psychological esteem benefits (Cummins 1986). Plus, obviously, the ability to communicate with a lot of people who speak a different language.

In fact, our society generally *values* bilingualism as a skill, and we spend much time and money attempting to teach additional languages to speakers of the majority language. As more than a few observers have pointed out, it might be more efficient to help children of (say) Korean immigrants to maintain their Korean while learning English than to try to teach Korean to monolingual English speakers at the university level.

As an aside: Elite trilingualism

The European School model, set up to teach the children of European Union officials (who move around a lot), involves at least three languages per student:

- The student's heritage language (Greek, for example) is used for instruction in primary school and is taught as a subject through high school.
- A "big" second language (French, German, or English) is taught as a subject in primary school and becomes the main language of instruction in high school.
- A third language is introduced as a subject in grade 8.
- A fourth language can be studied as a subject in the final two years of high school. (Housen 2002)

This second theme reminds us that whether we're talking about languages or dialects, the basic ideology underlying how things are supposed to happen in schools is the same: no matter how you come in, you're supposed to leave as part of the mainstream. The system isn't expected to change, or even to understand the sociolinguistic situation of the students. The onus to change is on the student.

what students take from school

So, what do students change into? What effect does education have on people's socio-linguistic behavior? It's important to keep in mind that when we talk about "education" in this regard, we usually mean successful completion of a certain level of schooling. To get to that point, people usually have had to adapt to the language and language ideologies of the school system. For many, including many middle-class children, this will have required very little adaptation at all. The language behaviors and ideologies that they brought with them from home were already very similar to those of the school ("A ducky!"), so they had an easier time in school and are more likely to have succeeded. For others, unless they're highly skilled dialect switchers (and very little in the school system will have encouraged them to maintain their home dialect), it's likely that their language use and ideologies have become more school-like than those of their less-educated peers.

And, of course, both of these successful groups are the people who will go on to become the teachers and professors and textbook writers of the future, and perpetuate the system. In other words, school is run by people who did well in school the way it is. As a result, these people will assume that school works fine, or that the ways in which it doesn't work can be fairly easily overcome through hard work, or changes in outlook and behavior.

When we talk about "education" as a social factor that influences people's language, then, we're using a broad label that includes how standard they were to start with, what experiences have been available to them, how willing to change to the standard they were, and their attitudes toward language varieties. We can see how this plays out here in Newfoundland. Clarke (1982), for example, found that of all the social groups who completed language attitude surveys about Newfoundland English, schoolteachers were the *least* likely to value local speech as a part of local identity. And Knee and Van Herk (2010) found that small-town adolescents who planned to go on to university had already reduced their use of salient local speech features to about one-third the rate of their non-university-bound friends and relatives. For those particular youth, university education will involve more than just classwork and ideology, as they'll have to leave their hometown to go to school, and thus will end up having different experiences, with different people, than the friends who stay behind. In this, they are similar to the Arabic-speaking students that Al-Wer (1997) describes, for whom university education has more sociolinguistic impact through the different experiences involved than through the education itself.

learning a language at school

For students learning another language at school, sociolinguistics and education interact in a different way. Research among learners of French in (majority-English) Ontario by Mougeon et al. (e.g., 2010) seems to show that there are certain fine points of sociolinguistic practice that people just don't get in school. Whether students were English speakers in French immersion programs, or French-ancestry students who learned French only in school, they didn't pick up on variable rules in the vernacular unless they also had contact with French in other domains of language use. Funnily enough, this seems to happen despite the fact that second language teaching researchers were among the first to pick up on sociolinguistic ideas like communicative competence (Hymes 1972), which Canale and Swain (1980: 20) define for second language learning as "a synthesis of knowledge of basic grammatical principles, knowledge of how language is used in social settings to perform communicative functions, and knowledge of how utterances and communicative functions can be combined according to the principles of discourse."

One explanation for the limited second language vernacular abilities of many school learners is that although teachers are aware of the stylistic range that their students might need, their own language ideologies or limited teaching time lead them to focus on the standard end of the language. This strategy probably comes from the (reasonable) belief that the social penalties incurred by second language learners for being too standard are smaller than the penalties for being not standard enough. I've certainly run into this in my own career. My French, while not entirely fluent, is very regionally accented and a bit non-standard, and when I teach university courses in French there are always a few students who wince and tell me, *Monsieur, on ne dit pas ça* ('Sir, one does not say that').

summing up

School is a venue where sociolinguistic concepts and practices can be observed at full volume, and where the consequences for misunderstanding sociolinguistic reality can be most serious. School is where young people develop much of their socioinguistic competence and repertoire. It's where language ideologies (and language varieties) collide in a high-stakes way, with standard ideologies and keepers of the institution encouraging a move toward the standard version of the majority language, and other speakers being marginalized.

Where to next?

I'm hesitant to make big predictions about the sociolinguistics of school, at least as far as it relates to how schools and teachers implement remedial programs or research findings. The bilingual-education pendulum is swinging so far and so hard that political scientists may be more competent to address the issue than sociolinguists. As far as research on the sociolinguistics of schools is concerned, this is currently a hot topic and is likely to stay that way, as schools and youth speech are such fertile areas for research, and the potential real-world applications of sociolinguistic findings are so large.

Spotlight: Talking nerdy

Bucholtz, Mary. "'Why be normal?' Language and identity practices in a community of nerd girls." *Language in Society* 28 (1999): 203–23.

Most of the language interaction that goes on in an average school day isn't between teachers and students, but between students and other students. This paper, from a community of practice (CofP) perspective, uses discourse analysis to see how a group of self-described nerd girls define themselves and their group by messing with ideas of standardness and hipness. Basically, they refuse to play by the rules of mainstream coolness determined by other students in the school.

Reading: After the introduction, the paper spends a long while contrasting CofPs and speech communities. You can understand the aims of the paper without reading this section (although it is a useful expansion of the ideas behind CofP). The next section relates that to gender studies. Then there's a section on how nerds fit into the jock–burnout continuum. After that, Bucholtz describes identity practices among a small group of high school nerds that she studied. My students who read the paper are impressed by how much she can get out of a couple of short conversations.

There's not much linguistic terminology to worry about here. The conventions of representing speech (especially overlapping speech) in discourse analysis may be new to you, but there's nothing in that to prevent your understanding. What *is* difficult for some readers is the amount of postmodern jargon, especially in the CofP section.

Links to other readings: When this first came out, the idea that nerds could be proud and/or female was much less part of public discourse than it is today, which may be why Bucholtz works harder to support her claims than she might have to in order to convince you (especially if you're a nerd girl yourself). If you liked the identity practice parts, check out Bucholtz and Hall's "Identity and interaction: A sociocultural linguistic approach" paper (2005).

Bucholtz has other papers on nerds; her 2001 article "The Whiteness of nerds: Superstandard English and racial markedness" was widely misinterpreted as claiming that Whiteness and smartness were the same, leading to a backlash in the mainstream media and online (check it out on any site you find – the summaries of the article are mostly straightforward, but the comments are almost entirely negative, and pretty hostile).

1. Find a cranky online site that expresses strong opinions (on either side) about bilingual education (don't worry, they won't be hard to find). The writers will probably claim that "studies" support their position. Find one of the studies they cite. See if it actually does support their position. Note any particular ways that the situation in the study might not be the same as whatever situation the cranky people are talking about.

2. Many Standard English speakers, especially at the university level, feel that it is unfairly hindering to be taught by teaching assistants with foreign accents. If you know people who feel that way, ask them if their attitude helps them sympathize with immigrant children who are taught by teachers who have different accents than the children's parents. (I'm not sure if this is an exercise or a rhetorical question, but you might at least start an interesting conversation about language ideology.)

3. Interview a professor, teaching assistant, or fellow student from a different language background about their linguistic experiences in academe. Has their language or accent ever been an issue? How so?

4. If you're a native (or very fluent) speaker of English, volunteer to read over and edit an assignment or paper written by a fellow student who's a non-native speaker, or less fluent. (This is obviously a nice thing to do, but it also becomes a useful learning experience if you choose to reflect on the process.)

5. If you're a fluent speaker of a language other than English, find somebody who doesn't speak that language and volunteer to summarize a piece of academic writing in "your" language that might be useful for their studies. It should probably be up to them to find the piece of writing in the first place, but you could help. (This, too, is a nice thing to do, but becomes a useful learning experience if you choose to reflect on the process.)

1. Have you been involved in any kind of bilingual education? If so, what kind? How did that go for you?

2. People sometimes say that going away to school "ruins" people's ability to speak in the vernacular, to "keep it real." What do you think?

3. Have you ever had your grammar corrected in school? What happened?

4. In your experience (or from what you hear from other people), do different disciplines in university (e.g., geography, math) have different tolerance levels for highly accented or otherwise second-language-sounding language in the classroom? If you do note differences, why do you think they exist?

5. Think back on your second language learning experiences (in the school system). How (if at all) were sociolinguistic issues addressed? For example, were some speech features described as formal, or restricted to particular genres or speakers?

6. Have you ever realized you'd gotten something wrong, sociolinguistically, in another language? What happened?

7. An argument against multilingual education is that children will get their different languages mixed up. Do you see anything in this chapter, or the chapter on multilingualism, that addresses that?

special extra discussion questions for students in education programs or faculties

1. How do your profs talk about bilingual education? For example, do they ever express frustration that research and practice can be so far apart?

2. If you've done a school placement or observation, how were speakers of different languages integrated into the classrooms you were in?

3. How does your university's education program address non-native-speaker students? Is there a separate class on how to teach them? Are they lumped in with other non-mainstream students, such as students with learning disabilities?

4. If you're studying at a university in a different country from where you went to school, are the answers to these questions different in the two countries? How so?

other resources

Multilingual education brings out the fighter in people, so researchers in the area often have strong viewpoints. For more, try Alatis and Staczek's *Perspectives on Bilingualism and Bilingual Education* (1985), Farr et al.'s *Ethnolinguistic Diversity and Education* (2010), or Skutnabb-Kangas et al.'s *Social Justice through Multilingual Education* (2009).

Heath's massively popular *Ways With Words: Language, Life, and Work in Communities and Classrooms* (1983) is an ethnography of how literacy works in a southern community. The classic variationist study of school as a sociolinguistic community is written up by Eckert in *Jocks and Burnouts: Social Categories and Identity in the High School* (1989) and *Linguistic Variation as Social Practice: The Linguistic Construction of Identity in Belten High* (2000). A description of some sociolinguistically informed techniques that have been tried in classrooms can be found in Rickford's "Using the vernacular to teach the standard," which you can read online at http://www.stanford.edu/~rickford/papers/VernacularToTeachStandard.html (accessed August 21, 2011).

Hornberger and McKay's *Sociolinguistics and Language Education* (2010) is aimed at applied linguists and educators.

You can read accessible and personalized accounts of what it's like to be a multilingual kid in a monolingual school setting in *Tongue Tied: The Lives of Multilingual Children in Public Schools*, edited by Santa Ana (2004).

Ferguson's *Language Planning and Education* (2006), as the title suggests, brings together many of the ideas covered in this and the previous chapter.

Journals include the *International Journal of Bilingual Education and Bilingualism*, http://www.tandf.co.uk/journals/1367-0050 (accessed August 21, 2011). Most journals about bilingualism or education will include work on bilingual education.

What is Sociolinguistics? 15

In this chapter:

- Applying what we know
- African American English
- Summing it all up

This book is not called *Language and Society*. It's called *What Is Sociolinguistics?* As part of that, it's supposed to be about how sociolinguists think and work, not just what they've discovered. So, what is sociolinguistics? The answer, it seems, is still "it depends who you ask." But another valid answer is "a bunch of things at the same time." Over the past 14 chapters, we've looked at different aspects of the relationship between language and society, and the different methods and theoretical positions associated with each of them. One of the biggest challenges for me has been deciding what goes where. Can we really talk about language planning without considering the role of language in education, probably the most influential domain of language planning? Can we consider ethnicity without class? Language contact without place?

The point of this last chapter is to try to draw these strands together, by investigating how different sociolinguistic approaches can tell us something useful about a single language variety – and vice versa. I chose African American English (AAE) to illustrate

What Is Sociolinguistics?, First Edition. Gerard Van Herk.
© 2012 Gerard Van Herk. Published 2012 by Blackwell Publishing Ltd.

this for a few reasons: it's a variety I've worked on, people in many countries are at least vaguely familiar with it through either personal experience or media, it's been addressed in major sociolinguistic debates, and most people understand the central role that AAE and its speakers have played in discussion of social issues. In fact, a cliché when people discuss inequality or representation is to replace the social distinction being discussed with Black/White, and then claim that whatever the other person said would be unacceptable in that context.

> ### As an aside: "Back of the book"
>
> Although I think that this approach will a useful learning exercise, I admit that I was a little hesitant about choosing to approach AAE this way, as this strategy has pushed most discussion of AAE to the back of the book, rather than integrating it throughout. On the upside, it should remind us all that we could take a similar approach to any sociolinguistic variety or situation.

the sociolinguistics of african american english

So, just by way of a reminder, when we talk about AAE we mean the language variety used, at least in informal contexts, by a majority of African slave descendants (Baugh 1991) in the United States. The central role of race in American public discourse has ensured AAE a central role in (American) sociolinguistics – one estimate is that six times as much has been written about AAE as about any other ethnic language variety (Schneider 1996: 3). All of that writing covers many of the same areas as our previous chapters. So let's have a look.

language/society/community

One of the strongest findings of early American sociolinguistic work, in the late 1960s and early 1970s, was the remarkable level of similarity across regional varieties of AAE, and the differences between AAE and other varieties. This argues, in classical sociolinguistic terms, that we should consider AAE speakers a speech community – they share norms about how the language works. Of course, within that (huge) speech community, we expect to see some internal diversity, as well as the effect of local communities of practice and social networks. See, for example, Edwards (1992), who shows that rates of use of AAE features vary depending on how much a speaker is plugged into local networks.

The language/dialect distinction has sometimes been contentious for AAE, with some people preferring terms like "African American Language" or "Ebonics" (Williams 1975), which foreground the ways that AAE is different from varieties of English. On linguistic grounds of mutual comprehensibility, though, most of us would describe AAE as a variety of English. Many researchers prefer the term "African American Vernacular English," to remind us that not every American with African ancestry uses all the features of the vernacular.

place

Some researchers argue that AAE is basically a regional (Southern) variety that became seen as an ethnic variety when millions of Southern AAE speakers moved into northern US cities early in the 1900s. This also helps explain the internal consistency of AAE in cities that are far from each other. Despite this consistency, there are still regional differences within AAE. The language spoken by many African Americans in coastal South Carolina and Georgia is distinct enough that it has its own name – Gullah – and is usually described as a creole. Elsewhere, we note regional pronunciation differences. For example, the NURSE and SQUARE vowels are merged in the AAE of St. Louis and parts of Maryland, a pronunciation that came to many people's attention through the work of St. Louis performer Nelly (and now you hear people all over say things like *I'm gettin' my hurr did*, 'I'm getting my hair done').

We might expect stronger regional distinctions to develop over time, as speakers in different cities move further generations away from their Southern roots. But some regional differences may have been there all along – in my thesis, I looked at letters written by African American settlers in Liberia in the mid-1800s, and already there were differences between writers from the Deep South and from farther north (Van Herk 2002). Some of these differences reflected different levels of use of features from the language of the surrounding White communities, a distinction that remains active today (see, for example, Mallinson & Childs, forthcoming).

And AAE is clearly influenced by *social* meanings of place and space. Racial residential segregation remains strong in many American cities, leading to the social isolation of AAE speakers from speakers of other varieties. Some research (such as Labov & Harris 1986) suggests that in some ways, AAE and other varieties are actually diverging – moving farther apart.

social status

The links between race, urbanization, and socio-economic status (SES) mean that many of the differences we observe between AAE and other varieties reflect differences in the economic and social opportunities available to their speakers, not just retained historical features. In fact, although the linguistic details differ, the social patterning of language variation among AAE speakers often reminds us of similar patterns in the language of lower-SES speakers elsewhere. This includes status differences *within* the African American community – Wolfram's (1969) study of Detroit AAE shows clear class distinctions in the use of particular non-standard features. One way that AAE may differ from some varieties in this respect is the greater emphasis placed on community membership and authenticity by some speakers. This requires speakers to affirm community membership even as they adopt features of the standard. Spears (1998, 1998) shows how speakers have constructed a Standard AAE that allows them to bridge this divide.

Variationists and others have done much work on the origins of AAE, partly to offset earlier inattention or ignorance. We don't all agree on where all the features of AAE came from: different researchers propose different levels of input from earlier English, dialects, language contact phenomena, creoles, and/or African languages. Sometimes our disagreements get messy and loud, but we do agree that AAE, like any other language variety, has a long pedigree, and that contemporary features reflect historical retentions or developments from them, rather than random errors.

Researchers also take advantage of AAE's non-mainstream status to study linguistic changes, which tend to happen much faster in varieties that don't have pundits insisting on how they should be written. For example, the future form *fixin' to*, as in *we're fixin' to leave*, moved very quickly in AAE to *finna* (Smith 2009) and even *fon* (the last part presumably by analogy with *gonna* and *gon'*, as in *they gon' tell you*).

With respect to age and the acquisition of sociolinguistic competence, recent work (Renn 2011) looks at AAE-speaking children and their ability to shift between dialects. It seems that the period between grades 1 and 6 (ages 6 and 11, roughly) is when most of the increase in dialect shifting happens. Renn encourages schools to consider this the important age group for making students overtly aware of the differences between their home and school languages, to improve their chances of academic success.

> ## As an aside: Ax me about history
>
> The first thing many non-speakers of AAE say when I tell them I work on earlier AAE is, "Why do they say *ask* wrong?" People are always surprised when I point out that this is one of the many features that AAE and Caribbean creoles retain from the English of past centuries. Earlier English allowed both *ask* and *aks*, just like English today allows *either* to be pronounced eye-thur or ee-thur. See, for example, this sentence from a letter by Margaret Paston, a woman of the gentry writing in the mid-1400s: *sche axyd me jf I had spokyn to my lady.*

---

culture and ethnicity

Earlier in this section, I seemed to be suggesting that a lot of what makes AAE distinct derives from its regional and class origins, rather than the ethnicity of its speakers. But this is not true for all aspects of AAE. Some aspects of African American speech, especially in the South, can be traced to African or creole (and thus ethnically determined) roots. These include semi-linguistic features like *suck-teeth*, which African Americans share with African and Caribbean people (Rickford & Rickford 1976), as well as words like *goober* or *pinder* ('peanut') or *benne* ('sesame') and, perhaps, some grammatical or pronunciation features (we're still arguing about that). The African roots are especially evident in Gullah – Turner (1949) traces scads of words, mostly names, back to African origins.

And, of course, once a linguistic form becomes *associated* with AAE, no matter where it came from, it gains ethnic connotations for speakers and listeners. Human resources people who hear somebody pronounce *ask* as *aks* and decide they'd be good janitors

(Henderson 2001, remember) aren't responding to the pronunciation's medieval origins, after all. And once a language feature picks up African American associations, speakers can use the feature to "borrow" those associations or connotations, even if they're not African American themselves. For example, young White male rap fans might want to borrow elements of street credibility or masculinity that they associate with AAE speakers (Cutler 1999).

gender and identity

Sociolinguists working on AAE have tended to go after the most non-standard speakers they can find. Especially in early work, these were often young urban males, sometimes gang-affiliated. This quest for authenticity has led to a masculinized view of the variety (although probably no more masculinized than work in traditional dialectology, seeking out old rural men). More recent work, with a stronger identity focus, has underlined the interactions between gender and ethnicity, so that what it means (linguistically) to be African American varies by gender, and what it means to be female varies by ethnicity. This broadening focus includes the publication, perhaps overdue, of a volume on African American women's language, from an identity perspective (Lanehart 2009).

style and code shifting

Research on style often observes similarities between the social forces influencing people's style shifting decisions and those involved in language shifting in bilingual communities: audience and speaker design, attention to speech, and all the components of SPEAKING. AAE style shifting can be seen as straddling the boundary between style shifting and code-switching, because AAE is a named (and sometimes marked) divergence from the standard (or vice versa, depending on how you look at it). Speakers using AAE and a more mainstream variety are drawing from their usual repertoire, but the components of that repertoire are seen as very distinct. Some researchers would consider this a type of code-switching. But Labov (1972b: 189) argues against that by analyzing a short passage where a 12-year-old African American speaker switches at an astonishing rate between grammatical and pronunciation forms associated with AAE (lower case in the example) and with Standard English (UPPER CASE). Sometimes a Standard grammatical form will have AAE pronunciation, or a single word will have pronunciations associated with the different varieties:

> An' den like IF YOU MISS ONESIES, de OTHuh person shoot to skelly; ef he miss, den you go again. An' IF YOU GET IN, YOU SHOOT TO TWOSIES. An' IF YOU GET IN TWOSIES, YOU GO TO tthreesies.

Labov says that this shows that what's going on here isn't really code-switching, but rather the speaker navigating the middle of his stylistic range. That's not to say that some switching isn't closer in form and intent to full-on code-switching, as there are contexts where either AAE or mainstream varieties are most called for.

interaction

In chapter 9, we discussed how differences in face needs between AAE-speaking custom-ers and Korean shopkeepers led to misunderstanding and distrust. But there is also a good deal of sociolinguistic work on other aspects of interaction in AAE, including speech acts. Mitchell-Kernan (1972) discusses a few: *signifying* – indirect language, often insulting; *loud-talking* – addressing someone loudly enough for others to hear; and *marking* – imitatively reporting another person's speech (I'm obviously simplifying the definitions here). All three speech acts involve a roundabout way of getting across a message, often (but not necessarily) negative. They work because the audience is aware of what the speaker is trying to do. In other words, these techniques are highly depend-ent on sociolinguistic context for their success.

language contact and creoles

How creole is AAE? Was it more creole in an earlier time? Many linguistic features of AAE sound like (and sometimes behave like) features found in creoles. Note in particu-lar the absence of the copula (the verb *be*) in sentences like *he gonna be sorry*, which AAE shares with many English-based creoles, but virtually no other English dialects. On the other hand, there are many other features of AAE and other varieties in the African diaspora that show up in traditional dialects with no African input, such as Newfound-land English. Scholars of AAE and creoles are often amazed when I tell them that many Newfoundlanders say things like *They're steady telling me that* or *She been left him* or *Give it to she*. And, of course, AAE lexical features are widespread in modern varieties of English, especially in youth slang.

attitudes and ideologies

I've already mentioned the strong negative attitudes toward AAE held by non-community members, revealed through matched guise techniques (Henderson 2001), and their real-world consequences (Purnell et al. 1999). Similar attitudes are also held by some people within the African American community, although results vary by age and time of the study: high school students favor Standard English guises in Hensley (1972), but chil-dren and pre-adolescents favor AAE guises in Linn and Piché (1982) and in Koch and Gross (1997), and adults have more negative views of AAE than youth do in Lovett and Neely (1997). In this, AAE seems to pattern like many other stigmatized varieties – it's people of the right age to be in the workforce who distance themselves most strongly from the non-standard.

language planning and education

A major component of language planning is the choice of the language (or language variety) in which schooling takes place. Given the perception many people seem to have of AAE, as the opposite of educated speech, it's no surprise that even the mention of AAE in discussions of education leads to strong reactions. There has been legal support for the idea of taking AAE-speaking children's home language variety into account in the school system since the famous (to sociolinguists) Ann Arbor trial of 1973, in which the judge ruled that not doing so contributed to students' school failure.

But in 1996, when the Oakland (California) school board proposed acknowledging the linguistic differences between AAE and Standard English in school efforts to teach standard English and literacy, public reaction was intense and largely negative. This was due, in large part, to the (mistaken) assumption that the board planned to *teach* AAE. People also objected to the board's use of the term "genetically based" (in the sense in which French is "genetically" descended from Latin), which implied that AAE use was racially determined. Although linguists came out strongly in support of an amended version of the school board's position, or at least the reasoning behind it, this turned into another of those situations where many in the mainstream (especially in the media) refused to acknowledge that linguists might know something useful about addressing language issues.

summing up (the book, not just the chapter)

If only to avoid ending the book with a complaint that nobody listens to linguists, let's briefly consider what we've covered since we started. The main thing that strikes me is how messy all of this is. Not just the book, but sociolinguistics as a discipline, and language and society as objects of study. Everything's complicated – far more complicated than the way I lay things out over fifteen chapters. This is a good thing, I think. As Wardhaugh (2006) reminds us, language is complex because it's a social thing, and society is complex. So any attempts to reduce it to formulas or approaches that don't acknowledge all that complexity seem a little suspicious.

That doesn't mean that we can't try to figure out what's going on, of course. What we can do is pick a subset of the whole big mess – maybe a particular community, or language feature, or time period – and use what we've learned from others to ask the right research questions. We hope that what we discover contributes to the larger pool of knowledge (especially if we luck into a situation that offers possible answers to difficult questions), but we accept that we might just end up describing how things work in a particular place and time, for particular speakers.

If this sounds like I'm advocating for tiny research, it's probably because I am. There *are* big studies waiting to be done, studies that need money and people and expertise and equipment. But you, the reader, have the potential to contribute something useful to sociolinguistic knowledge right now (the money and equipment can come later).

You're a member of one or more sociolinguistic communities. You know something about the attitudes and norms of the communities that you deal with. And, I hope, you're developing the heightened awareness and skills needed to understand and explain them. Everybody's a potential sociolinguist. Go find out some stuff. Let me know how it goes.

All the best,

Gerard

---

exercises

1. Pick any two topics (chapter titles) from this book. Consider how they relate to each other.
2. Write a letter to future readers of this book, or future students of the course that you have read it for. Give them advice on what to look out for, how do get more out of it, or how to do well.
3. Pick another language variety and take the same approach to it as we have here for AAE. Which of the topics covered in the book seem to be the most relevant to understanding the sociolinguistics of the variety that you chose?
4. Google "ebonics humor." How much of it is actually about AAE (Ebonics)? What racial attitudes are evident in the choices of the humor writers? (For more on this, you might want to read the chapter "Ebonics 'humor'" in Rickford and Rickford's *Spoken Soul: The Story of Black English* (2000).)
5. Ask people what makes AAE distinct. Notice what kinds of things they mention.

---

discussion

1. Let's assume you read this book because you had to, for a course. If somebody asked you to explain what you've learned (or at least been exposed to) in the course, what would you say? Have your attitudes toward any aspects of language and society changed during the course?
2. What aspects of sociolinguistics do you wish you knew more about?
3. If you were to study a community (or some other sociolinguistic topic), which would it be? What would you want to find out?
4. If your home community has very few African Americans, are there still African American speech features or words that people use – maybe even translated into another language? (Yes, I'm talking to you, Koreans!) What social connotations (if any) do these features have? Are they used more by particular people in the community?
5. Have a look back at the discussion questions in chapter 1. Would your comments be different now than they were when you started this book or course?

other resources

Rickford and Rickford's *Spoken Soul: The Story of Black English* (2000) is a readable exploration of AAE. There are more "difficult" (theoretical) sociolinguistic books by Baugh, Green, Lanehart, Mufwene, Poplack and Tagliamonte, Rickford, and Wolfram and Thomas.

Ramirez et al.'s *Ebonics: The Urban Education Debate* (2005) collects writings on the Ebonics controversy.

Studies of AAE show up in a range of journals, including:

American Speech, http://americanspeech.dukejournals.org (accessed August 31, 2011).
Language Variation and Change, http://journals.cambridge.org/action/displayJournal?jid =LVC (accessed August 31, 2011).
Journal of Pidgin and Creole Languages, http://www.benjamins.com/#catalog/journals/jpcl (accessed August 31, 2011).

There's also a whole parallel universe of discussion of AAE in journals devoted to literature or education.

There's a page of resources on AAE at http://linguistlist.org/topics/ebonics (accessed August 21, 2011).

Check out *Word*, the online journal of AAE, at http://africanamericanenglish.com (accessed August 21, 2011).

Glossary

Terms in SMALL CAPITALS within definitions are also defined in this glossary.

accent: Linguists use this term to refer to a speaker's pronunciation (PHONETICS and/or PHONOLOGY) while non-linguists sometimes use it as a synonym for DIALECT. Accents can INDEX where a speaker is from and/or reveal social information, such as social class or level of education.

accommodation: Changing your speech STYLE to sound more like the people you are speaking with.

accommodation theory: A theory that tries to explain why people change their STYLE of speaking to sound more like their INTERLOCUTORS (cf. Giles 1973 and Giles and Powesland 1975).

acrolect: A term used in CREOLE studies to refer to the least creole-like, or most STANDARD or prestigious VARIETY. See also BASILECT, CREOLE CONTINUUM, MESOLECT.

actuation problem: Determining why a particular linguistic change happens when it does.

address forms: See FORMS OF ADDRESS.

adjacency pair: Used in CONVERSATION ANALYSIS, particularly ETHNOGRAPHY OF COMMUNICATION, to refer to a single stimulus-plus-response sequence by participants, that is, one in which a specific type of utterance by one speaker is followed by a specific type by someone else.

adolescent peak: The observation that some VARIANTS (especially incoming variants) are actually most used by adolescents, not by the youngest group.

after perfect: A grammatical means of describing a (usually recent) completed event in Irish (and consequently Newfoundland) English, so that *I'm after doing it* is the equivalent of *I have just done it*.

age grading: When differences between age groups repeat as each generation ages, that is, when all speakers in a particular community favor a particular VARIANT at one age and then a different variant at another. People sometimes change their (reported) behavior over the years as their life situation changes.

What Is Sociolinguistics?, First Edition. Gerard Van Herk.
© 2012 Gerard Van Herk. Published 2012 by Blackwell Publishing Ltd.

agentive: A word borrowed from traditional grammar that, in this field, suggests that there's an active doer or chooser at work. In this framework, people actively perform aspects of their identity, such as GENDER, on the basis of a combination of their own background and experiences and the way they relate to social expectations (by either challenging them or conforming to them).

anti-languages: The LANGUAGE used by oppositional subcultures within a society, usually used to reverse or twist the STANDARD meaning of words for social or political ends (cf. Halliday 1978), such as Rasta talk or I-talk in Rastafarian communities.

apparent time hypothesis: Based on the assumption that people's basic grammar changes very little during adulthood, apparent time studies compare speakers of different ages in a particular community and use this information to describe change over time. Thus, if older speakers are different from younger speakers, it is assumed that this is because change has taken place in the community. Many sociolinguistic studies use this methodology, as opposed to REAL TIME STUDIES.

argot: A specialized type of SLANG, often originally associated with thieves' talk.

aspiration: People often try to talk like who they *want* to be (cf. Chambers 1995, 2009). There's also a linguistic meaning of *aspiration*, about how a consonant is produced.

asymmetrical bilingualism: A bilingual situation in which the less POWERFUL linguistic groups are expected to adopt the LANGUAGE of the powerful group in order to access education or government services or jobs.

attention to speech: Labov (1972b) suggests that different levels of formality result from the amount of attention a speaker pays to the act of speaking. In some activities, such as reading aloud, speakers pay more attention to their speech, while in others, such as talking with friends, they are less attentive.

audience design: Derived from research on interaction, particularly ACCOMMODATION THEORY, audience design theory proposes that speakers STYLE SHIFT on the basis of who they are speaking with or who might overhear them, that is, their audience members (cf. Bell 1984).

Bajan: Also known as Barbadian English, Bajan is sometimes described as a MESOLECTAL or near-ACROLECTAL English-based CREOLE.

basilect: A term used in CREOLE studies to refer to the most creole-like VARIETY, that is, the most distant from the ACROLECT. See also CREOLE CONTINUUM.

borrowed prestige: Speakers' setting and the role they're playing can lead them to use LANGUAGE features associated with a particular class (cf. Labov 1966). See also PRESTIGE, OVERT PRESTIGE, COVERT PRESTIGE.

borrowings: A linguistic form, such as a word, taken from one LANGUAGE or DIALECT and incorporated into another, such that monolingual speakers of the borrowing language use it, sometimes with new associations. Once a word is truly borrowed, it loses its associations with the original language, and is adapted to the pronunciation and word formation rules of the borrowing language.

brokers: People who participate in multiple COMMUNITIES OF PRACTICE and bring ideas from one into the other, that is, people who introduce innovations to their SOCIAL NETWORKS.

Canadian Raising: A PHONOLOGICAL process found in Canadian English (and some other VARIETIES), in which the MOUTH and PRICE vowels (see table 3.2) are pronounced differently when preceding a voiceless consonant in the same syllable, in words like *hike* and *stout*. It's the root of the American STEREOTYPE that Canadians say *oot and aboot* for *out and about*.

caste: In societies where mobility is more difficult and linguistic boundaries are more rigid, social groups, or castes, tend to be fixed, for example, traditional (Hindu) Indian social structure.

categorical: The opposite of PROBABILISTIC, categorical rules are absolute, that is, they apply every time that they can apply.

change from above: Change in a SPEECH COMMUNITY that takes place above the level of conscious awareness and is often subject to overt commentary. It is introduced by the dominant social class.

change from below: Change in a SPEECH COMMUNITY that takes place below the level of conscious awareness and is typically not subject to social commentary. It may be introduced by any social class.

closings: In CONVERSATION ANALYSIS, closings end the interaction. See also OPENINGS, TURN-TAKING.

code: A term often used to mean "LANGUAGE" or "language VARIETY", especially in the term "CODE-SWITCHING." Also, in Saville-Troike and Klefgen (1989), the content and form of an INTERACTION.

code-switching: A common occurrence in bilingual and multilingual communities, code-switching refers to instances in which people alternate between at least two LANGUAGES or language VARIETIES in a single conversation (across sentences or clause boundaries). Sometimes called *code-mixing*. See also EMBEDDED LANGUAGE, MATRIX LANGUAGE.

coining: Creating new words, often through compounding.

communicative competence: Native speakers' ability to produce and understand grammatically acceptable and situationally appropriate sentences. See also PERFORMANCE, SOCIOLINGUISTIC COMPETENCE.

communities of choice: Communities that people choose to belong to, as opposed to communities of circumstance.

community of practice (CofP): Unit of analysis, introduced to SOCIOLINGUISTICS by Penelope Eckert and Sally McConnell-Ginet in their work on LANGUAGE and GENDER, that looks at a smaller analytical DOMAIN than SOCIAL NETWORKS. A community of practice is characterized by mutual engagement, a jointly negotiated enterprise, and a shared repertoire; for example, Eckert's work on jocks and burnouts.

competence: A distinction drawn by Chomsky (1965) (vs. PERFORMANCE) that refers primarily to what speakers know about LANGUAGE. See also COMMUNICATIVE COMPETENCE, SOCIOLINGUISTIC COMPETENCE.

consultant: People from the SPEECH COMMUNITY who are willing to be recorded. Same as INFORMANT.

contact: When speakers of a LANGUAGE or language VARIETY interact with speakers of a different language or language variety.

contrastive analysis: A method, now little used in second language acquisition, that focuses on the similarities and differences between two VARIETIES. In the context of the book's discussion, students are trained to notice the precise ways in which the STANDARD is different from the LANGUAGE they use outside of school.

convergence: ACCOMMODATION toward your INTERLOCUTORS, that is, trying to sound more like the people you're talking to.

conversation analysis: Among other things, this method looks at the sequential organization of conversation and how participants manage the conversation using strategies like TURN-TAKING. Conversation analysis allows researchers to search large collections of recorded natural speech to discover patterns in the distribution of utterances.

co-occurrence restrictions: Constraints on which forms or STYLES can be used together.

corpus (plural corpora):   A collection, usually large, of LANGUAGE in use, that can be adapted to allow linguistic analysis.

corpus linguistics: A linguistic research method based on the QUANTITATIVE analysis of collections of naturally occurring LANGUAGE data, usually very large.

corpus planning: A type of LANGUAGE PLANNING concerned with the internal structure of the LANGUAGE, with choosing between available VARIANTS within that language in order to build up a language to the point it can be used for all the requirements of a modern society. Also known as *language development.*

covert prestige: A norm or target that speakers unconsciously orient to, with a sort of hidden positive evaluation that speakers give to (usually NON-STANDARD) forms. The linguistic equivalent of *street credibility* (cf. Trudgill 1972). See also BORROWED PRESTIGE, OVERT PRESTIGE, PRESTIGE.

creole: A LANGUAGE VARIETY that develops out of a PIDGIN in a language CONTACT situation. Unlike a pidgin, a creole is spoken as a first language of some community or group of speakers, and can be used in the entire range of social settings. See also CREOLE CONTINUUM.

creole continuum: Subvarieties of CREOLES fall along a continuum, ranging from BASILECT, the least STANDARD, to ACROLECT, the most standard. MESOLECT VARIETIES fall in the middle.

critical discourse analysis (CDA):   The underlying assumption of this practice is that texts promote or reproduce ideologies, and that people can be trained to critically read these texts, to be aware of what these texts are doing to them. Also known as CRITICAL LANGUAGE AWARENESS.

critical language awareness: See CRITICAL DISCOURSE ANALYSIS.

crossing: When speakers use LANGUAGE features or linguistic STYLES associated with another ethnic group (cf. Rampton 1995).

crossover effect: In formal situations, speakers using PRESTIGE VARIANTS even more often than the group above them, the people they were presumably trying to emulate. See also HYPERCORRECTION, LINGUISTIC INSECURITY.

decreolization: A reduction in the number of CREOLE features in the speech of an individual or community.

dense: A term used to describe the number of connections within a SOCIAL NETWORK. In a low-density network, people know a central member but not each other. In a high-density network, members know and interact with each other. See also MULTIPLEX.

descriptive: A non-evaluative approach to LANGUAGE that is focused on how language is actually used, without deciding if it is "right" or "wrong." Contrasted with PRESCRIPTIVE.

dialect: A term that tends to refer to subvarieties of a single LANGUAGE. Non-linguists sometimes use the term as a synonym for ACCENT, though dialects can differ in terms of not only pronunciation but also words, word and sentence structure, and meaning. See also VARIETY.

dialect atlas: A collection of maps of a given area that show the distribution of various linguistic features.

dialect leveling: The process by which the regional features of the speech of a group of people CONVERGE toward a common norm over time.

dialectology: The study of regional differences in LANGUAGE.

difference model: The idea that GENDER differences in LANGUAGE reflect different cultures of conversation (cf. Tannen 1990). See also DOMINANCE MODEL.

diglossia: A situation in which two distinctly different LANGUAGE VARIETIES co-exist in a SPEECH COMMUNITY, acting as social REGISTERS, in which the high variety is used in formal situations and the low variety among friends (cf. Ferguson 1959).

diphthong: A vowel sound that starts as one sound and ends as another, for example the vowel sound in *bite*, which starts out somewhat like the PALM vowel and ends up somewhat like the FLEECE vowel. See also MONOPHTHONG.

direct indexing: A linguistic feature directly indexes something with social meaning when it is CATEGORICAL and exclusive, for example, using *he* to refer to a man (cf. Ochs 1992). See also INDIRECT INDEXING.

directive function: LANGUAGE used to try to get someone to do something (cf. Hymes 1974a; Malinowski 1923). See also EXPRESSIVE FUNCTION, PHATIC FUNCTION, REFERENTIAL FUNCTION, SPEECH ACT.

discourse: An extended LANGUAGE interaction, that is, longer than a sentence. Also, the study of such interaction.

Discourse (capital D):   A society's way of talking about something that reflects underlying assumptions of the dominant group; these tend to become seen as "common sense" and thus are barely noticeable, despite the influence they have.

discourse analysis: An examination of the structure of a conversation, looking for linguistic regularities.

discourse marker: A word or phrase that isn't really part of sentence structure, but that helps an INTERACTION along. Examples include *well, y'know, I mean, like, know what I'm sayin'?*

discrete: VARIANTS that are clearly distinct from one another, as opposed to GRADIENT. Examples of discrete VARIABLES are the choice between fricative or stop for *th* (*this thing* vs. *dis ting*) or between *going to* and *will* for future marking.

divergence: ACCOMMODATION away from your INTERLOCUTORS, that is, trying to sound less like the people you're talking to.

domain: The social or institutional context of LANGUAGE use.

dominance model: The idea that GENDER differences in LANGUAGE reflect differences in access to POWER (cf. Tannen 1990; Lakoff 1972). See also DIFFERENCE MODEL.

dragging: From GENDER studies, when people use features that both they and their audience know are associated with another group (e.g., the other gender).

dual-language programs: When two LANGUAGES are used for instruction for a fairly long period.

elaborated code: Elaborated codes, typically associated by Bernstein (1961a, 1972) with the middle-class and broader, less MULTIPLEX SOCIAL NETWORKS. Involves STANDARD SYNTAX, complex sentences, preposi-tions, lots of "I," a wide range of adjectives and adverbs, and a lot of qualifying LANGUAGE. See also RESTRICTED CODE.

embedded language: The non-dominant LANGUAGE in CODE-SWITCHING (cf. Myers-Scotton 1993a). See also MATRIX LANGUAGE.

embedding problem: Determining the particular combinations of social and linguistic behaviors in which change happens.

empiricist: The philosophy or approach that we only trust evidence that we find out there in the real world. That is, that knowledge comes through sensory experience.

enclaves: A distinctly bounded geographic area in which many residents share an ethnicity or other social characteristic.

enregisterment: A process through which a linguistic feature or repertoire becomes a socially recognized REGISTER (cf. Agha 2003).

equivalence constraint: A proposed constraint on CODE SWITCHING. Simplified version: switching tends to happen where the sentence structure just before and just after the switch are possible in both LANGUAGES involved.

ethnic hypercorrection: When people use a feature associated with their ethnic group even less often than non-members of the group.

ethnography: A branch of anthropology that deals with the scientific description of individual cultures.

ethnography of communication: The study of DISCOURSE in relation to extralinguistic VARIABLES that identify the social basis of communication using the same sort of methods that anthropologists might use to study other aspects of a culture.

ethnolect: An ethnic VARIETY of a LANGUAGE or DIALECT.

ethnolinguistic vitality (EV):   Rooted in the social psychology of language (cf. Giles et al. 1977), this term refers to how widely a LANGUAGE or VARIETY associated with a particular culture or ethnicity is spoken.

ethnonym: A name or term for an ethnic group.

expanding circle: In descriptions of World Englishes (e.g., Kachru 1985), areas where English does not have an official role but is still widely spoken, as a foreign LANGUAGE, to tourists, or as a shared language of communication, for example, China. See also INNER CIRCLE, OUTER CIRCLE.

expressive function: Language used to express feelings (cf. Hymes 1974a; Malinowski 1923). See also DIRECTIVE FUNCTION, PHATIC FUNCTION, REFERENTIAL FUNCTION, SPEECH ACT.

eye dialect: The use of NON-STANDARD spellings to represent pronunciations of individual words that match those of almost all English speakers, for example, *duz* (*does*), *wurd* (*word*).

face: An individual's public self-image or social persona (cf. Brown & Levinson 1987; Goffman 1955). See also FACE WANTS, NEGATIVE FACE, POLITENESS THEORY, POSITIVE FACE.

face threatening acts: Actions that threaten people's FACE WANTS, forcing the speaker or hearer to choose whether to use POSITIVE POLITENESS or NEGATIVE POLITENESS in response. See also FACE, NEGATIVE FACE, POLITENESS THEORY, POSITIVE FACE.

face wants: The desire to protect one's POSITIVE FACE and NEGATIVE FACE. Also called *face needs*. See also FACE.

fleeing: Avoiding linguistic features associated with another social group.

folk etymology: A change in a word's form based on a mistaken understanding of its meaning or composition.

forms of address: The way in which conversation participants call (or address) each other.

free morpheme constraint: A proposed constraint on CODE SWITCHING. Simplified version: switching can't happen between bound morphemes, word parts that can't stand on their own.

free variation: A term used when the speaker's choice between forms (or VARIANTS) is completely arbitrary and unpredictable. Opposite of STRUCTURED VARIATION.

gender: A socially constructed identity, rather than a biological category. (Contemporary English speakers often use the word *gender* to mean biological sex.)

gender paradox: Emerging from Labov's (2001) principles I, Ia, and II, the idea that women are more likely to use STANDARD forms and lead in CHANGES FROM ABOVE, but are also leaders in CHANGES FROM BELOW the level of awareness (like vowel shifts), which are not necessarily toward higher-PRESTIGE forms.

genre: A category of LANGUAGE use recognized and usually named by the SPEECH COMMUNITY, for example, *crime novel, sermon*. Sometimes confused with REGISTER. See also STYLE.

gradient: VARIABLES that are best measured on a continuous range of values, such as vowel height. See also DISCRETE.

grammatical gender: In some LANGUAGES, such as French and German, a way of classifying nouns, usually as feminine, masculine, or neuter.

Great Vowel Shift (GVS):   A major pronunciation change that took place in England between 1450 and 1750 involving the raising and DIPHTHONGIZATION of most of the vowels of English. It is part of what separates Middle and Modern English.

habitus: Socially learned ways of being that are so ingrained that we don't notice them (cf. Bourdieu 1977).

heritage language: A LANGUAGE that is acquired by individuals raised in homes where the region's dominant language is not (exclusively) spoken.

heterosexual marketplace: The (media-driven) institutionalization of heterosexuality and traditional gender (cf. Eckert 1996).

heuristic: Guidelines for how to approach a research problem.

high involvement style: In CONVERSATION ANALYSIS, a type of interaction involving frequent turn changes, interruption, and overlapping speech.

homosocial: A term used to refer to situations involving same-sex groups or relationships that are (presumed to be) non-sexual, such as fraternities, prisons, and religious orders.

honorific: A FORM OF ADDRESS expressing respect and esteem.

hypercorrection: When people go beyond the highest-STATUS group in using new PRESTIGE features, often a sign of LINGUISTIC INSECURITY, typically when someone middle-class uses a higher-class VARIANT reflecting their desire for upward mobility (cf. Labov 1972b). Also, when people "over-apply" a linguistic rule that's not part of their own VARIETY, for example, pronouncing *hearse* as *hearst* because you know that STANDARD English speakers don't pronounce *first* as *firs'*, like you do. See also CROSSOVER EFFECT.

hyperstyle variable: A VARIABLE where there's more VARIATION within an individual, across STYLES, than there is between individuals of different social backgrounds.

ideology: In linguistics, this term refers to LANGUAGE attitudes or perceptions of language.

immersion: A teaching method in which students who speak one LANGUAGE (usually the socially dominant one) are taught content in another language by (bilingual) teachers.

implicational scale: A scale or ordering that implies that a feature associated with a particular point will also be associated with all points to one side of it.

indexing: See DIRECT INDEXING and INDIRECT INDEXING.

indicator: A VARIABLE that is "below the radar," meaning that it can show differences by age or social group and is often associated with particular characteristics, but is not subject to STYLE SHIFTING. See also MARKER, STEREOTYPE.

indirect indexing: A linguistic feature indirectly indexes something with social meaning when it is not CATEGORICALLY associated with that meaning, but rather is linked to another meaning that is itself linked to that social meaning (cf. Ochs 1992). This definition confuses even me. Go to the text and read examples, and it'll make more sense. See also DIRECT INDEXING.

informant: See CONSULTANT.

inner circle: Areas in which English is an OFFICIAL LANGUAGE and the first language of most people, for example, New Zealand, the United States, Great Britain (cf. Kachru 1985). See also EXPANDING CIRCLE, OUTER CIRCLE.

interaction: A relationship between two or more individuals. In SOCIOLINGUISTICS, it's usually pretty much a synonym for "conversation."

interlocutor: The person with whom you are speaking.

intra-speaker: Within the speaker. Intra-speaker VARIATION is the difference in the way a single speaker talks in two or more different situations.

isogloss: An imaginary boundary or line drawn on a map that separates particular linguistic features, for example, the line across England separating northerners who pronounce the STRUT and FOOT vowels roughly the same from southerners who don't.

isogloss bundle: Many ISOGLOSSES occurring in the same area, likely representing a major DIALECT boundary.

jargon: A REGISTER associated with a particular occupation or activity often develops its own special vocabulary items. Jargon can involve special terms or specialized meanings for existing words. Jargon makes communication more effective for in-group members and can also exclude non-members of a group from participation or understanding.

language: The act of speaking, writing, or signing in a particular situation. See PERFORMANCE.

language bioprogram hypothesis: The argument that similarities among CREOLES arise because all children have access to an innate biological program that leads them to restructure the very basic input of each PIDGIN in the same way.

language death: A complete LANGUAGE SHIFT in which the original LANGUAGE is no longer used by anyone, anywhere.

language maintenance: The study of how LANGUAGES survive, or the continuing use of a (minority) language in the face of a more regionally, socially, or politically dominant language.

language myth: Widely held beliefs about LANGUAGE (that are usually not supported by empirical evidence).

language planning: Conscious efforts by government, society, organizations, etc. to affect the role and STATUS of LANGUAGES. See also LANGUAGE POLICY.

language planning ideologies: The four main motivations for LANGUAGE PLANNING or LANGUAGE POLICY: linguistic assimilation, linguistic pluralism, vernacularization, and internationalization (cf. Cobarrubias 1983).

language policy: Sometimes used synonymously with LANGUAGE PLANNING, language policy refers to the goals underlying the language planning process.

language shift: The gradual replacement of one LANGUAGE by another as the primary language of communication and socialization within a SPEECH COMMUNITY (cf. Weinreich 1953).

language subordination process: From Lippi-Green (1997), the process by which some LANGUAGE VARIETIES are built up and others are put down.

lexical gap: When a particular LANGUAGE doesn't have a word for a particular concept (and thus usually adopts a word from another language), for example, *schadenfreude*.

lexical set: A way of identifying vowels using a set of words in which they occur as opposed to a linguistic symbol (cf. Wells 1982). For example, "the STRUT vowel" is shorthand for "all the words that in most VARIETIES of English are pronounced with the same vowel as in the word *strut*."

lexicon: The vocabulary of a particular LANGUAGE.

lexifier language: The LANGUAGE that supplies most of the vocabulary (i.e., LEXICON) for a PIDGIN or CREOLE.

Likert scale: A scale often used in questionnaires, usually to let respondents indicate how much they agree with or accept a particular statement.

lingua franca: The LANGUAGE used when people who speak different languages need to interact on a regular basis, but have languages that are not MUTUALLY INTELLIGIBLE.

linguistic constraint: A linguistic factor that governs the choice of a particular VARIANT.

linguistic insecurity: The force hypothesized to drive people to use a VARIANT that is thought to be prestigious or correct and that is not part of their own casual speech (cf. Labov 1972b). See also CROSSOVER EFFECT, HYPERCORRECTION.

linguistic isolation: When speakers of a DIALECT or LANGUAGE are cut off from other VARIETIES and have retained older features, so that their variety has developed differently from their sister ones.

linguistic market: The importance of STANDARD LANGUAGE in the social and economic life of the speaker (cf. Sankoff & Laberge 1978).

marked: A very noticeable and often-discussed linguistic element. There's also a linguistic meaning of *marked*: with affixes (so *jump* is UNMARKED, but *jumped* is marked).

marker: A VARIABLE that speakers are less aware of than a STEREOTYPE, but whose use they can control in STYLE SHIFTING. Markers can be affected by a SPEECH COMMUNITY's norms. See also INDICATOR.

matched guise test: A test designed to gauge unexpressed LANGUAGE attitudes by asking subjects to rate recorded speakers on a scale according to traits like social class, intelligence, and friendliness; however, subjects are actually listening to the same speaker or speakers several times, using different ACCENTS or speaking different LANGUAGES (cf. Lambert et al. 1960; Lambert 1967).

matrix language: The dominant LANGUAGE in CODE-SWITCHING (cf. Myers-Scotton 1993b). See also EMBEDDED LANGUAGE.

mentalist: The philosophy or approach that describes how LANGUAGE is represented in the mind.

mesolect: A term used in CREOLE studies to refer to the intermediate VARIETY between BASILECT and ACROLECT. See also CREOLE CONTINUUM.

metaphorical code-switching: When CODE-SWITCHING is used as a sociolinguistic resource, rather than just to respond to context.

Michif: An example of a MIXED LANGUAGE still spoken in and near Manitoba among the Métis, people of mixed Cree and French ancestry.

mixed language: A LANGUAGE that shares components of two or more languages, generally in equal proportions.

monophthongs: A pure vowel sound, spoken in a single place of articulation, with no change in quality, for example, *bat* as opposed to *bite*. See also DIPHTHONG.

morphology: The structure of words or patterns of word formation in a LANGUAGE or language VARIETY. Also the study of these patterns.

multiplex: A term used to describe SOCIAL NETWORKS in which members have multiple connections with one another. The opposite of a uniplex network. See also DENSE.

mutual intelligibility: If people speaking different VARIETIES (of LANGUAGES or DIALECTS) can understand each other, their varieties are mutually intelligible.

nativization: When a word borrowed from another LANGUAGE is changed so that it behaves like a word from our language.

negative face: The want of every adult community member to be left alone, to not be imposed on, to be unimpeded (cf. Brown & Levinson 1987). See also FACE, FACE WANTS, POLITENESS THEORY, POSITIVE FACE.

negative politeness: Ways of interacting with people using negative strategies such as minimizing interactions or apologizing for bothering someone (cf. Brown & Levinson 1987). See also FACE, FACE WANTS, NEGATIVE FACE, POLITENESS THEORY, POSITIVE POLITENESS.

no-naming: Addressing somebody or getting someone's attention without using any ADDRESS FORM at all (cf. Ervin-Tripp 1972).

nonce borrowings: Individual words from another LANGUAGE that are inserted, often being changed to obey the rules of the MATRIX LANGUAGE. See also CODE-SWITCHING.

non-standard: VARIETIES of a LANGUAGE other than the STANDARD.

NORMs: An acronym for "non-mobile older rural males." These speakers are believed to have retained the most traditional speech and are consequently the focus of many DIALECTOLOGY studies.

official language: A LANGUAGE declared the language of a particular region or country as a result of legislation. See also STATUS PLANNING.

openings: In CONVERSATION ANALYSIS, openings begin the interaction. See also CLOSINGS, TURN-TAKING.

outer circle: Areas in which English is historically important as the result of colonial history and plays a large role in public life but is not the first LANGUAGE of the majority (cf. Kachru 1983). Examples include former British colonies in Africa and South Asia. See also EXPANDING CIRCLE, INNER CIRCLE.

overt prestige: Positive or negative assessments of VARIANTS that are in line with the dominant norms associated with sounding "proper" and that people are aware of, often coinciding with the norms of the media, educational institutions, or higher socio-economic classes. See also BORROWED PRESTIGE, COVERT PRESTIGE, PRESTIGE.

panel study: A REAL TIME STUDY that looks at the same members of a SPEECH COMMUNITY at two (or more) points in time, for example, 20 years apart. See also TREND STUDY.

paralinguistic channel cues: Cues (including tempo, pitch, volume, breathing rate, and laughter) that seem to correlate with casual speech.

participant observation: A fieldwork strategy in which the researcher becomes a part of the community, to whatever degree that's possible or permitted, in order to observe it. This usually involves intense engagement with the community over an extended period of time, in some role that makes sense in the context.

passing: From DISCOURSE on ethnicity, when people adopt (linguistic and other) behaviors from another group in order to be taken as authentic members of that group.

performance: What speakers actually produce when speaking (which might be full of false starts, errors, hesitations, and other such "noise," as well as switches between DIALECTS). See also COMMUNICATIVE COMPETENCE.

performative: Typically used in discussion of GENDER, the idea that actions and speech acquire constitutive force and are used to create a particular gender identity (cf. Butler 1990).

phatic function: The use of LANGUAGE to express empathy or SOLIDARITY (cf. Hymes 1974a; Malinowski 1923). Also known as *phatic language*. See also DIRECTIVE FUNCTION, EXPRESSIVE FUNCTION, RAPPORT STYLE, REFERENTIAL FUNCTION, SPEECH ACT.

phonetics: The study of the sounds of human speech, looking primarily at the physical properties of speech sounds. See also PHONOLOGY.

phonology: A major area of linguistics that studies the systematic way in which sounds are arranged to create syllables, words, and other linguistic forms. See also PHONETICS.

physical isolation: A DIALECT or LANGUAGE can be physically or geographically isolated from others, for example, by being on an island.

pidgin: A LANGUAGE VARIETY that is stripped down to its essentials, that is, not very linguistically complex. Pidgins arise in language CONTACT situations, for example, trade, and are used as a LINGUA FRANCA. Often a precursor or early stage of CREOLES, pidgins tend to have a fairly developed vocabulary and basic linguistic structure but, unlike creoles, pidgins are not spoken as a first language and are used in limited social settings. See also CREOLE CONTINUUM.

politeness theory: Based on the notion of FACE, politeness theory argues that people use strategies of POSITIVE POLITENESS and NEGATIVE POLITENESS to negotiate personal interactions (cf. Brown & Levinson 1987). See also FACE WANTS, NEGATIVE FACE.

political correctness: A term originally used in a self-deprecating way within progressive groups. Now popular among defenders of the social status quo to describe (and disparage) social changes and the people who advocate them.

positive face: The desire of every adult community member that their wants be desirable to at least some others, that is, to be valued (cf. Brown & Levinson 1987). See also FACE, FACE WANTS, NEGATIVE FACE, POLITENESS THEORY.

positive politeness: Ways of interacting with people using positive strategies such as friendliness, compliments, and approval (cf. Brown & Levinson 1987). See also FACE, FACE WANTS, NEGATIVE FACE, NEGATIVE POLITENESS, POLITENESS THEORY.

power: An unequal or non-reciprocal relationship between two or more speakers, predicting who (or whose norms) will dominate an interaction.

prescriptive: An approach to LANGUAGE that is focused on rules of correctness, that is, how language "should" be used. Contrasted with DESCRIPTIVE.

prestige: VARIANTS associated with higher-STATUS groups are considered prestige forms. See also BORROWED PRESTIGE, COVERT PRESTIGE, OVERT PRESTIGE.

probabilistic: The opposite of CATEGORICAL, probabilistic constraints are not absolute but rather tendencies in one direction.

proto-pidgin: Part of the RELEXIFICATION HYPOTHESIS, this is the template LANGUAGE into which the actual words of different LEXIFIER LANGUAGES are slotted. See also CREOLE, PIDGIN.

qualitative: Usually smaller-scale intensive research, using methods like interviewing and ETHNOGRAPHY, that aims to study meanings and motivation, rather than large-scale QUANTITATIVE frequencies or correlations.

quantitative: Research that counts or measures stuff. In SOCIOLINGUISTICS, this is usually research that looks at frequencies of use and statistical tests of correlations between a linguistic behavior and some other characteristic.

rapport style: Using LANGUAGE to build and maintain relationships.

real time study: A study that samples a SPEECH COMMUNITY at two or more points in time.

reciprocal naming: An expression of SOLIDARITY, as when friends call each other by their first names.

referential function: Language used to convey information from the speaker to the hearer (cf. Hymes 1974a; Malinowski 1923). See also DIRECTIVE FUNCTION, EXPRESSIVE FUNCTION, PHATIC FUNCTION, REPORT STYLE, SPEECH ACT.

register: A VARIETY of LANGUAGE used in a particular social or economic setting, for example, legal or academic register. See also GENRE.

reified: Made into a concrete thing.

relexification hypothesis: The argument that similarities among CREOLES arise because creoles all over the world have developed from a single template LANGUAGE, which acted as a sort of structural frame into which the actual words of different LEXIFIER LANGUAGES were slotted. See also PIDGIN.

report style: Using LANGUAGE to communicate factual information.

restricted code: Restricted codes, typically associated by Bernstein (1961a, 1972) with the working class and closed, MULTIPLEX SOCIAL NETWORKS (but also accessible to the middle class). Involves NON-STANDARD grammatical constructions that are short, simple, and often unfinished, with few conjunctions, little subordination, dislocated presentation of information, fewer adverb and adjective types, infrequent impersonal pronoun subjects, and frequent comprehension requests. See also ELABORATED CODE.

rhotic: A term used to describe English DIALECTS in which the /r/ following a vowel is pronounced. Also known as *r-ful*. (Dialects that do not pronounce /r/ after vowels are *non-rhotic*.)

salient/salience: Usually refers to a noticeable VARIANT – one that stands out due to physiological, social, and/or psychological factors.

Sapir–Whorf hypothesis: A theory about LANGUAGE and thought that argues that the way a particular language describes the world actually affects its speakers' view of reality.

scripts: In Saville-Troike and Klefgen (1989), the social expectations that people bring to an interaction.

self-fulfilling prophecy: A prophecy that causes itself to become true. The term is often used in education to suggest that high teacher expectations for a particular student lead to success for that student.

shibboleth: When the pronunciation of a single word becomes a STEREOTYPE of a SPEECH COMMUNITY, such as Jamaicans supposedly saying *mon* for *man*.

situational code-switching: When CODE-SWITCHING is constrained by the social context. Also known as *domain-based code-switching.*

slang: Words that are new to a LANGUAGE, or old words or phrases with new meanings. Slang is usually associated with younger speakers and tends to be short-lived.

social category: A way of grouping people by traits that are relatively fixed, such as class, gender, or ethnicity, or open to active PERFORMANCE and construction, like identity.

social constraint: A social factor like sex or age that governs the use of a particular VARIANT.

social distance: Degree of intimacy or familiarity between INTERLOCUTORS.

social hypercorrection: When speakers overdo what they see as the linguistic requirements of a situation (usually in the direction of formality or use of STANDARD VARIANTS).

social isolation: A DIALECT or LANGUAGE can be socially isolated by conventions or attitudes, for example, by class or race prejudice.

social mobility: The ability to move between social classes, often determined by how defined class roles are in a particular culture.

social network: The different groups of people that each of us has interacted with over the years. Each of us participates in multiple networks; our networks are connected through the members that they share, and some of our connections are stronger than others. See also DENSE, MULTIPLEX.

social relationships: How each of us, as social beings, adapt our LANGUAGE to suit the situation and the audience. Often contrasted with social characteristics, the socially relevant traits that we are seen to possess.

societal multilingualism: When multiple LANGUAGES co-exist in a single community.

sociolect: A subset of LANGUAGE used by a particular social group or class. Sometimes called *social* DIALECT.

sociolinguistic competence: The skills and resources needed to be a competent member of a SPEECH COMMUNITY, who can use LANGUAGE grammatically and also appropriately in different contexts. See also COMMUNICATIVE COMPETENCE, PERFORMANCE.

sociolinguistic interview: An interview with different components, to elicit different STYLES of speech, usually in a one-on-one context. The term is also used to refer to an interview conducted for sociolinguistic research.

sociolinguistic norms: A combination of expressed attitudes and variable linguistic behavior shared by all members of a SPEECH COMMUNITY.

sociolinguistics: The study of how LANGUAGE and social factors interact.

sociology of language: The branch of sociology concerned with LANGUAGE. Unlike SOCIOLINGUISTICS, this approach studies the social contexts of language without recourse to analysis of linguistic structure.

solidarity: Closeness or intimacy, or shared STATUS.

speaker agency: The ability of speakers to control what they do and to make conscious choices.

speaker design: Speakers using different STYLES to present themselves differently.

speech act: A communicative activity or utterance that does something. See also DIRECTIVE FUNCTION, EXPRESSIVE FUNCTION, PHATIC FUNCTION, REFERENTIAL FUNCTION.

speech community: A group of people who are in habitual CONTACT with one another, who share a LANGUAGE VARIETY and social conventions, or SOCIOLINGUISTIC NORMS, about language use.

speech event: A group of SPEECH ACTS or interactions.

speech situation: The circumstances and context surrounding the use of speech.

sprachbund: A group of (usually unrelated) LANGUAGES that have become more similar because of geographical proximity.

stable variation: VARIATION without change; when multiple VARIANTS survive for a long period, without one replacing the other.

standard: The codified VARIETY of a LANGUAGE, that is, the language taught in school, used in formal writing, and often heard from newscasters and other media figures who are trying to project authority or ability.

status: Social positions that society assigns to its members, or the differences between social groups, in terms of the PRESTIGE associated with them by others.

status planning: A type of LANGUAGE PLANNING concerned with choosing between available LANGUAGES or language VARIETIES and promoting one over another, often including the declaration of an OFFICIAL LANGUAGE. Also known as *language determination*.

stereotype: A VARIABLE that is socially MARKED, that is, very noticeable and often discussed. See also INDICATOR, MARKER.

stigma: A negative association, something viewed pejoratively.

structured immersion programs: Where students who don't speak the dominant LANGUAGE are taught that language and taught in that language.

structured variation: A term used when the speaker's choice between forms (or VARIANTS) is linked to other factors. Opposite of FREE VARIATION.

style: Intra-speaker ("within the speaker") VARIATION as opposed to variation across groups.

style shifting: An individual's speech changes according to differences in INTERLOCUTOR(s), social context, personal goals, or external factors.

substrate: A VARIETY that has influenced the structure or use of another, more dominant variety. See also SUPERSTRATE.

superstrate: A VARIETY that has influenced the structure or use of another, less dominant variety, as evidenced by the influences of LANGUAGES like English and Arabic on other languages. See also SUBSTRATE.

supralocal: A term used to refer to the level "above the local," in which speakers adopt the LANGUAGE features of the nearest large city, leading to a clumping of tiny DIALECT areas into bigger ones.

syntax: A LANGUAGE's sentence structure. Also the study of this structure.

T form: Originally named from the French *tu*, a FORM OF ADDRESS in many LANGUAGES used reciprocally among family and close friends or to people of lower STATUS (cf. Brown & Gilman 1960). See also V FORM.

trend study: A REAL TIME study that studies different members of a SPEECH COMMUNITY at different times, for example, talking to people who are 20, 40, and 60 now and then other people who are 20, 40, and 60 twenty years in the future. See also PANEL STUDY.

turn-taking: Part of CONVERSATION ANALYSIS that looks at how speakers share the conversational floor, or right to speak.

uniformitarian principle: The idea that the general properties of LANGUAGE and language change have been the same throughout history and we are thus able to look at the changes going on today and assume that the same kind of forces were at play in the past.

unmarked: The opposite of MARKED, that is, a linguistic feature that does not get noticed. There's also a linguistic meaning of *unmarked*: without affixes, as in *jump* vs. *jumped*.

unstable multilingualism: Temporary or fleeting instances of social multilingualism.

V form: Originally named from the French *vous*, a FORM OF ADDRESS in many LANGUAGES used among people who are not close or to people of higher STATUS (cf. Brown & Gilman 1960). See also T FORM.

variable: The abstract representation of a source of VARIATION, realized by at least two VARIANTS, for example, *gonna* and *will* are variants of the variable *future temporal reference*.

variant: The different expressions, or actual realizations, of a VARIABLE, for example, pronouncing the suffix *-ing* as "ing" or "in."

variation: Different ways of doing something.

variationist: A researcher who focuses on VARIATIONIST SOCIOLINGUISTICS.

variationist sociolinguistics: The study of LANGUAGE use by describing and explaining the distribution of VARIABLES according to social and linguistic characteristics, with a strong focus on quantitative analysis.

variety: A value-neutral term for any LANGUAGE or DIALECT.

Whiteness: A term from social sciences that emphasizes that Whiteness, like other ethnic characteristics, is marked and nameable. White privilege is said to gain its power in part from the fact that Whiteness is usually *not* examined or seen as a separate, noticeable thing.

Bibliography

Abdulaziz, Mohamed H. "East Africa (Tanzania and Kenya)." In *English Around the World: Sociolinguistic Perspectives*, ed. Jenny Cheshire, 391–401. Cambridge: Cambridge University Press, 1991.

Adams, Michael. *Better Happy than Rich? Canadians, Money and the Meaning of Life*. Toronto: Penguin, 2000.

Agha, Asif. "The social life of cultural value." *Language and Communication* 23 (2003): 231–73.

Alatis, James E., and John J. Staczek, eds. *Perspectives on Bilingualism and Bilingual Education*. Washington, DC: Georgetown University Press, 1985.

Alim, Samy, Awad Ibrahim, and Alastair Pennycook, eds. *Global Linguistic Flows: Hip Hop Cultures, Identities, and the Politics of Language*. Mahwah, NJ: Lawrence Erlbaum, 2009.

Al-Wer, Enam. "Arabic between reality and ideology." *International Journal of Applied Linguistics* 7, no. 2 (1997): 251–65.

Ammon, Ulrich. "The present dominance of English in Europe." *Sociolinguistica* 8 (1994): 1–14.

Andersen, Elaine S. *Speaking with Style: The Sociolinguistic Skills of Children*. London and New York: Routledge, 1992.

Andrzejewski, Bogumil W. "The implementation of language planning in Somalia: A record of achievement." *Language Planning Newsletter* 6, no. 1 (1980): 1 and 4–5.

Assiri, Ahmad. "Sociolinguistic variation in Rijaal Alma?, Saudi Arabia." Presented at Change and Variation in Canada II, Ottawa, ON, June 21–2, 2008.

Atagi, Eriko. "Are you a native speaker? The role of ethnic background in the hallucination of foreign accents on native speakers." Presented at NWAVE 32, Philadelphia, PA, 2003.

Atkinson, Dwight. "A critical approach to critical thinking in TESOL." *TESOL Quarterly* 31 (1997): 71–94.

Austin, J. L. *How to Do Things with Words*. London: Oxford University Press, 1962.

Bailey, Benjamin H. "Communication of respect in service encounters between immigrant Korean retailers and African American customers." Master's thesis, University of California at Los Angeles, 1996.

Bailey, Guy, Natalie Maynor, and Patricia Cukor-Avila, eds. *The Emergence of Black English: Texts and Commentary*. Amsterdam: John Benjamins, 1991a.

Bailey, Guy, Tom Wikle, Jan Tillery, and Lori Sand. "The apparent time construct." *Language Variation and Change* 3 (1991b): 241–64.

Baker, Carolyn. "Literacy practices and social relations in classroom reading events." In *Towards a Critical Sociology of Reading Pedagogy*, eds. Carolyn Baker and Allan Luke, 161–90. Amsterdam: John Benjamins, 1991.

Bakhtin, Mikhail. "Discourse in the novel." In Mikhail Bakhtin, *The Dialogic Imagination*, ed. Michael Holquist,

What Is Sociolinguistics?, First Edition. Gerard Van Herk.
© 2012 Gerard Van Herk. Published 2012 by Blackwell Publishing Ltd.

trans. Caryl Emerson and Michael Holquist, 259–422. Austin: University of Texas Press, 1981 (1st pub. 1935).

Bakhtin, Mikhail. "The problem of speech genres." In Mikhail Bakhtin, *Speech Genres and Other Late Essays*, eds. Caryl Emerson and Michael Holquist, trans. Vern W. McGee, 60–102. Austin: University of Texas Press, 1986 (1st pub. 1953).

Bakir, Murtadha. "Sex differences in the approximation to standard Arabic: A case study." *Anthropological linguistics* 28 (1986): 3–9.

Bakker, Peter, and Maarten Mous, eds. *Mixed Languages: 15 Case Studies of Language Intertwining*. Amsterdam: IFOTT, 1994.

Baron, Naomi S. *Always On: Language in an Online and Mobile World*. Oxford and New York: Oxford University Press, 2008.

Barrett, Rusty. "Supermodels of the world, unite! Political economy and the language of performance among African American drag queens." In *Beyond the Lavender Lexicon: Authenticity, Imagination, and Appropriation in Lesbian and Gay Languages*, ed. William Leap, 207–26. Amsterdam: Gordon and Breach, 1995.

Barrett, Rusty. "Markedness and styleswitching in performances by African American drag queens." In *Codes and Consequences: Choosing Linguistic Varieties*, ed. Carol Myers-Scotton, 139–61. New York: Oxford University Press, 1998.

Basso, Keith H. "To give up on words: Silence in Western Apache culture." In *Language and Social Context: Selected Readings*, ed. Pier Paolo Giglioli, 67–86. New York: Penguin, 1972.

Basso, Keith H. *Portraits of "The Whiteman": Linguistic Play and Cultural Symbols among the Western Apache*. Cambridge and New York: Cambridge University Press, 1979.

Bauer, Laurie, and Peter Trudgill, eds. *Language Myths*. New York: Penguin, 1998.

Baugh, John. "The politicization of changing terms of self-reference among American slave descendants." *American Speech* 66, no. 2 (1991): 133–46.

Baugh, John. *Out of the Mouths of Slaves*. Austin: University of Texas Press, 1999.

Baugh, John. "Linguistic profiling." In *Black Linguistics: Language, Society, and Politics in Africa and the Americas*, eds. Sinfree Makoni, Geneva Smitherman, Arnetha F. Ball, and Arthur K. Spears, 155–68. London: Routledge, 2003.

Beattie, James. *The Theory of Language*. Menston: Scolar Press, 1968 (1st pub. 1788).

Bell, Allan. "Language style as audience design." *Language in Society* 13 (1984): 145–204.

Bell, Allan. "Style in dialogue: Bakhtin and sociolinguistic theory." In *Sociolinguistic Variation: Theories, Methods, and Applications*, eds. Robert Bayley and Ceil Lucas, 90–109. Cambridge: Cambridge University Press, 2007.

Bell, Allan, and Gary Johnson. "Towards a sociolinguistics of style." *University of Pennsylvania Working Papers in Linguistics* 4 (1997): 1–12.

Bereiter, Clark, and Seigfried Engelmann. *Teaching Disadvantaged Children in the Preschool*. Englewood Cliffs, NJ: Prentice Hall, 1966.

Bernstein, Basil. "Social class and linguistic development: A theory of social learning." In *Education, Economy and Society*, eds. A. H. Halsey, Jean Floud, and C. Arnold Anderson, 288–314. New York: Free Press, 1961a.

Bernstein, Basil. "Social structure, language and learning." *Educational Research* 3 (1961b): 163–76.

Bernstein, Basil. "A sociolinguistic approach to socialization with some reference to educability." In *Directions in Sociolinguistics: Ethnography of communication*, eds. John Gumperz and Dell Hymes, 465–97. New York: Holt, Rinehart & Winston, 1972.

Bialystok, Ellen. "Influences of bilingualism on metalinguistic development." *Second Language Research* 3 (1987): 154–66.

Biber, Douglas, and Edward Finegan. "Drift in three English genres from the 18th to the 20th centuries: A multidimensional approach." In *Corpus Linguistics, Hard and Soft*, eds. Merja Kyto, Ossi Ihalainen, and Matti Rissanen, 83–101. Amsterdam: Rodopi, 1988.

Biber, Douglas, and Edward Finegan, eds. *Sociolinguistic Perspectives on Register*. Oxford: Oxford University Press, 1994.

Blake, Renée. "All o' we is one? Race, class and language in a Barbados community." PhD dissertation, Stanford University, 1997.

Blom, Jan-Petter, and John Gumperz. "Social meaning in linguistic structures: Code switching in northern Norway." In *Directions in Sociolinguistics: The Ethnography of Communication*, eds. John Gumperz and Dell Hymes, 407–34. New York: Holt, Rinehart & Winston, 1972.

Blommaert, Jan. *Discourse: A Critical Introduction*. Cambridge: Cambridge University Press, 2005.

Blondeau, Hélène, Naomi Nagy, Gillian Sankoff, and Pierrette Thibault. "La couleur locale du français des

Anglo-Montréalais." In *L'Acquisition de la Variation par les Apprenants du Français Langue Seconde*, eds. Jean-Marc Dewaele and Raymond Mougeon, 73–100. Paris: L'Association Encrages, 2002.

Bloomfield, Leonard. "A set of postulates for the science of language." *Language* 2 (1926): 153–64.

Boas, Franz. *Handbook of American Indian Languages*. Washington, DC: Smithsonian Institution, 1911.

Boberg, Charles. "Sex, gender, and the phonetics of Canadian English." Presented at NWAV 35, Ohio State University, Columbus, 2006.

Bodine, Ann. "Androcentrism in prescriptive grammar: singular 'they', sex-indefinite 'he', and 'he or she.'" *Language in Society* 4 (1975): 129–46.

Bonfiglio, Thomas Paul. *Race and the Rise of Standard American*. Berlin and New York: Mouton, 2002.

Bourdieu, Pierre. *Outline of a Theory of Practice*. Cambridge: Cambridge University Press, 1977.

Bourdieu, Pierre. *Distinction: A Social Critique of the Judgement of Taste*, trans. R. Nice. London: Routledge and Kegan Paul, 1984 (1st pub. 1979).

Bourdieu, Pierre. *State Nobility*. Cambridge: Polity, 1998.

Bourdieu, Pierre, and Luc Boltanski. "Le titre et le poste: Rapports entre le système de production et le système de reproduction." *Actes de la Recherche en Sciences Sociales* 2 (1975): 95–107.

Bourhis, Richard, and Howard Giles. "The language of intergroup distinctiveness." In *Language, Ethnicity, and Intergroup Relations*, ed. Howard Giles, 119–35. London: Academic Press, 1977.

Bradley, John. "Men speak one way, women another." In *Language and Gender: A Reader*, ed. Jenny Coats, 26–35. London: Blackwell, 1998.

Britain, David. "Dialect and space: A geolinguistic study of speech variables in the Fens." PhD dissertation, University of Essex, 1991.

Britain, David. "Space and spatial diffusion." In *The Handbook of Variation and Change*, eds. J. K. Chambers, Peter Trudgill, and Natalie Schilling-Estes, 603–37. Oxford: Blackwell, 2002.

Brown, Penelope, and Stephen C. Levinson. *Politeness: Some Universals in Language Usage*. Cambridge: Cambridge University Press, 1987.

Brown, Roger, and Albert Gilman. "The pronouns of power and solidarity." In *Style in Language*, ed. Thomas A. Sebeok, 156–76. Cambridge, MA: MIT Press, 1960.

Brun, Auguste. *Parlers Régionaux, France Dialectale et Unité Française*. Paris: Didier, 1946.

Bucholtz, Mary. "Geek the girl: Language, femininity, and female nerds." In *Gender and Belief Systems: Proceedings of the Fourth Berkeley Women and Language Conference*, eds. Natasha Warner, Jocelyn Ahlers, Leela Bilmes, Monica Oliver, Suzanne Wertheim, and Mel Chen, 119–31. Berkeley: Berkeley Women and Language Group, 1998.

Bucholtz, Mary. "'Why be normal?' Language and identity practices in a community of nerd girls." *Language in Society* 28 (1999): 203–23.

Bucholtz, Mary. "The Whiteness of nerds: Superstandard English and racial markedness." *Journal of Linguistic Anthropology* 11, no. 1 (2001): 84–100.

Bucholtz, Mary. *White Kids: Language, Race, and Styles of Youth Identity*. New York: Cambridge University Press, 2011.

Bucholtz, Mary, and Kira Hall. "Identity and interaction: A sociocultural linguistic approach." *Discourse Studies* 7, no. 4–5 (2005): 585–614.

Butler, Judith. *Gender Trouble: Feminism and the Subversion of Identity*. New York: Routledge, 1990.

Cameron, Deborah. "Performing gender identity: Young men's talk and the construction of heterosexual masculinity." In *Language and Masculinity*, eds. Sally Johnson and Ulrike Hanna Meinhof, 45–64. Malden, MA: Blackwell, 1997.

Cameron, Deborah, and Don Kulick. *Language and Sexuality*. Cambridge: Cambridge University Press, 2003.

Cameron, Deborah, and Don Kulick, eds. *The Language and Sexuality Reader*. London: Routledge, 2006.

Canale, Michael, and Merrill Swain. "Theoretical bases of communicative approaches to second language teaching and testing." *Applied Linguistics* 1, no. 1 (1980): 1–47.

Carranza, Michael A., and Ellen B. Ryan. "Evaluative reactions of adolescents toward speakers of standard English and Mexican American accented English." *International Journal of the Sociology of Language* 8 (1975): 3–102.

Cedergren, Henrietta. "The spread of language change: Verifying inferences of linguistic diffusion." *Georgetown University Round Table on Language and Linguistics* (1988): 45–60.

Chambers, J. K. "Dialect acquisition." *Language* 68 (1992): 673–705.

Chambers, J. K. *Sociolinguistic Theory: Linguistic Variation and its Social Significance*. Oxford: Blackwell, 1995, 2009.

Chambers, J. K. "Dynamics of dialect convergence." *Journal of Sociolinguistics* 6 (2002): 117–30.

Chambers, J. K., and Peter Trudgill. *Dialectology*. Cambridge: Cambridge University Press, 1980.

Chambers, J. K., Peter Trudgill, and Natalie Schilling-Estes, eds. *The Handbook of Language Variation and Change*. Malden, MA: Blackwell, 2002.

Charity, Ann. "Regional differences in low SES African-American children's speech in the school setting." *Language Variation and Change* 19 (2007): 281–93.

Charity, Ann H., Hollis S. Scarborough, and Darion M. Griffin. "Familiarity with school English in African American children and its relation to early reading achievement." *Child Development* 75, no. 5 (2004): 1340–56.

Cheshire, Jenny. *Variation in an English Dialect: A Sociolinguistic Study*. Cambridge: Cambridge University Press, 1982.

Childs, Becky, and Christine Mallinson. "African American English in Appalachia: Dialect accommodation and substrate influence." *English World-Wide* 25 (2004): 27–50.

Childs, Becky, Gerard Van Herk, and Jennifer Thorburn. "Safe harbour: Ethics and accessibility in sociolinguistic corpus building." *Corpus Linguistics and Linguistic Theory* 7, no. 1 (2011): 163–80.

Chomsky, Noam. *Aspects of the Theory of Syntax*. Cambridge: MIT Press, 1965.

Choy, Wayson. *The Jade Peony*. Vancouver: Douglas & McIntyre, 1995.

Clarke, Sandra. "Sampling attitudes to dialect varieties in St. John's." In *Languages in Newfoundland and Labrador*, ed. Harold Paddock, 90–105. St. John's, Newfoundland: Memorial University of Newfoundland, 1982.

Clarke, Sandra. "Newfoundland English: Phonology." In *A Handbook of Varieties of English. Vol. 1: Phonology*, eds. Bernd Kortmann, Edgar W. Schneider, Clive Upton, Rajend Mesthrie, and Kate Burridge, 95–110. Berlin and New York: Mouton, 2004.

Clarke, Sandra. *Newfoundland and Labrador English*. Edinburgh: Edinburgh University Press, 2010a.

Clarke, Sandra. "Newfoundland and Labrador English." In *The Lesser-Known Varieties of English*, eds. Edgar Schneider, Daniel Schreier, Peter Trudgill, and Jeffrey P. Williams, 72–91. New York: Cambridge University Press, 2010b.

Clarke, Sandra, Ford Elms, and Amani Youssef. "The third dialect of English: Some Canadian evidence." *Language Variation and Change* 7 (1995): 209–28.

Clyne, Michael. *Community Languages: The Australian Experience*. Cambridge: Cambridge University Press, 1991.

Clyne, Michael. "Multilingualism." In *The Handbook of Sociolinguistics*, ed. Florian Coulmas, 301–14. Oxford: Blackwell, 1997.

Coates, Jennifer. *Language and Gender: A Reader* (2nd edn). Malden, MA: Blackwell, 2011 (1st pub. 1998).

Cobarrubias, Juan. "Ethical issues in status planning." In *Progress in Language Planning: International Perspectives*, eds. Juan Cobarrubias and Joshua A. Fishman, 41–85. Berlin: Mouton de Gruyter, 1983.

Cooper, Robert Leon. *Language Planning and Social Change*. Cambridge: Cambridge University Press, 1989.

Coulmas, Florian. "Language adaptation." In *Language Adaptation*, ed. Florian Coulmas, 1–25. Cambridge: Cambridge University Press, 1989.

Coulmas, Florian, ed. *The Handbook of Sociolinguistics*. Oxford: Blackwell, 1997.

Coulmas, Florian. *Sociolinguistics: The Study of Speakers' Choices*. Cambridge: Cambridge University Press, 2005.

Coupland, Justine, Nikolas Coupland, Howard Giles, and Karen Henwood. "Formulating age: Dimensions of age identity in elderly talk." *Discourse Processes* 14 (1991): 87–106.

Coupland, Nikolas. "Style-shifting in a Cardiff work-setting." *Language in Society* 9 (1980): 1–12.

Coupland, Nikolas. "The social differentiation of functional language use: A sociolinguistic investigation of travel agency talk." PhD dissertation, UWIST, 1981.

Coupland, Nikolas. "Accommodation at work: Some phonological data and their implications." *International Journal of the Sociology of Language* 46 (1984): 49–60.

Coupland, Nikolas. "Language, situation, and the relational self: Theorizing dialect-style in sociolinguistics." In *Style and Sociolinguistic Variation*, eds. Penelope Eckert and John Rickford, 185–210. Cambridge: Cambridge University Press, 2001

Coupland, Nikolas, and Adam Jaworski, eds. *The New Sociolinguistics Reader*. Basingstoke: Palgrave, 2009.

Coupland, Nikolas, Justine Coupland, and Howard Giles. *Language, Society and the Elderly: Discourse, Identity, and Ageing*. Oxford: Blackwell, 1991.

Crago, M. "Communicative interaction and second language acquisition." *TESOL Quarterly* 26 (1992): 487–506.

Cross, Robert, Andrew Parker, and Lisa Sasson, eds. *Networks in the Knowledge Economy*. New York: Oxford University Press, 2003.

Crystal, David. *English as a Global Language*. Cambridge: Cambridge University Press, 1997.

Crystal, David. *Language Death*. Cambridge: Cambridge University Press, 2000.

Cummins, Jim. "The role of primary language development in promoting educational success for language-minority students." In *Schooling and Language-Minority Students: A Theoretical Framework*, ed. Charles F. Leyba, 1–49. Los Angeles: California State University; Evaluation, Dissemination and Assessment Center, 1981.

Cummins, Jim. "Empowering minority students: A framework or intervention." *Harvard Educational Review* 56, no. 1 (1986): 18–36.

Cummins, Jim. "From multicultural to anti-racist education: An analysis of programmes and policies in Ontario." In *Minority Education: From Shame to Struggle*, eds. Tove Skutnabb-Kangas and Jin Cummins, 127–57. Philadelphia: Multilingual Matters, 1988.

Cummins, Jim. "The empowerment of Indian students." In *Teaching American Indian Students*, ed. Jon Reyhner, 3–12. Norman, OK: University of Oklahoma Press, 1992.

Cunningham, P. M. "Teacher's correction responses to Black-dialect miscues which are non-meaning-changing." *Reading Research Quarterly* 12 (1976–7): 635–53.

Cutler, Cecilia A. "Yorkville Crossing: White teens, hip hop and African American English." *Journal of Sociolinguistics* 3/4 (1999): 428–42.

de Beauvoir, S. *Le Deuxième Sexe*. Paris: Gallimard, 1949.

DeCamp, David. "Toward a generative analysis of a post-creole speech continuum." In *Pidginization and Creolization of Languages*, ed. Dell Hymes, 349–70. Cambridge: Cambridge University Press, 1971.

Dorian, Nancy. "Language shift in community and individual: The phenomenon of the Laggard semi-speaker." *International Journal of the Sociology of Language* 25 (1980): 85–94.

Dorian, Nancy. *Language Death: The Life and Cycle of a Scottish Gaelic Dialect*. Philadelphia: University of Pennsylvania Press, 1981.

Dressler, Wolfgang, and Ruth Wodak-Leodolter. "Language preservation and language death in Brittany." *International Journal of the Sociology of Language* 12 (1977): 33–44.

Dubois, Betty, and Isabel Crouch. "The question of tag questions in women's speech: They really don't use more of them." *Language in Society* 4 (1975): 289–94.

Dubois, Sylvie, and Barbara Horvath. "Let's tink about dat: Interdental fricatives in Cajun English." *Language Variation and Change* 10, no. 3 (1998): 245–61.

Dubois, Sylvie, and Barbara Horvath. "When the music changes, you change too: Gender and language change in Cajun English." *Language Variation and Change* 11, no. 3 (1999): 287–313.

Dubois, Sylvie, William Gautreau, Howard Margot, Megan Melançon, and Tracy Veler. "The quality of French spoken in Louisiana: Linguistic attitudes toward the varieties of French in Cajun communities." *SECOL Review* 19 (1995): 126–50.

Duranti, Alessandro, ed. *Linguistic Anthropology: A Reader* (2nd edn). Malden, MA: Wiley-Blackwell, 2009.

Eckert, Penelope. *Jocks and Burnouts: Social Categories and Identity in the High School*. New York: Teachers College Press, 1989.

Eckert, Penelope. "Entering the heterosexual marketplace: Identities of subordination as a developmental imperative." *Working Papers on Learning and Identity* 2 (1994).

Eckert, Penelope. "Age as a sociolinguistic variable." In *The Handbook of Sociolinguistics*, ed. Florian Coulmas, 151–67. Oxford: Blackwell, 1996.

Eckert, Penelope. *Linguistic Variation as Social Practice: The Linguistic Construction of Identity in Belten High*. Malden, MA: Blackwell, 2000.

Eckert, Penelope, and Sally McConnell-Ginet. "Think practically and look locally: Language and gender as community-based practice." *Annual Review of Anthropology* 21 (1992): 461–90.

Eckert, Penelope, and Sally McConnell-Ginet. "New generalisations and explanations in language and gender research." *Language in Society* 28, no. 2 (1999): 185–203.

Eckert, Penelope, and Sally McConnell-Ginet. *Language and Gender*. New York: Cambridge University Press, 2003.

Eckert, Penelope, and John Rickford. *Style and Sociolinguistic Variation*. Cambridge: Cambridge University Press, 2001.

Edwards, John. "Judgments and confidence reactions to disadvantaged speech." In *Language and Social Psychology*, eds. Howard Giles and Robert N. St. Clair, 22–44. Baltimore: University Park Press, 1979.

Edwards, John. *Multilingualism*. London: Routledge, 1994.

Edwards, Walter. "Sociolinguistic behavior in a Detroit inner-city Black neighbourhood." *Language in Society* 21 (1992): 93–115.

Ekka, Francis. "Men's and women's speech in Kṛrux." *Linguistics* 81 (1972): 25–31.

Ellegård, Alvar. *The Auxiliary do: The Establishment and Regulation of Its Use in English*. Stockholm: Almqvist & Wikwell, 1953.

Ervin-Tripp, Susan M. "Sociolinguistic rules of address." In *Sociolinguistics*, eds. J. B. Pride and Janet Holmes, 225–40. Harmondsworth: Penguin, 1972.

Fairclough, Norman. *Language and Power*. New York: Longman, 1989.

Farr, Marcia, Lisya Seloni, and Juyoung Song. *Ethnolinguistic Diversity and Education*. New York: Routledge, 2010.

Fasold, Ralph. *The Sociolinguistics of Society*. Oxford: Blackwell, 1984.

Fasold, Ralph. *The Sociolinguistics of Language*. Oxford: Blackwell, 1990.

Ferguson, Charles A. "Diglossia." *Word* 15 (1959): 325–40.

Ferguson, Charles A. "Language development." In *Language Problems of Developing Nations*, eds. Joshua. A. Fishman, Charles. A. Ferguson, and Jyotirindra Dasgupta, 27–35. New York: John Wiley & Sons, 1968.

Ferguson, Gibson. *Language Planning and Education*. Edinburgh: Edinburgh University Press, 2006.

Finegan, Edward, and John R. Rickford, eds. *Language in the USA: Themes for the Twenty-First Century*. Cambridge: Cambridge University Press, 2004.

Fischer, John L. "Social influences on the choice of a linguistic variant." *Word* 14 (1958): 47–56.

Fish, Jefferson. "Why isn't there a French race?" http://www.psychologytoday.com/blog/looking-in-the-cultural-mirror/201010/why-isnt-there-french-race (accessed August 30, 2011), 2010.

Fishman, Joshua. "Language maintenance and language shift as fields of inquiry." *Linguistics* 9 (1964): 32–70.

Fishman, Joshua. "What is reversing language shift (RLS) and how can it succeed?" *Journal of Multilingual and Multicultural Development* 11 (1990): 5–36.

Fishman, Joshua. *Reversing Language Shift: Theoretical and Empirical Foundations of Assistance to Threatened Languages*. Clevedon: Multilingual Matters, 1991.

Fishman, Pamela. "Interactional shitwork." *Heresies* 1 (1980): 99–101.

Fishman, Pamela. "Interaction: The work women do." In *Language, Gender and Society*, eds. Barrie Thorne, Cheris Kramarae, and Nancy Henley, 89–101. London and Tokyo: Newbury House, 1983.

Fonollosa, Marie-Odile. "The representation of spoken French in Québec theater." Presented at NWAVE-XXIV, University of Pennsylvania, 1995.

Fought, Carmen. *Chicano English in Context*. New York: Palgrave Macmillan, 2003.

Fought, Carmen. *Language and Ethnicity: Key Topics in Sociolinguistics*. New York: Cambridge University Press, 2006.

Fowler, Joy. *The social stratification of (r) in New York City department stores, 24 years after Labov*. Unpublished manuscript, NewYork University, New York City, 1986.

Frangoudaki, Anna. "Greek societal bilingualism of more than a century." *International Journal of the Sociology of Language* 157 (2002): 101–7.

Freed, Alice F., and Alice Greenwood. "Women, men and type of talk: What makes the difference." *Language in Society* 25, no. 1 (1996): 1–26.

Gal, Susan. *Language Shift: Social Determinants of Language Change in bilingual Austria*. New York: Academic Press, 1979.

Garcia, Ofelia. "Bilingual education." In *The Handbook of Sociolinguistics*, ed. Florian Coulmas, 405–20. Oxford: Blackwell, 1997.

Gardner, Matt Hunt. "The in-crowd and the 'oat-casts': Diphthongs and identity in a Cape Breton high school." Presented at NWAV 39, San Antonio, TX, November 4–6, 2010.

Gauchat, Louis. "'L'unité phonetique dans le patois d'une commune." In *Aus Romanischen Sprachen und Literaturen: Festschrift Heinrich Morf*, 175–232. Halle: Niemeyer, 1905.

Geertz, Clifford. *The Religion of Java*. Chicago: University of Chicago Press, 1960.

Genesee, Fred, G. Richard Tucker, and Wallace E. Lambert. "Communication skills of bilingual children." *Child Development* 46, no. 4 (1975): 1010–14.

Giles, Howard. "Accent mobility: A model and some data." *Anthropological Linguistics* 15 (1973): 87–105.

Giles, Howard, and Nikolas Coupland. *Language: Contexts and Consequences*. Pacific Grove, CA: Brooks/Cole, 1991.

Giles, Howard, and Peter F. Powesland. *Speech Style and Social Evaluation*. London: Academic Press, 1975.

Giles, Howard, Richard Bourhis, and D. M. Taylor. "Toward a theory of language in ethnic group relations." In *Language Ethnicity and Intergroup Relations*, ed. Howard Giles, 307–49. London: Academic Press, 1977.

Goffman, Erving. "On face-work: An analysis of ritual elements in social interaction." *Psychiatry: Journal for the Study of Interpersonal Processes* 18 (1955): 213–31.

Gordon, Raymond, Jr., ed. *Ethnologue: Languages of the World*, (15th edn). Dallas: SIL International, 2005.

Gray, John. *Men Are from Mars, Women Are from Venus*. New York: HarperCollins, 1992.

Green, Lisa J. *African American English: A Linguistic Introduction*. New York: Cambridge University Press, 2002.

Greenfield, Patricia. "Oral and written language: The consequences for cognitive development in Africa, the United States and England." *Language and Speech* 15 (1972): 169–78.

Gregersen, Frans, Marie Maegaard, and Nicolai Pharao. "The long and short of (æ)-variation in Danish: A panel study of short (æ)-variants in Danish in real time." *Acta Linguistica Hafniensia* 41 (2009): 64–82.

Gross, Richard D. *Psychology: The Science of Mind and Behaviour*. London: Hodder & Stoughton, 1992.

Gumperz, John. "The speech community." In *International Encyclopedia of the Social Sciences*, ed. David Sills, 381–6. New York: Macmillan, 1968.

Gumperz, John. "The communicative competence of bilinguals." *Language in Society* 1, no. 1 (1972): 143–54.

Haas, Mary R. "Men's and women's speech in Koasati." *Language* 20 (1944): 142–9.

Haeri, Niloofar. *The Sociolinguistic Market of Cairo*. London: Kegan Paul, 1997.

Haeri, Niloofar. *Sacred Language, Ordinary People*. New York: Palgrave, 2003.

Hall, Kira. "Lip service on the fantasy lines." In *Gender Articulated*, eds. Kira Hall and Mary Bucholtz, 183–216. New York and London: Routledge, 1995.

Halliday, M. A. K. *Language as a Social Semiotic: The Social Interpretation of Language and Meaning*. Caulfield East, Victoria: Edward Arnold, 1978.

Harrington, Jonathan, Sallyanne Palethorpe, and Catherine Watson. "Does the queen speak the Queen's English?" *Nature* 408 (2000a): 927–8.

Harrington, Jonathan, Sallyanne Palethorpe, and Catherine Watson. "Monophthongal vowel changes in received pronunciation: An acoustic analysis of the queen's Christmas broadcasts." *Journal of the International Phonetic Association* 30 (2000b): 63–78.

Harrington, Jonathan, Sallyanne Palethorpe, and Catherine Watson. "Deepening or lessening the divide between diphthongs? An analysis of the queen's annual Christmas broadcasts." In *A Figure of Speech: A Festschrift for John Laver*, eds. William. J. Hardcastle and Janet Mackenzie Beck, 227–61. Mahwah, NJ: Lawrence Erlbaum, 2005.

Haugen, Einar. "Language conflict and language planning." In *Sociolinguistics*, ed. William Bright, 50–71. The Hague: Mouton, 1966a.

Haugen, Einar. *Language Conflict and Language Planning: The Case of Modern Norwegian*. Cambridge, MA: Harvard University Press, 1966b.

Haugen, Einar. *Blessings of Babel: Bilingualism and Language Planning*. Berlin: Mouton, 1987.

Hazen, Kirk. "The family." In *The Handbook of Language Variation and Change*, eds. J. K. Chambers, Peter Trudgill, and Natalie Schilling-Estes, 500–25. Malden, MA: Blackwell, 2002.

Heath, Shirley Brice. *Ways with Words: Language, Life, and Work in Communities and Classrooms*. Cambridge: Cambridge University Press, 1983. (Republished 1996.)

Henderson, Anita. "Is your money where your mouth is? Hiring managers' attitudes toward African-American Vernacular English." PhD dissertation, University of Pennsylvania, 2001.

Hensley, Anne. "Black high school students' reactions to Black speakers of Standard and Black English." *Language Learning* 22, no. 2 (1972): 253–9.

Hickey, Raymond. "The Atlantic edge: The relationship between Irish English and Newfoundland English." *English World-Wide* 23, no. 2 (2002a): 281–314.

Hickey, Raymond. *A Source Book for Irish English*. Amsterdam: John Benjamins, 2002b.

Hickey, Raymond, ed. *Motives for Language Change*. Cambridge: Cambridge University Press, 2003.

Hickey, Raymond. *Handbook of Language Contact*. Chichester and Malden, MA: Wiley-Blackwell, 2010.

Hill, Jane, and Kenneth Hill. *Speaking Mexicano: Dynamics of Syncretic Language in Central Mexico*. Tucson: University of Arizona Press, 1986.

Hill, Mike. "'Souls undressed': The rise and fall of the new Whiteness studies." *Review of Education/Pedagogy/Cultural Studies* 20, no. 3 (1998): 229–39.

Hodge, Robert W., Paul M. Siegel, and Peter H. Rossi. "Occupational prestige in the United States, 1925–63." *American Journal of Sociology* 70 (1964): 286–302.

Hoffmann, Fernand. "Triglossia in Luxemburg." In *Minority Languages Today*, eds. Einar Haugen, J. Derrick McClure, and Derick Thomson. Edinburgh: Edinburgh University Press, 1981.

Hoffman, Micol, and James Walker. "Ethnolects and the city: Ethnic orientation and linguistic variation in Toronto English." *Language Variation and Change* 22 (2010): 37–67.

Holm, John, and Susanne Michaelis, eds. *Contact Languages: Critical Concepts in Language Studies*. New York: Routledge, 2008.

Holmes, Janet. *An Introduction to Sociolinguistics*. London and New York: Longman, 1992.

Holmes, Janet, Allan Bell, and Mary Boyce. *Variation and Change in New Zealand English: A Social Dialect Investigation*. Project Report to the Social Sciences Committee of the Foundation for Research, Science and Technology. Wellington: Department of Linguistics, Victoria University of Wellington, 1991.

Hornberger, Nancy, and Sandra McKay, eds. *Sociolinguistics and Language Education*. Bristol: Multilingual Matters, 2010.

Horvath, Barbara. *Variation in Australian English*. New York and Cambridge: Cambridge University Press, 1985.

Housen, Alex. "Processes and outcomes in the European schools model of multilingual education." *Bilingual Research Journal* 26, no. 1 (2002): 45–64.

Hudson, Liam. *Frames of Mind*. Harmondsworth: Penguin, 1968.

Hymes, Dell. "On communicative competence." In *Sociolinguistics*, eds. J. B. Pride and Janet Holmes, 269–93. Harmondsworth: Penguin, 1972.

Hymes, Dell. *Foundations in Sociolinguistics: An Ethnographic Approach*. Philadelphia: University of Pennsylvania Press, 1974a.

Hymes, Dell. "Ways of speaking." In *Explorations in the Ethnography of Speaking*, eds. Richard Bauman and Joel Sherzer, 433–51. Cambridge: Cambridge University Press, 1974b.

Hymes, Dell, William Bittle, and Harry Hoijer. *Studies in Southwestern Ethnolinguistics: Meaning and History in the Languages of the American Southwest*. The Hague and Paris: Mouton, 1967.

Ignatiev, Noel. *How the Irish Became White*. New York: Routledge, 1995.

Jackson, George. *Popular Errors in English Grammar, Particularly in Pronunciation, Familiarly Pointed Out: For the Use of Those Persons Who Want Either Opportunity or Inclination to Study This Science*. London: Effingham Wilson, 1830.

James, Deborah, and Sandra Clarke. "Women, men, and interruptions: A critical review." In *Gender and Conversational Interaction*, ed. Deborah Tannen, 231–81. New York and Oxford: Oxford University Press, 1993.

James, Deborah, and Janice Drakich. "Understanding gender differences in amount of talk." In *Gender and Conversational Interaction*, ed. Deborah Tannen, 281–312. New York: Oxford University Press, 1993.

Jernudd, Bjorn. "Language planning as a kind of language treatment." In *Language Planning: Current Issues and Research*, eds. Joan Rubin and Roger Shuy, 11–23. Washington, DC: Georgetown University Press, 1973.

Johnstone, Barbara. "Pittsburghese shirts: Commodification and the enregisterment of an urban dialect." *American Speech* 84 (2009): 157–75.

Kachru, Braj B. "Standards, codification and sociolinguistic realism: The English language in the outer circle." In *English in the World: Teaching and Learning the Language and Literatures*, eds. Randolph Quirk and Henry G. Widdowson, 11–30. Cambridge: Cambridge University Press, 1985.

Kachru, Braj B., Yamuna Kachru, and Cecil L. Nelson, eds. *The Handbook of World Englishes*. Malden, MA, and Oxford: Blackwell, 2006.

Kachru, Yamuna, and T. K. Bhatia. "The emerging 'dialect' conflict in Hindi: A case of glottopolitics." *International Journal of the Sociology of Language* 16 (1978): 47–56.

Keenan, Elinor. "Conversation and oratory in Vakinankaratra, Madagascar." PhD dissertation, University of Pennsylvania, 1974.

Kerswill, Paul. "Children, adolescents and language change." *Language Variation and Change* 8 (1996): 177–202.

Key, Mary Ritchie. *Male/Female Language: With a Comprehensive Bibliography*. New York: Scarecrow Press, 1975.

Kiesling, Scott F. "Language, gender, and power among fraternity men." PhD dissertation, Georgetown University, 1996.

Kiesling, Scott F. "Dude." *American Speech* 79, no. 3 (2004): 281–305.

Kiesling, Scott F. "Variation, stance and style: Word-final -er, high rising tone, and ethnicity in Australian English." *English World-Wide* 26, no. 1 (2005): 1–42.

King, Ruth. *The Lexical Basis of Grammatical Borrowing.* Philadelphia and Amsterdam: John Benjamins, 2000.

King, Ruth, and Sandra Clarke. "Contesting meaning: *Newfie* and the politics of ethnic labeling." *Journal of Sociolinguistics* 6 (2002): 537–58.

Kloss, Heinz. "'Abstand languages' and 'Ausbau languages.'" *Anthropological Linguistics* 9 (1967): 29–41.

Knee, Sarah, and Gerard Van Herk. "Stop and go (away): Linguistic consequences of non-local aspirations among small-town Newfoundland youth." Presented at NWAV 39, San Antonio, TX, November 4–6, 2010.

Koch, Lisa M., and Alan Gross. "Children's perceptions of Black English as a variable in intraracial perception." *Journal of Black Psychology* 23, no. 3 (1997): 215–26.

Koerner, E. F. K. *Toward a History of American Linguistics.* London and New York: Routledge, 2002.

Kontra, Miklós. "Class over nation. Linguistic hierarchies eliminated: The case of Hungary." *Multilingua* 11 (1992): 217–21.

Kortmann, B., Schneider, E., Burridge, K., Mesthrie, R., and Upton, C., eds. *A Handbook of Varieties of English. Vol. 2.* Berlin and New York: Mouton, 2004.

Kovac, Ceil, and H. D. Adamson. "Variation theory and first language acquisition." In *Variation Omnibus*, eds. David Sankoff and Henrietta Cedergren, 403–10. Carbondale, IL: Linguistic Research, 1981.

Kroch, Anthony. "Toward a theory of social dialect variation." *Language in Society* 7 (1978): 17–36.

Kroch, Anthony. "Reflexes of grammar in patterns of language change." *Language Variation and Change* 1 (1989): 199–244.

Labov, William. "The social motivation of a sound change." *Word* 19 (1963): 273–309.

Labov, William. *The Social Stratification of English in New York City.* Washington, DC: Center for Applied Linguistics, 1966. (2nd ed. 2006.)

Labov, William. "The study of language in its social context." *Studium Generale* 23 (1970): 30–87.

Labov, William. *Language in the Inner City: Studies in the Black English Vernacular.* Philadelphia: University of Pennsylvania Press, 1972a.

Labov, William. *Sociolinguistic Patterns.* Philadelphia: University of Pennsylvania Press, 1972b.

Labov, William. "Academic ignorance and black intelligence." *Atlantic Monthly*, June (1972c):. 59–67.

Labov, William. "On the use of the present to explain the past." In *Proceedings of the 11th International Congress of Linguists*, ed. Luigi Heilmann, 825–51. Bologna: Il Mulino, 1974.

Labov, William. "The social origins of sound change." In *Locating Language in Time and Space*, ed. William Labov, 251–66. New York: Academic Press, 1980.

Labov, William. "The child as linguistic historian." *Language Variation and Change* 1 (1989): 85–97.

Labov, William. "The intersection of sex and social class in the course of linguistic change." *Language Variation and Change* 2 (1990): 205–54.

Labov, William. *Principles of Linguistic Change. Vol. 1: Internal Factors.* Oxford: Blackwell, 1994.

Labov, William. *Principles of Linguistic Change. Vol. 2: Social Factors.* Oxford: Blackwell, 2001.

Labov, William. "The social stratification of (r) in NYC department stores." In William Labov, *The Social Stratification of English in New York City* (2nd edn), 40–57. Cambridge: Cambridge University Press, 2006 (1st pub. 1966).

Labov, William. *Principles of Linguistic Change. Vol. 3: Cognitive and Cultural Factors.* Oxford: Blackwell, 2010.

Labov, William, and Wendell Harris. "De facto segregation of Black and White vernaculars." In *Diversity and Diachrony*, ed. David Sankoff, 1–24. Amsterdam: John Benjamins, 1986.

Labov, William, Sherry Ash, and Charles Boberg. *Atlas of North American English: Phonetics, Phonology, and Sound Change.* Berlin: Mouton, 2006.

Labov, William, Malcah Yaeger, and R. Steiner. *A Quantitative Study of Sound Change in Progress.* Philadelphia: U.S. Regional Survey, 1972.

Lakoff, Robin. "Language in context." *Language* 48, no. 4 (1972): 907–27.

Lakoff, Robin. "Language and woman's place." *Language and Society* 2 (1973): 45–79.

Lakoff, Robin. "The social context of language use." Presented at the Linguistic Summer Institute, Ann Arbor, 1973.

Lakoff, Robin. *Language and Woman's Place.* New York: Harper & Row, 1975.

Lakoff, Robin. *Language and Woman's Place: Text and Commentaries.* London: Oxford University Press, 2004.

Lambert, Wallace E. "A social psychology of bilingualism." *Journal of Social Issues* 23 (1967): 91–108.

Lambert, Wallace E., Richard C. Hodgson, Robert C. Gardner, and Samuel Fillenbaum. "Evaluative reactions to spoken languages." *Journal of Abnormal and Social Psychology* 60 (1960): 44–51.

Lanehart, Sonja L., ed. *Sociocultural and Historical Contexts of African American English*. Philadelphia: John Benjamins, 2001.

Lanehart, Sonja. L., ed. *African American Women's Language: Discourse, Education, and Identity*. Newcastle upon Tyne: Cambridge Scholars, 2009.

Lange, Deborah. "Using *like* to introduce constructed dialogue: How *like* contributes to discourse coherence." Master's thesis, Georgetown University, 1988.

Laosa, Luis M. "What languages do bilingual children use and with whom? Research evidence and implications for education." Presented at the National Convention of Teachers of English to Speakers of Other Languages (TESOL), Los Angeles, CA, 1975.

Lave, Jean, and Etienne Wenger. *Situated learning: Legitimate Peripheral Participation*. Cambridge and New York: Cambridge University Press, 1991.

Leet-Pellegrini, Helena M. "Conversational dominance as a function of gender and expertise." In *Language and Social Psychological Perspectives*, eds. H. Giles, P. Robinson, and P. Smith. New York: Pergamon, 1980.

Lenneberg, Eric Heinz. *Biological Foundations of Language*. New York: John Wiley & Sons, 1967.

Leonard, Tom. *Intimate Voices: Writing 1965–83*. Newcastle upon Tyne: Galloping Dog, 1984.

Levitski, Olga. "Trilingual code-switching as communication strategy: Russian Israelis in Toronto." MA thesis, York University, 2005.

Lewis, G. "Bilingualism and bilingual education: The ancient world to the Renaissance." In *Bilingual Education: An International Sociological Perspective*, ed., J. A. Fishman, 150–200. Rowley, MA: Newbury House, 1976.

Li Wei. *Three Generations, Two Languages, One Family: Language Choice and Language Shift in a Chinese Community in Britain*. Clevedon: Multilingual Matters, 1994.

Li Wei and Melissa G. Moyer, eds. *The Blackwell Guide to Research Methods in Bilingualism and Multilingualism*. Oxford: Blackwell, 2008.

Lieberson, Stanley. "Bilingualism in Montréal: A demographic analysis." In *Advances in Sociology of Language. Vol. 2*, ed. Joshua A. Fishman, 231–54. The Hauge: Mouton, 1972.

Lieberson, Stanley. "Procedures for improving sociolinguistic surveys of language maintenance and language shift." *International Journal of the Sociology of Language* 25 (1980): 11–27.

Ligon, Richard. *A True and Exact History of the Island of Barbados*. London: Frank Cass, 1970 (1st pub. 1657).

Lindenfeld, Jacqueline. *Speech and Sociability at French Urban Marketplaces*. Amsterdam and Philadelphia: John Benjamins, 1990.

Linn, Michael D., and Gene Piché. "Black and White adolescent and preadolescent attitudes toward Black English." *Research in the Teaching of English* 16, no. 1 (1982): 53–69.

Lippi-Green, Rosina. *English with an Accent: Language, Ideology and Discrimination in the United States*. London: Routledge, 1997.

Lovett, Marilyn, and Joneka Neely. "On becoming bilingual." *Journal of Black Psychology* 23, no. 3 (1997): 242–4.

Macaulay, Ronald K. S. *Locating Dialect in Discourse: The Language of Honest Men and Bonnie Lasses in Ayr*. New York: Oxford University Press, 1991.

MacKay, Donald G., and David C. Fulkerson. "On the comprehension and production of pronouns." *Journal of Verbal Learning and Verbal Behavior* 18 (1979): 661–73.

Mahlau, Axel. "Some aspects of the standardization of the Basque language." In *Standardization of National Languages: Symposium on Language Standardization*, eds. Utta von Gleich and Ekkehard Wolff, 79–94. Hamburg: UNESCO Institute for Education, 1991.

Malinowski, Bronislaw. "The problem of meaning in primitive language." In *The Meaning of Meaning*, eds. Charles K. Ogden and I. A. Richards, 451–510. London: Routledge & Kegan Paul, 1923.

Mallinson, Christine, and Becky Childs. "The language of Black women in the Smoky Mountain region of Appalachia." In *Language Variety in the South: Historical and Contemporary Perspectives*, eds. Michael D. Picone and Catherine Evans Davies. Tuscaloosa: University of Alabama Press, forthcoming.

Marx, Karl, and Friedrich Engels. Manifesto of the Communist Party, 1848. In *Selected Works. Vol. 1*, Karl Marx and Friedrich Engels, 98–137. Moscow: Progress Publishers, 1969.

McIntyre, Joseph. "Lexical innovation in Hausa (Niger, Nigeria)." In *Standardization of National Languages*, eds. Utta von Gleich and Ekkehard Wolff, 11–20. Hamburg: UNESCO, 1991.

Mather, Patrick-André. "The social stratification of /r/ in New York City: Labov's department store study revisited." Journal of English Linguistics *(in press)*.

Mendoza-Denton, Norma. "Pregnant pauses: Silence and authority in the Hill–Thomas hearings." In *Gender Articulated: Language and the Socially Constructed Self*, eds.

Kira Hall and Mary Bucholtz, 51–68. London: Routledge, 1994.

Mendoza-Denton, Norma. *Chicana/Mexican Identity and Linguistic Variation: An Ethnographic and Sociolinguistic Study of Gang Affiliation in an Urban High School*. PhD dissertation, Stanford University, California, 1997.

Mendoza-Denton, N., and Stefanie Jannedy. "Implementation of super-low tones in Latina Gang girl speech." Presented at Perceiving and Performing Gender Conference, Keil, Germany, 1998.

Mesthrie, Rajend, and Rakesh M. Bhatt. *World Englishes: The Study of New Linguistic Varieties*. Cambridge: Cambridge University Press, 2008.

Mesthrie, Rajend, Joan Swann, Ana Deumert, and William Leap. *Introducing Sociolinguistics* (2nd edn). Edinburgh: Edinburgh University Press, 2009.

Meyerhoff, Miriam. *Introducing Sociolinguistics*. London and New York: Routledge, 2006.

Meyerhoff, Miriam, and Nancy Niedzielski. "The globalisation of vernacular variation." *Journal of Sociolinguistics* 7, no. 4 (2003): 534–55.

Meyerhoff, Miriam, and Erik Schleef, eds. *The Routledge Sociolinguistics Reader*. Routledge, 2010.

Michnowicz, Jim. "El habla de Yucatám: Final [m] in a dialect in contact." In *Selected Proceedings of the Third Workshop on Spanish Sociolinguistics*, eds. Jonathan Holmquist, Augusto Lorenzino, and Lotfi Sayahi, 38–43. Somerville, MA: Cascadilla Proceedings Project, 2007.

Milroy, Lesley. *Language and Social Networks* (2nd edn). Oxford: Blackwell, 1987 (1st pub. 1980).

Milroy, Lesley, and Matthew Gordon. *Sociolinguistics: Method and Interpretation*. Oxford: Blackwell, 2003.

Mitchell-Kernan, Claudia. "Signifying and marking: Two Afro-American speech acts." In *Directions in Sociolinguistics: The Ethnography of Communication*, eds. John Gumperz and Dell Hymes, 161–79. New York: Academic Press, 1972.

Mitford, Nancy, ed. *Noblesse Oblige: An Enquiry into the Identifiable Characteristics of the English Aristocracy*. London: Hamish Hamilton, 1956.

Modaressi-Tehrani, Yahya. "A sociolinguistic analysis of Modern Persian." PhD dissertation, University of Kansas, 1978.

Mougeon, Raymond, Terry Nadasdi, and Katherine Rehner. *The Sociolinguistic Competence of Immersion Students*. Bristol: Multilingual Matters, 2010.

Mufwene, Salikoko, John Rickford, Guy Bailey, and John Baugh, eds. *African American English: Structure, History and Use*. New York: Routledge, 1998.

Mugglestone, Lynda. *"Talking Proper": The Rise of Accent as Social Symbol* (2nd edn). Oxford: Oxford University Press, 2003.

Mukherjee, Bharati. *Jasmine*. New York: Fawcett Crest, 1989.

Myers-Scotton, Carol. *Duelling Languages: Grammatical Structure in Codeswitching*. Oxford: Clarendon Press, 1993a.

Myers-Scotton, Carol. "Common and uncommon ground: Social and structural factors in codeswitching." *Language in Society* 22 (1993b): 475–503.

Nevalainen, Terttu. "Negative concord as an English 'vernacular universal': Social history and linguistic typology." *Journal of English Linguistics* 34, no. 3 (2006): 257–78.

Nichols, Patricia C. "Linguistic options and choices for Black women in the rural South." In *Language, Gender and Society*, eds. Barrie Thorne, Cheris Kramarae, and Nancy Henley, 54–68. Cambridge, MA: Newbury House, 1983.

Niedzielski, Nancy. "The effect of social information on the perception of sociolinguistic variables." *Journal of Language and Social Psychology* 18 (1999): 62–85.

Niedzielski, Nancy, and Dennis Preston. *Folk Linguistics*. Berlin: Mouton De Gruyter, 2000.

Oakley, Ann. *The Sociology of Housework*. Oxford: Martin Robertson, 1974.

Ochs, Elinor. "Norm makers and norm breakers in Malagasy society." In *Explorations in the Ethnography of Speaking*, eds. Richard Baumann and Joel Sherzer, 125–43. Cambridge: Cambridge University Press, 1974.

Ochs, Elinor. "Indexing gender." In *Rethinking Context: Language as an Interactive Phenomenon*, eds. Alessandro Duranti and Charles Goodwin, 335–58. Cambridge: Cambridge University Press, 1992.

Ogbu, John. *Minority Education and Caste: The American System in Cross-Cultural Perspective*. New York: Academic Press, 1978.

Omari, Osama. "A sociophonetic study of interdental variation in Jordanian Arabic." Presented at Aldrich Interdisciplinary Conference, St. John's, NL, March 21–2, 2009.

Parasher, S. V. "Mother tongue–English diglossia: A case study of educated Indian bilinguals' language use." *Anthropological Linguistics* 22, no. 4 (1980): 151–62.

Parris, Samantha. "The reanalysis of a traditional feature in industrial Cape Breton." Presented at Change and Variation in Canada III, Ottawa, ON, June 20–1, 2009.

Patrick, Peter. *Urban Jamaican Creole: Variation in the Mesolect*. Amsterdam: John Benjamins, 1999.

Paulston, Christina Bratt, and Richard Tucker, eds. *Sociolinguistics: The Essential Readings*. Malden, MA: Blackwell, 2003.

Payne, Arvilla. "Factors controlling the acquisition of the Philadelphia dialect by out-of-state children." In *Locating Language in Time and Space*, ed. William Labov, 143–78. Orlando, FL: Academic Press, 1980.

Pearlmann, J. "Historical legacies: 1840–1920." *Annals of the American Academcy of Political and Social Science* 508 (1990): 27–37.

Pegge, Samuel. *Anecdotes of the English Language: Dialect of London*. London: J. Nichols, Son and Bentley, 1814 (1st pub. 1803).

Pendakur, Ravi, and John Kralt. *Ethnicity, Immigration and Language Shift*. Ottawa: Policy and Research, Multiculturalism Sector, 1991.

Pennycook, Alastair. *Global Englishes and Transcultural Flows*. London and New York: Routledge, 2007.

Phillipson, Robert. *Linguistic Imperialism*. Oxford: Oxford University Press, 1992.

Pilkington, Jane. "'Don't try and make out that I'm nice!' The different strategies women and men use when gossiping." *Wellington Working Papers in Linguistics* 5 (1992): 37–60.

Placencia, María E. "Inequality in address behavior at public institutions in La Paz, Bolivia." *Anthropological Linguistics* 43, no. 2 (2001): 198–217.

Podesva, Robert. "On constructing social meaning with stop release bursts." Paper presented at Sociolinguistics Symposium 15, Newcastle upon Tyne, 2004.

Pope, Jennifer. "The social history of a sound change on the island of Martha's Vineyard, Massachusetts: Forty years after Labov." Master's thesis, University of Edinburgh, 2002.

Poplack, Shana. "Sometimes I'll start a sentence in Spanish y termino en español: Toward a typology of codeswitching." *Linguistics* 18 (1980): 581–618.

Poplack, Shana. "Contrasting patterns of codeswitching in two communities." In *Aspects of Bilingualism: Proceedings from the Fourth Nordic Symposium on Bilingualism, 1984*, eds. Erling Wande, Jan Anward, Bengt Nordberg, Lars Steensland, and Mats Thelander, 51–76. Uppsala: Borgström, 1987.

Poplack, Shana. "The inherent variability of the French subjunctive." In *Theoretical Analyses in Romance Linguistics*, eds. C. Laeufer and T. Morgan, 235–63. Amsterdam: John Benjamins, 1991.

Poplack, Shana, ed. *The English History of African American English*. Oxford: Blackwell, 2000.

Poplack, Shana, and Anne St-Amand. "A real-time window on 19th century vernacular French: The *Récits du Français québécois d'Autrefois*." *Language in Society* 36, no. 5 (2007): 707–34.

Poplack, Shana, and Sali Tagliamonte. *African American English in the Diaspora*. Oxford: Blackwell, 2001.

Poplack, Shana, Rebecca Malcolmson, Molly Love, and Rocío Pérez-Tattam. "Ideology vs. usage: English as a minority language." Presented at NWAV 33, University of Michigan, Ann Arbor, 2004.

Power, Suzanne. "Beyond the /t/: Sociophonetic variation in the frication of word-final oral stops in Placentia, Newfoundland." Presented at Methods in Dialectology 14, London, ON, August 2–6, 2011.

Preston, Dennis. "The Li'l Abner syndrome: Written representations of speech." *American Speech* 60, no. 4 (1985): 328–36.

Preston, Dennis. "Language with an attitude." In *The Handbook of Language Variation and Change*, eds. J. K. Chambers, Peter Trudgill, and Natalie Schilling-Estes, 40–66. Malden, MA: Blackwell, 2002.

Preston, Dennis, and George M. Howe. "Computerized generalizations of mental dialect maps." In *Variation in Language: NWAV-XV at Stanford*, eds. Keith M. Denning, Sharon Inkelas, Faye C. McNair-Knox, and John R. Rickford, 361–78. Stanford: Department of Linguistics, Stanford University, 1987.

Pullum, Geoffrey. *The Great Eskimo Vocabulary Hoax and Other Irreverent Essays on the Study of Language*. Chicago: University of Chicago Press, 1991.

Purnell, Thomas, William Idasrdi, and John Baugh. "Perceptual and phonetic experiments on American English dialect identification." *Journal of Language and Social Psychology* 18, no. 1 (1999): 10–31.

Queneau, Raymond. *Exercises in Style*. New York: New Directions, 1947.

Rahman, Jacquelyn. "Golly gee! The construction of middle-class characters in the monologues of African-American comedians." Presented at NWAVE 32, Philadelphia, PA, 2003.

Ramirez, J. David., Terrence G. Wiley, Gerda de Klerk, Enid Lee, and Wayne E. Wright, eds. *Ebonics: The Urban Education Debate*. Clevedon: Multilingual Matters, 2005.

Rampton, Ben. *Crossing: Language and Ethnicity among Adolescents*. London: Longman, 1995.

Ray, Punya Sloka. "Language standardization." In *Language Problems of Developing Nations*, eds. Joshua A. Fishman, Charles Albert Ferguson, and Jyotirindra Dasgupta, 754–65. New York: John Wiley & Sons.

Renn, Jennifer. "Patterns of style in the language of African American children and adolescents." *Proceedings of the Boston University Conference on Language Development* (2011): 513–25.

Reynolds, Katsue Akiba. "Female speakers of Japanese in transition." In *Language and Gender: A Reader*, ed. Jennifer Coates, 299–308. Oxford: Blackwell, 1998.

Ricento, Thomas. "Historical and theoretical perspectives in language policy and planning." *Journal of Sociolinguistics* 4, no. 2 (2000): 196–213.

Ricento, Thomas. *An Introduction to Language Policy: Theory and Method*. Malden, MA: Blackwell, 2006.

Rickford, John R. "Variation in a creole continuum: Quantitative and implicational approaches." PhD dissertation, University of Pennsylvania, 1979.

Rickford, John R. *African American Vernacular English: Features, Evolution, and Educational Implications*. Malden, MA: Blackwell, 1999.

Rickford, John. "Implicational scales." In *The Handbook of Language Variation and Change*, eds. J. K. Chambers, Peter Trudgill, and Nathalie Schilling-Estes, 142–67. Malden, MA: Blackwell, 2002.

Rickford, John R., and F. McNair-Knox. "Addressee- and topic- influenced style shift: A quantitative sociolinguistic study." In *Sociolinguistic Perspectives on Register*, eds. D. Biber and E. Finegan, 235–76. New York, Oxford University Press, 1994.

Rickford, John R., and Angela E. Rickford. "Cut-eye and suck teeth: African words and gestures in new world guise." *Journal of American Folklore* 89, no. 353 (1976): 194–309.

Rickford, John R., and Angela E. Rickford. "Dialect readers revisited." *Linguistics and Education* 7 (1995): 107–28.

Rickford, John R., and Russell Rickford. *Spoken Soul: The Story of Black English*. New York: John Wiley & Sons, 2000.

Roberts, Julie. *The Acquisition of Variation: (-t,d) Deletion and (ing) Production in Pre-School Children*. Institute for Research in Cognitive Science (IRCS) Report 96–09. Philadelphia: University of Pennsylvania, 1996.

Robins, R. H., and Eugenius M. Uhlenbeck, eds. *Endangered Languages*. Oxford: Berg, 1991.

Romaine, Suzanne. *The Language of Children and Adolescents*. Oxford: Blackwell, 1984.

Romaine, Suzanne. *Language in Society: An Introduction to Sociolinguistics*. Oxford: Oxford University Press, 2000.

Rose, Mary. Language, place and identity in later life. PhD dissertation, Stanford University, 2006.

Ross, Alan S. C., "Linguistic class-indicators in present-day English." *Neuphilologische Mitteilungen (Helsinki)* 55 (1954): 113–49.

Rubin, Donald. "Nonlanguage factors affecting undergraduates' judgments of nonnative English-speaking teaching assistants." *Research in Higher Education* 33, no. 4 (1992): 511–31.

Rubin, Joan. "Language planning: Discussion of some current issues." In *Language Planning: Current Issues and Research*, eds. Joan Rubin and Roger Shuy, 16–17. Washington, DC: Georgetown University Press, 1973.

Rubin, Joan. "Spanish language planning in the United States." In *Spanish Language Use and Public Life in the United States*, eds. Lucía Elías-Olivares, Elizabeth A. Leone, René Cisneros, and John R. Gutiérrez, 133–52. Berlin and New York: Mouton, 1985.

Russell, John. "Networks and sociolinguistic variation in an African urban setting." In *Sociolinguistic Variation in Speech Communities*, ed. Suzanne Romaine, 125–44. London: Edward Arnold, 1982.

Sankoff, David, and Suzanne Laberge. "Statistical dependence among successive occurrences of a variable in discourse." In *Linguistic Variation, Models and Methods*, ed. David Sankoff, 119–26. New York: Academic Press, 1978.

Sankoff, Gillian, and Henrietta Cedergren. "Some results of a sociolinguistic study of Montréal French." In *Linguistic Diversity in Canadian Society*, ed. Regna Darnell, 61–87. Edmonton: Linguistic Research, 1971.

Santa Ana, Otto, ed. *Tongue-Tied: The Lives of Multilingual Children in Public Schools*. Lanham, MD: Rowman & Littlefield, 2004.

Santa Ana, Otto, and Claudia Parodi. "Modeling the speech community: Configuration and variable types in the Mexican Spanish setting." *Language in Society* 27, no. 1 (1998): 23–51.

Sarkar, M., and L. Winer. "Multilingual codeswitching in Québec rap: Poetry, pragmatics and performativity."

International Journal of Multilingualism 3, no. 3 (2006): 173–200.

Saville-Troike, M., and Kleifgen, J.. "Culture and language in classroom communication." In *English across Cultures, Cultures across English: A Reader in Cross-Cultural Communication*, eds. O. Garcia and R. Otheguy, 83–102. Berlin: Mouton de Gruyter, 1989.

Schatz, Henriëtte F. *Plat Amsterdams in its Social Context: A Sociolinguistic Study of the Dialect of Amsterdam.* Amsterdam: P. J. Meertens-Instituut voor Dialectologie, Volkskunde en Naamkunde, 1986.

Schilling-Estes, Natalie. "Investigating 'self-conscious' speech: The performance register in Ocracoke English." *Language in Society* 27 (1998): 53–83.

Schilling-Estes, Natalie. "Investigating stylistic variation." In *The Handbook of Language Variation and Change*, eds. J. K. Chambers, Peter Trudgill, and Natalie Schilling-Estes, 375–401. Malden, MA: Blackwell, 2002.

Schilling-Estes, Natalie, and Walt Wolfram. "Alternative models for dialect death: Dissipation vs. concentration." *Language* 75, no. 3 (1999): 486–521.

Schneider, Edgar. *Focus on the USA*. Philadelphia: John Benjamins, 1996.

Schneider, Edgar. "Cataloguing the pronunciation variants of world-wide English." Presented at Methods in Dialectology XII, Moncton, New Brunswick, 2005.

Schneider, Edgar. *Postcolonial English*. Cambridge: Cambridge University Press, 2007.

Scott, James. *Weapons of the Weak: Everyday Forms of Peasant Resistance*. New Haven: Yale University Press, 1985.

Sedlak, P. *The Kenyan Language Setting*. Washington, DC: Academy for Educational Development, 1983.

Serpell, Robert. "The cultural context of language learning: Problems confronting English teachers in Zambia." In *Language Planning and English Language Teaching*, ed. C. Kennedy, 92–106. London: Prentice Hall, 1989.

Sherzer, Joel. *Kuna Ways of Speaking: An Ethnographic Perspective*. Austin: University of Texas Press, 1983.

Shields-Brodber, Kathryn. "Dynamism and assertiveness in the public voice: Turn-taking and code-switching in radio talk shows in Jamaica." *Pragmatics* 2, no. 4 (1992): 487–504.

Siegel, Jeff. *The Emergence of Pidgin and Creole Languages*. Oxford and New York: Oxford University Press, 2008.

Silva-Corvalán, Carmen. "The gradual loss of mood distinctions in Los Angeles Spanish." *Language Variation and Change* 6 (1994): 255–72.

Silverstein, Michael. "Shifters, linguistic categories, and cultural description." In *Meaning in Anthropology*, eds. K. Basso and H. A. Selby, 11–56. Albuquerque: School of American Research, University of New Mexico Press, 1976.

Silverstein, Michael. "Monoglot 'standard' in America: Standardization and metaphors of linguistic hegemony." In *The Matrix of Language: Contemporary Linguistic Anthropology*, eds. Donald Brenneis and Ronald H. S. Macaulay, 284–306. Boulder, CO: Westview Press, 1996.

Silverstein, Michael. "Indexical order and the dialectics of sociolinguistic life." *Language and Communication* 23, nos. 3–4 (2003): 193–229..

Simmons-McDonald, Hazel, and Ian Robertson, eds. *Exploring the Boundaries of Caribbean Creole Languages*. Jamaica: University of the West Indies Press, 2006.

Singler, John Victor, and Silvia Kouwenberg, eds. *The Handbook of Pidgin and Creole Studies*. Malden, MA: Blackwell, 2008.

Skutnabb-Kangas, Tove, and Robert Phillipson, eds. *Linguistic Human Rights: Overcoming Linguistic Discrimination*. Berlin and New York: Mouton, 1995.

Skutnabb-Kangas, Tove, Robert Phillipson, Ajit Mohanty, and Minati Panda, eds. *Social Justice through Multilingual Education*. Bristol: Multilingual Matters, 2009.

Smakman, Dick. *Standard Dutch in the Netherlands. A Sociolinguistic and Phonetic Description*. Utrecht: LOT, 2006.

Smith, K. Aaron. "The history of *be fixing to*: Grammaticization, sociolinguistic distribution and emerging literary space." *English Today* 25, no. 1 (2009): 12–18.

Spears, Arthur. "African-American language use: Ideology and so-called obscenity." In *African American English: Structure, History, and Use*, eds. Salikoko S. Mufwene, John R. Rickford, Guy Bailey, and John Baugh, 226–50. London and New York, Routledge: 1998.

Spolsky, Bernard. *Language Policy*. Cambridge: Cambridge University Press, 2004.

Sridhar, Kamal. "Speech acts in an indigenized variety: Sociocultural values and language variation." In *English around the World: Sociolinguistic Perspectives*, ed. Jenny Cheshire, 308–18. Cambridge: Cambridge University Press, 1991.

Sridhar, Kamal. "Societal multilingualism." In *Sociolinguistics and Language Teaching*, eds. Sandra Lee McKay and Nancy Hornberger, 47–70. Cambridge: Cambridge University Press, 1996.

Statistics Canada. *Population Estimates by First Official Language Spoken*. Ottawa: Statistics Canada, Housing and Social Statistics Division and Language Studies, 1989.

Steinberg, Danny D., Hiroshi Nagata, and David P. Aline. *Psycholinguistics: Language, Mind and World* (2nd edn), Danny D. Steinberg, Hiroshi Nagata, and David P. Aline. Harlow: Pearson, 2001.

Sussman, Steve, Pallav Pokhrel, Richard D. Ashmore, and B. Bradford Brown. "Adolescent peer group identification and characteristics: A review of literature." *Addictive Behaviors* 32 (2007): 1602–27.

Tabouret-Keller, Andrée. "Sociological factors of language maintenance and language shift: A methodological approach based *Language Problems of Developing Nations*, eds. Joshua A. Fishman, Charles A. Ferguson, and Jyotirindra Dasgupta, 107–18. New York: John Wiley & Sons, 1968.

Tagliamonte, Sali. *Analysing Sociolinguistic Variation*. Cambridge: Cambridge University Press, 2006.

Tagliamonte, Sali, and Alexandra D'Arcy. "Peaks beyond phonology: Adolescence, incrementation, and language change." *Language* 85 (2009): 58–108.

Tajfel, Henri. *Differentiation between Social Groups: Studies in the Social Psychology of Intergroup Relations*. London: Academic Press, 1978.

Takahara, Kumiko. "Female speech patterns in Japanese." *International Journal of the Sociology of Language* 92 (1991): 61–85.

Tannen, Deborah. *Conversational Style: Analyzing Talk among Friends*. Norwood, NJ: Ablex, 1984.

Tannen, Deborah. *You Just Don't Understand: Women and Men in conversation*. New York: William Morrow, 1990.

Timm, Lenora. "Bilingualism, diglossia, and language shift in Brittany." *International Journal of the Sociology of Language* 25 (1980): 29–41.

Tollefson, James. *Language Policies in Education: Critical Issues*. Mahwah, NJ: Lawrence Erlbaum, 2001.

Trechter, Sara, and Mary Bucholtz. "White noise: Bringing language into Whiteness studies." *Journal of linguistic Anthropology* 11, no. 1 (2001): 3–21.

Trudgill, Peter. "Sex, covert prestige and linguistic change in the urban British English of Norwich." *Language in Society* 1, no. 2 (1972): 175–95.

Trudgill, Peter. *The Social Differentiation of English in Norwich*. Cambridge: Cambridge University Press, 1974.

Trudgill, Peter. "Linguistic accommodation: Sociolinguistic observations on a sociopsychological theory." In *Papers from the Parasession on Language and Behavior*, eds. Roberta Hendrick, Carrie Masek, and Mary Frances Miller, 218–37. Chicago: Chicago Linguistics Society, 1981.

Trudgill, Peter. *Sociolinguistics: An Introduction to Language and Society*. Harmondsworth: Penguin, 1983.

Trudgill, Peter. *Dialects in Contact*. Oxford: Blackwell, 1986.

Trudgill, Peter. *New-Dialect Formation: The Inevitability of Colonial Englishes*. Edinburgh: Edinburgh University Press, 2004.

Trudgill, Peter, and Jenny Cheshire, eds. *The Sociolinguistics Reader. Vol. 1: Multilingualism and Variation*. London: Edward Arnold, 1998.

Trudgill, Peter, and George Tzavaras. "Why Albanian-Greeks are not Albanians: Language shift in Attica and Biotia." In *Language, Ethnicity and Intergroup Relations*, ed. Howard Giles, 171–84. New York: Academic Press, 1977.

Tucker, G. Richard, and Wallace E. Lambert. "White and Negro listeners' reactions to various American English dialects." *Social Forces* 47 (1969): 463–8.

Turner, Lorenzo Dow. *Africanisms in the Gullah Dialect*. Chicago: University of Chicago Press, 1949.

Urciuoli, Bonnie. *Exposing Prejudice: Puerto Rican Experiences of Language, Race, and Class*. Boulder, CO: Westview Press, 1996.

Van de Velde, Hans, Marinel Gerritsen, and Roeland van Hout. "The devoicing of fricatives in Standard Dutch: A real-time study based on radio recordings." *Language Variation and Change* 8 (1996): 149–75.

Van Herk, Gerard. *A Message from the Past: Past Temporal Reference in Early African American Letters*. PhD dissertation, University of Ottawa, 2002.

Van Herk, Gerard. "Barbadian lects: Beyond meso." In *Contact Englishes of the Eastern Caribbean*, eds. M. Aceto and J. Williams, 241–64. Amsterdam: John Benjamins, 2003.

Van Herk, Gerard. "Getting past participles to function: /t,d/ in early African American English (AAE)." Presented at NWAV 33, University of Michigan, Ann Arbor, 2004.

Van Herk, Gerard. "Regional variation in 19th-century African American English." In *Language Variety in the South: Historical and Contemporary Perspectives*, eds. M. D. Picone and C. Evans Davies, 380–410. Tuscaloosa: University of Alabama Press, 2011.

Van Herk, Gerard, and the Ottawa Intensifier Project. "That's so tween: Intensifier use in on-line subcultures."

Presented at NWAV 35, Columbus, November 9–12, 2006.

Van Herk, Gerard, and Shana Poplack. "Rewriting the past: Bare verbs in the Ottawa Repository of Early African American Correspondence." *Journal of Pidgin and Creole Languages* 18, no. 2 (2003): 1–36.

Van Herk, Gerard, Becky Childs, and Matthew Sheppard. "Work that -s! Drag queens, gender, identity, and traditional Newfoundland English." Presented at NWAV 37, Houston, TX, November 6–9, 2008.

Voloshinov, Valentin. *Marxism and the Philosophy of Language*, trans. Ladislav Matejka and I. R. Titunik. New York and London: Seminar Press, 1973 (1st pub. 1929).

Wardhaugh, Ronald. *Proper English: Myths and Misunderstandings about Language*. Oxford: Blackwell, 1999.

Wardhaugh, Ronald. *An Introduction to Sociolinguistics*. Malden, MA: Blackwell, 2006.

Weinreich, Uriel. *Languages in Contact: Findings and Problems*. New York: Publications of Linguistic Circle of New York, 1953.

Weinreich, Uriel. *Languages in Contact*. The Hague: Mouton, 1963.

Weinreich, Uriel, William Labov, and Marvin Herzog. "Empirical foundations for a theory of language change." In *Directions for Historical Linguistics*, eds. W. Lehmann and Y. Malkiel, 95–198. Austin: University of Texas Press, 1968.

Weinstein, Brian. "Language planning in Francophone Africa." *Language Problems and Language Planning* 4, no. 1 (1980): 55–77.

Wells, John. C. *Accents of English*. Cambridge and New York: Cambridge University Press, 1982.

Wenger, Etienne. *Communities of Practice: Learning, Meaning, and Identity*. Cambridge: Cambridge University Press, 1998.

West, Candace, and Don Zimmerman. "Small insults: A study of interruptions in cross-sex conversations between unacquainted persons." In *Language, Gender and Society*, eds. Barrie Thorne, Cheris Kramarae, and Nancy Henley, 103–17. Cambridge, MA: Newbury House, 1983.

Widdowson, Henry. "Norman Fairclough: *Discourse and Social Change* (Book Review)." *Applied Linguistics* 16, no. 4 (1995): 510–16.

Williams, Frederick. "Some research notes on dialect attitudes and stereotypes." In *Variation in the Form and Use of Language: A Sociolinguistics Reader*, ed. Ralph Fasold, 354–69. Washington, DC: Georgetown University Press, 1983.

Williams, Robert. *Ebonics: The True Language of Black Folks*. St Louis, MO: Institute of Black Studies, 1975.

Winford, Donald. *An Introduction to Contact Linguistics*. Malden, MA: Blackwell, 2003.

Wodak, Ruth. *Gender and Discourse*. London: Sage, 1997.

Wolfram, Walt. *A Sociolinguistic Description of Detroit Negro Speech*. Washington, DC: Center for Applied Linguistics, 1969.

Wolfram, Walt, and Natalie Schilling-Estes. *American English: Dialects and Variations* (2nd edn). Malden, MA: Blackwell, 2006.

Wolfram, Walt, and Erik R. Thomas. *The Development of African American English*. Malden, MA: Blackwell, 2002.

Woods, Howard B. "A socio-dialectology of the English spoken in Ottawa: A study of sociological and stylistic variation in Canadian English." PhD dissertation, University of British Columbia, 1979.

Woolard, Kathryn A., and Bambi Schieffelin. "Language ideology." *Annual Review of Anthropology* 23 (1994): 55–82.

Youssef, Valerie. "Marking solidarity across the Trinidad speech community: The use of *an ting* in medical counselling to break down power differentials." *Discourse and Society* 4, no. 3 (1993): 291–306.

Zhang, Xiaoheng. *Dialect MT: A Case Study between Cantonese and Mandarin*. Unpublished paper, Hong Kong Polytechnic University, n.d.

Zimmerman, Don, and Candace West. "Sex roles, interruptions and silences in conversation." In *Language and Sex: Difference and Dominance*, eds. Barrie Thorne and Nancy Henley, 105–29. Rowley, MA: Newberry House: 1975.

Index

What Is Sociolinguistics?, First Edition. Gerard Van Herk.
© 2012 Gerard Van Herk. Published 2012 by Blackwell Publishing Ltd.

Index compiled by Terry Halliday